The Piggy Bank Murder

To Sharon 5-20-03
Enjoy
Your pool buddy
Tom Walsh

The Piggy Bank Murder

*A Story Based On An Actual Murder And Trial
With Trial Proceedings from Actual Court
Transcripts It Places The Reader In the Jury Box*

Tom Walsh

iUniverse, Inc.
New York Lincoln Shanghai

The Piggy Bank Murder

All Rights Reserved © 2003 by Thomas J. Walsh

No part of this book may be reproduced or transmitted in any form or by any means, graphic, electronic, or mechanical, including photocopying, recording, taping, or by any information storage retrieval system, without the written permission of the publisher.

iUniverse, Inc.

For information address:
iUniverse, Inc.
2021 Pine Lake Road, Suite 100
Lincoln, NE 68512
www.iuniverse.com

All rights reserved, including the right of reproduction in whole or in part in any form.
First edition 2003

ISBN: 0-595-26960-5

Printed in the United States of America

To my mother, Mary MacNeill Duder

Contents

Introduction 1
Chapter 1 3
Chapter 2 8
Chapter 3 10
Chapter 4 13
Chapter 5 16
Chapter 6 19
Chapter 7 25
Chapter 8 29
Chapter 9 58
Chapter 10 62
Chapter 11 73
Chapter 12 81
Chapter 13 85
Chapter 14 97
Chapter 15 116
Chapter 16 132
Chapter 17 135
Chapter 18 148

CHAPTER 19	164
CHAPTER 20	170
CHAPTER 21	184
CHAPTER 22	200
CHAPTER 23	213
CHAPTER 24	243
CHAPTER 25	252
CHAPTER 26	259
CHAPTER 27	264
CHAPTER 28	271
CHAPTER 29	275
CHAPTER 30	290
CHAPTER 31	292
CHAPTER 32	300
CHAPTER 33	317

Acknowledgements

I wish to express my sincere gratitude and appreciation to the people who took the time to grant interviews for this true story: the doctors, attorneys, undertakers, coroners, store keepers, the people who knew Dorothy, her employer at the bank, the tradesmen who worked on the new house, the people who employed Agnes to mind their children, Mr. Demeusy of the Hartford Courant for all the copy, to the court stenographers for their assistance, and especially a heartfelt thanks to my good friend Melanie Barlow, for her insight.

Introduction

The Piggy Bank Murder, a true account of a murder and resulting court trial, took place in Connecticut, in 1965. It was Connecticut's most famous murder trial, because two defendants were suspect at the same time.

The trial was complicated because of several factors. The State Police Major, who was in charge of the investigation, was a hard-hitting cop with a tendency to make his own rules. He not only resorted to deception and subterfuge, he also used what he called his "Bag of Tricks" in the performance of his duty, and was proud of it to the point where he actually admitted it under oath. He violated the rights of the accused, and in some situations actually tried to trick them into a confession. This philosophy was in direct opposition to that of the entire State Police force. Subsequently he was despised by not only his fellow State Police Officers, but by many attorneys as well.

To compound the issue, the defense Attorney and the prosecuting attorney were constantly at each others throat every day of the trial causing undo delays.

The poor grammar used by the attorneys and the indecisive judge, with his long winded convoluted statements, only exacerbated.situation.

Although a considerable amount of dialog may appear to be poorly written and grammatically incorrect, all the court room text is nevertheless factual, having been taken from actual court transcripts.

A "nail-set" is mentioned throughout the story, and for those readers not accustomed to carpenter tools, a definition is in order. A "nail-set" is a metal tool used in finish carpentry work, measuring approximately three inches in length and similar in appearances to a ballpoint pen. Once a nail is driven into wood, so that the head of the nail is within approximately 1/32 of an inch from the surface, the pointed end of the "nail-set" is placed at the head of the nail; the opposite end of the "nail set" is given a slight blow with a hammer, thus driving the nail below the surface of the wood. The resulting cavity is filled with wood putty.

1

"Dottie's in the back yard, dead, and I can't find the baby!," he screamed out loud as he pounded on the door of the neighbor's house across the road. This hysterical outburst jolted Mr. and Mrs. Robert J. Stadler, Jr. from their dinner table. Mr. Stadler rushed to the back door, and grabbed the frantic young man by the shoulders. "Try to control yourself. Tell us what happened." Incoherently, the man related the gruesome findings. As soon as Mrs. Stadler heard what had happened, she telephoned the State Police; she then joined her husband across the road. Dorothy Thompson, a thirty-year-old wife and mother, was lying on the ground almost under the partially finished sun deck, brutally murdered. Mr. Stadler frantically searched every room in the house until he found the baby upstairs safe and sound with her grandmother.

State Police Capt. Thomas O'Brien and Doctor Owen Murphy, the medical examiner from Simsbury, responded to the call. Close examination showed that Mrs. Thompson had been stabbed in the back, throat and chest with a meat carving fork. Her skull was crushed, one eye had popped out, and the other collapsed. Initially she was also hanged by the neck with an electrical cord, and the body was suspended over the edge of the sun deck. The dead weight of the body was too much for the sloppy makeshift arrangement of the electrical cord, which was attached to the deck by a "nailset". The "nailset" pulled loose and the body dropped about ten feet to the ground below. Dr. Murphy removed the wire from Mrs. Thompson's neck. His impression was that the blows to the skull were made with a small sledge hammer. The stomach and lower part of the body appeared to be crushed with a rock. Examination of the house showed that Mrs. Thompson had been ironing, with a shirt partially ironed, still on the ironing board. Three of the five rooms on the first floor were spattered with blood. There was a large pool of blood on the kitchen floor, extending to the adjoining rooms, and out onto the sun deck. It was obvious from the streaks of blood on the floor, that the body had been dragged through the house, out onto the sun deck, and dropped to the ground.

Mrs. Stadler, trying to control her tears and gather her composure said, "I've known Dottie for years, she was a lovely quiet girl. We graduated from Gilbert High School together in 1953, and she was the organist at St. Paul's Lutheran Church in New Hartford." The victim's parents, Mr. and Mrs. Asa Burdick, owners and operators of the Burdick Apple Orchards, were well liked and highly respected residents of New Hartford. It was obvious that Dottie had inherited her parent's grace and dignity. Before her marriage to Arnfin Thompson, she was employed as a teller at the Riverside Bank in New Hartford.

State Trooper Enrico Soliani had arrived on the scene, and assisted Doctor Murphy in removing the body from the yard. It was then released to Mr. John Shea, director of the John Shea Funeral Home in New Hartford. Lt. Cleveland Fussenich who accompanied Trooper Soliano in the cruiser asked, "You say Mr. Thompson, you can't find the baby?" Without answering the State Troopers question, Arnfin Thompson mechanically walked to the front hall of the house, and upstairs to his mother's apartment. Two-year-old Christa was asleep in her grandmothers apartment. Sixty four year old Mrs. Agnes Thompson sat quietly as she told the police she had not heard any disturbance, and was in her room all afternoon. She gave the impression that she was unaware of the tragedy that had struck her daughter-in-law. A brief check of the household determined that the only missing item from the Thompson home was a piggy bank.

A house-to-house investigation was started immediately, however, none of the neighbors had seen anything unusual. Unlike property in the city, country neighbors are not close to one another. Typical properties usually consists of several acres. The land the Thompson's purchased, and on which they built their house, was almost directly across the road from the Stadlers'.

Visitors and picnickers frequently traveled along route 219 to enjoy the magnificent scenery of the roadside and the hills. On a typical summer day, mountain laurel blossoms, and evergreens glisten with dew, and feathery white clouds caress the blue sky. It was especially beautiful by the Barkhamsted Reservoir that is surrounded by state forests. The State Troopers, therefore, had a vast area to cover, and the comments of those interviewed included, "No, there wasn't a stranger in sight, nor any automobiles going up or down the road" or, "The only signs of life were the cows grazing in the fields or ponies romping in the meadows." This could have been the result of the fact, that it was only two days before the start of school vacation, and the mothers were busy with plans for graduation parties and other duties that kept then indoors

The day was hot and humid in the city, but up in the hills of this little town of Barkhamsted (population 1,700), the air was crisp and delightful. On this day, however, on route 179, in the Washington Hill section of Barkhamsted, there was a vicious murderer who brutally snuffed out the life of a young woman as she stood in her own kitchen at the ironing board ironing one of her husband's shirts.

Her husband was Arnfin Thompson, thirty two years old, of medium height, pale complexion and dark haired. At the time of the murder he was employed at Carpenter Brick Co. in South Windsor, Connecticut. His work day started at 8:30 in the morning, but he usually left the house a little before 8:00 to drive to the office about thirty miles distant. He seldom returned home for lunch, and was in the habit of staying out for dinner three, or four nights a week. His excuse to Dorothy was that he had to work late. She, therefore, devoted most of her time to the baby. She had a car but rarely traveled any farther than the Hayes store in town, or to her parent's home in New Hartford, close by.

Arnfin spent weekends working on the house. Although it was a small Cape Cod measuring only 24' x 34', of wood frame construction, with a cut stone front and clapboard exterior, there was still considerable finish work to be completed. This house had a simple floor plan with a front to back living room, a dining room, two bedrooms and a bathroom on the first floor. The second floor consisted of two bedrooms and a bath room, that were converted to an apartment for Agnes Thompson, Arnfin's mother. There was also a full size walk-out basement. Arnfin had accomplished most of the construction by himself. However, the heating and plumbing work was contracted to the local firm of Thordjorn "Tobey" Solberg, a tradesman of excellent reputation and former landlord of the Thompsons. The Thompsons originally rented a cottage in the rear of the Solberg property when they were married in 1959. They remained there until moving into their 'dream home', that had now become a nightmare. Harry Solberg, a high school student, helped his father in the business after school. During summer vacation he also helped Arnfin with the framing and studding of the house.

As is customary in a time of crises, the residents of small towns and some outsiders as well, usually cluster around in small groups, exchanging opinions and rumors with considerable impartiality. This town was no different. The facts of the murder were not as yet established, however, murderer, or murderess was already on trial in absentia. Fingers may not have pointed, but heads nodded agreement when certain names were mentioned.

This normally sedate rural scene was now in a state of turmoil. State Troopers, members of the news media, ambulance attendants, and the medical examiner were shuttling back and forth, each one intent upon his particular job, and apparently oblivious to the milling crowd.

The blackness of early evening in the country was violated by flood lights, flashing lights on the Police Cruisers, and popping flashbulbs; a scene reminiscent of TV movies. Many people lingered until early morning, rooted to the spot by morbid curiosity. I have heard it said that it takes a lot of living to become a woman. Dorothy Thompson's womanhood, however, was short-lived and violently terminated.

2

Hayes', the only general store in East Hartland, has been owned and operated by the same family for many years. Its success was due to the friendly atmosphere, courteous service,and personal attention, especially to meat orders. Families patronizing this store came from all directions from a distance of ten to fifteen miles to do business with Russell Hayes and his wife. Hayes' store boasted another unique feature, an imported food section, catering to the Norwegian trade, including: Reindeer meatballs, Fiskekaker (fish cakes), Frukt Kompott, (Norwegian fruit desserts), Svis Kompott, and apricot-prune. The store hours are, 7:30 A.M., to 8:00 P.M. It was at this store that Dorothy Thompson purchased her groceries and sundry items.

Customers lingered outside this same store day after day discussing the murder; the biggest news to hit this small community since the floods of 1955. The more they talked, the more bewildered they became. They even worked themselves into a state of nervous excitement. The fear of going back to an empty house was dominant. Conversations covered every imaginative scenario such as; "Who could do this to Dottie?, Why would she keep the doors locked if she was afraid of her mother-in-law?, If she was afraid of her, why keep herself locked in with her?" One woman was overheard saying, "If I were afraid of someone who was living in my house, I would keep the doors unlocked. So if there was trouble, I could grab the baby and run." Another said, "If the doors were locked, and I screamed for help, how could anyone come to my rescue?" Another woman added, "I have heard that Dottie was afraid of her. But, would a woman as meticulous as Agnes make such a mess? Would she be able to stay there all afternoon and look at blood all over the floors?" "Agreed," said an older woman, "And if Christa saw her grandmother kill her mama, she would be hysterical with fright, and wouldn't let her grandmother touch her. Instead, the child was holding on to her, and didn't want to go with the aunt. No youngster would want to stay with a person who hurt her mommy." Then the inevitable question arose. What did Christa see? What did the child mean when she repeated, "She killed her. She killed her." How would a child that young know if anybody was killed?

The men who stopped at the gas pumps in front of Hayes' store on their way home, didn't ask "Who?" They asked, "What's new?" They were all hoping for a quick solution to the crime, so their wives wouldn't be afraid to stay home alone during the day. The community of East Hartland, West Hartland and Hartland, is populated largely by hardworking, church going Swedish and Norwegian families, who pride themselves in their crafts, and believe in giving a good days work for a reasonable wage. For relaxation they attend church socials or read their bibles. At the Lutheran church on route 20, the parishioners now discussed in detail the court proceedings, the police investigations, and the house-to-house investigations. Needless to say,there were many opinions. What everyone did agree on, however, was that there must be many things that townspeople were afraid to tell the investigators. One woman said, "The night before the murder my daughter was visiting and reminiscing with a friend whom she had not seen since they were together in college. They didn't noticed the late hour until I phoned her and suggested she start for home."

Route 179 is a dark, hilly and curvy country road, with little, or no traffic, and as she was driving home around midnight, a man ran in front of her car waving her to stop. She frantically tried to get pass him, however, he kept running back and forth in an attempt to keep her from passing. Fortunately, my husband always instructed the girls to keep their car doors and windows locked at night, especially when driving alone. So she remained cool, and rammed the accelerator to the floor, nearly running him over as she raced by. She was, in fact, so busy trying to get away, she was unable to identify him.

3

The murder scene was cordoned of by the State Troopers to prevent everyone except the troopers and investigators, from tromping through the crime scene. The night of the murder, Christa went with her aunt and uncle to their house in New Hartford. Agnes Thompson who had been a patient two years ago, was escorted by a police woman and two State Troopers to the Connecticut Valley Mental Hospital in Middletown, where she was to remain for a period of ten months.Although she was a suspect, she nevertheless had not been indicted. The investigation was more tedious and took longer than normal due to the distance between homes or farms, some of which occupy hundreds of acres. The only two houses near each other on this stretch of RT. 179 are the Thompsens' and Stadlers'.

Patiently, and painstakingly, the troopers questioned everyone who had been working in the area on the day of the murder. Truck drivers whose daily route took them into the area, commuters who passed the murder scene on their way to and from the city, and delivery men who know everyone on their route. In spite of their extensive leg work, nobody reported anything unusual. One frightened woman in the store said to Mr. Hayes, "There must be someone, somewhere who saw something." As it turned out, one alert citizen, a man who passed the Thompson house on his way to work in Hartford on the afternoon shift, reported seeing a black 1959 Ford parked in front of the Thompson house at about the time of the murder.

Friday afternoon, Dorothy Thompson was buried from St. Paul's Lutheran Church, in New Hartford; the same church where she had played the organ for many services. Funeral director, John Shea said, "In all the years I've been in this business, I've never seen anything like it. I've have hundreds of accident cases, burn victims, even people thrown through windshields in automobile accidents, but this is the first time I have ever cried when I looked at a body Whoever did this to Dottie must be a maniac." While friends and neighbors were attending the service, State Troopers working surreptitiously, scrutinized the crowds in the church, and at the gravesite.

In the meantime, back on route 179 in Barkhamsted, State Troopers discovered a large red-stained hammer, 110 feet to the rear of the house. Capt. O'Brien described it as a "stone hammer" weighing about 5 pounds, with a wood handle 18 inches long. The Troopers also found a red earring, and a white, blood stained, shoelace in the driveway of the murder scene.

The highway naturally became a Mecca of morbid onlookers. They would drive up as far as East Hartland and then return for a second look. Most of the townspeople stayed close to home, and those who never locked their doors, were now routinely locking doors and windows.

It was a frightening experience, to say the least, for those country people who were in the habit of taking care of each others livestock and homes whenever a neighbor went away for a day or so. Now they were trying to remember to keep everything locked. It was not unusual to overhear comments such as, "As long as I have lived in my house, I have never had a key or kept anything locked up." Now they're going to the village to buy new locks. The local women were afraid to go home from work after dark. They would wait until someone was available to escort them from the car to the house. Going into barns or garages after dark was no longer an option. Everyone was afraid of the darkness of night, in spite of the fact the murder occurred during the day.

The darkness, or the unknown, seems to intensify fear. Occurrences such as a violent storm in the middle of the night, seems more terrifying than one just as fierce during daylight. First Selectman, Hubert Callahan said, "Everyone in town is shocked and dumbfounded. We all knew Dottie, we were all friends."

This was the first murder in Barkhamsted since 1914, when County Commissioner Hubert B. Case was murdered in his store in Barkhamsted Hollow. He was attacked on November 28, and died on November 29. Two suspects, by the names of Williams and Roe were convicted of the crime and hanged one year later, almost to the day, November 16, 1915

4

Mr. William Flagg a Metropolitan Water District patrolman, whose route normally took him along route 179 and around the reservoir sat watching the eleven o'clock news, too distraught to relax. He wondered why the newscasters had to go into such gruesome details of the murder of Dottie, whom he had dated before she married Arnfin. The thoughts of Dottie being so brutally murdered was enough to make one's "skin crawl". They were close friends, before and after her marriage, now she was dead. The newscaster said, "The State Troopers were appealing to everyone to report anything they might have seen, that might be relevant." This appeal jogged his memory. He called the State Police., identified himself, and explained that he lived in Winsted. He reported to the tooper, "It was about one thirty in the afternoon, and I was on routine patrol headed south. As I passed the Thompsen house, a black 59 Ford, heading north towards East Hartland, was just coming to a stop in front of it." There was a pause while the Trooper caught up with his notes. Then Mr. Flagg continued, "I had a particular reason to look carefully at this car and its occupant. About two weeks ago we had a case of indecent exposure at the reservoir beach, and the fellow in question had a 1959 Ford; that's why I happened to notice it. Through the rearview mirror I saw a man walking around in front of the car. He was about five feet ten, or eleven, well built, wearing a pink shirt and gray slacks."

"Slow up a bit. I'm trying to get all this down.", said the tooper. Mr. Flagg continued, "He was about thirty years old and wore glasses. I didn't think this was the man involved in the beach incident, so I drove on. I didn't note the license plate number.

The Dorothy Thompsen murder was still the feature story in all the Hartford area daily and weekly newspapers. The search for the owner, or driver of the 1959 black Ford intensified.

Arnfin Thompsen had neglected his mail for weeks. There were more important things to do, but now, he thought it was about time he drove to the East Hartland Post Office. The Postmaster said, "Your box is stuffed, Arnie, I knew you wouldn't be at the house, so I was going to call you at the office. How are you getting along?" They chatted as Arnfin cleared out the box, and put the mail in a paper bag the Postmaster had provided. Arnfin sat in the car sorting the bag of mail. One letter in particular attracted his attention, because his name and address was printed in large letters. It was postmarked Winsted, Connecticut and dated June 17. He opened it, and his blood ran cold as he read the large printed contents:

> I liked your wife, she worked with me at the bank. I told her if I couldn't have her no-one would. She didn't believe me. It took a long time, but I succeeded in what I planned. Soon I will kill the baby, so no sign of her will remain in my mind. I stabed her with a fork. I stomped on her face, then I draged her through the house with an electrical cord, then I used a hammer to pound in the skike to hang her. She fell to the ground, then I bashed her head in several times with a large rock. I used a nabors car, a dark blue 58 Ford hardtop. I wanted to take her with me Away from here but she wouldn't go. My car was too old and ran too poorly so I stold someones on the way to her house. Pretty smooth except she wouldn't go with me. I'll kill the baby someday soon. I'll kill the baby too, and my wife.

Arnfin read, and reread the letter, thinking, this must be a prank. He paid particular attention to the spelling. Electric is spelled properly, but stabbed is spelled stabed, and neighbor is spelled nabor. Succeeded is spelled properly, but he says he stold the car.

Arnfin put the letter in his pocket and started the car, but wasn't sure where to go. Would it be wise to say nothing? Or should he show it to his minister, the family, or one of the troopers? He decided that the State Troopers would have the experience and facilities to trace such things. He drove back to Barkhamsted and gave the letter to the State Trooper who was guarding the property. He then proceeded to his friends house in South Windsor, confident he had done the right thing.

5

In his office on the third floor of the Connecticut State Police building, Major Sam Rome sat at his desk reading the letter that had been delivered from the Canaan Barracks. The major was really pissed because he wasn't called in on the case immediately. In Connecticut a case doesn't go automatically to the Chief of Detectives. Commissioner Leo J. Mulcahy established the rule that Major Rome must wait to be assigned, even in a murder case. "This letter is from a fucking crank," the major shouted, "This sick bastard has written everything that was in the news. He's not the fucking murderer. Return this to the Canaan Barracks, and tell them we'll do everything we can to help them find the sender. Any stupid bastard, who would threaten the life of a baby, is a fucking psychopath."

The sergeant picked up the letter and returned it to the Canaan Barracks. The State Troopers didn't appreciate having The Hartford Division of Detectives stepping in on their case, especially Sam Rome. There was not only professional jealousy but above all, personal pride involved. It was no secret they hated his guts, so it's easy to understand why they were disgusted when the major was assigned to the Thompsen case. Major Sam Rome, as any resident of Connecticut who reads the Hartford newspapers will tell you, is any police departments worst nightmare. He uses unscrupulous tactics to get a confession at any cost. If he tricks a suspect into a confession, and it was proven later that the suspect was actually guilty, he would then use that as an excuse for justification of his methods. Defense lawyers also hated him. It's a common belief that the Mafia has a price on his head. He has been quoted as saying he never goes to bed without a gun under his pillow. His house is wired with security alarms, and he never sits near a window. Ask any cop about Major Rome, and the answer typically will be," He's an uncompromising hard-nosed prick cop, just out for attention and a bust."

Major Rome, and Sergeant Orlando Ragazzi left for a meeting with Captain O'Brien, Lt. Fussenich, the officers from his own division, and the men from the Canaan Barracks. Rome examined the police photos, read the investigators reports, studied the autopsy report, then said, "Let's go to the house. I want to get oriented and see for myself where this victim was 'iced'." When he arrived at the scene, he stood in the hallway and looked around. From there he went to the bedrooms and the dining room. He then went upstairs, to see the small apartment where Agnes lived. While up there, he looked out the windows towards the woods. Back downstairs, he went out to the yard, and into the woods.

The friction between the officers intensified as soon as Major Rome said, "Agnes is the goddamn killer. She was there all afternoon, and if anyone came she would hear them". Lieutenant Fussenich said, "I disagree with you. Agnes Thompsen is a little sixty four year old woman who doesn't weigh much more than a hundred and fifteen. She's not much over five feet tall and isn't strong enough to lift a nineteen pound rock."

Major Rome ordered a complete search of the house and woods. He came back with some men at night and scanned all the clothes in Agnes's closets with an ultraviolet light that would detect blood stains on clothing, even after they had been washed. They were looking for any bit of evidence including bloodstains, fingerprints, or an instrument of any kind that might be construed to be the murder weapon. What frustrated him most was not finding the piggy bank. He then brought in a metal detector, and after testing it to determine if it would react to coins, he ordered the entire area searched, including the yard and adjacent woods. They found nothing except empty beer cans. Then he ordered the ground dug up where there were fresh looking spots. All they found were more cans. He was becoming more frustrated by the hour. He then shouted to the men, "Call in the 'Honey Wagon', I want the frigging septic tank pumped out."

The next day Rome called Arnfin Thompsen and said, "I want you to come with me, Lieutenant Fussenici and Sergeant Ragazzi, to the hospital. I have to talk to your mother." The doctor agreed that Agnes was well enough to be interviewed, provided that the nurse would be present in the room with Agnes. He also stipulated that who ever was to do the interviewing would have to use a microphone in the next room. Arnfin, Fussenich and Ragazzi were allowed to stay. Agnes was lucid, and she talked about her husband dying when she was a young woman, and the hard time she had trying to support her two children. The doctor brought Agnes a glass of milk and suggested they take a short break. The major tried to get her to concentrate on the day of the murder, not on the raising of her children. At the mention of Dorothy's name, Agnes got up and walked around. She became irritated as she repeated the dialogue she had with the officers at the house. When Rome disputed the statements, she said, "It's a lie, It's a lie, I want to leave." Major Rome could see that his constant hammering was getting him nowhere, so he finally gave up, thanked the doctor, and said they would return.

Rome's next visit was with Dorothy's parents, and he ran into a similar situation. There was nothing new they could add, his visit was fruitless. From there he went to the home of Dorothy's sister to talk to Christa. His attempt at questioning a two year old was not only stupid, but also fruitless. She couldn't tell him anything, she just cried for her mother.

6

Litchfield is one of Connecticut's most picturesque towns located in the foothills of the Berkshires. Before the murder of Agnes Thompsen, it retained the same appearance it had in the nineteenth century, and is still unique in its variety of tastes and interests.

Weekend entertaining, especially in summer, was typically a "cookout" on the back lawn, or a Friday evening dinner in one of the colonial mansions. Up until the time of the murder, it was not unusual for guests from other countries to mingle with prominent residents. Now there were news reporters from Hartford, other large Connecticut cities, and from adjoining states, as well as photographers, magazine writers, authors, the curious, and the thrill seekers. All were waiting for the inquest. But now the atmosphere had changed. This influx of strangers in town caused an enigma among the business men, shopkeepers, and restaurant owners. The question they toyed with was: Would the extra dollars resulting from these outsiders patronizing the local businesses compensate for the resulting confusion? Obviously the small town thinking had warped their judgment.

Finally the inquest began. In June, a week after the murder, Dr. Abraham Stolman, pathologist for the State Department of health investigating the case, said, "There is one piece of evidence upon which the technicians have not reached a firm conclusion. I don't wish to hold an inquest and reach a conclusion which will hurt the investigation." Mrs. Agnes Thompsen was escorted into the courtroom by Major Rome and a nurse from the hospital. She was to be represented by public defender Henry C. Campbell, appointed to her by Coroner Guion.

Dr. Lincoln Opper, who performed the autopsy, testified, "It is my opinion that Dorothy Thompsen knew her killer. There were no defense wounds on the mutilated body. She was stabbed several times with both table and carving forks, beaten on the head with a sledge hammer, and strangled with a length of an electrical cord. Any one of the injuries would have been enough to kill this frail young woman, who weighed only 115 pounds." The doctor paused for a few seconds, wiped his forehead and continued, "The killer stabbed Mrs. Thompsen over the left side of the neck with the table fork, which became bent and wasn't useable after many blows. Then the killer plunged the large carving fork into the woman's back penetrating both lungs, and from there to her shoulders. She probably fell to the floor, and then she was hit over the head with the sledgehammer, and in the face over the left eye. The blow crushed her skull, and a large rock crushed the abdomen."

Dr. Owen Murphy, the medical examiner from the Town of Simsbury, was the next witness. The first questions about the condition of the body were almost the same as Dr. Opper had answered. Then Dr. Murphy was asked, "What was the condition of the mother-in-law, Mrs. Agnes Thompsen, when you talked with her after the discovery of the murder?"

"She was warm and full of joy and happiness." She said, "Dr. Murphy, I am awful glad to see you." "She obviously was in a grandiose state of mind, stimulated by some action of religious origin between her and her Maker. She seemed subconsciously looking for a reward, as though she had rendered some service. That's the attitude I felt." Then Dr. Murphy was asked, "Is Agnes Thompsen strong enough to lift the body of the deceased?," The answer was, "Yes." Is she strong enough to lift this nineteen pound boulder, which was dropped on the victim." Again, Dr. Murphy answered, "Yes."

It was now lunch time, and Agnes Thompsen was escorted to an adjoining room. The officers stayed with her while the nurse went out for some food. One officer said, "Agnes is oblivious to the seriousness of the inquest. She acts as if it was happening to someone else." At two o'clock the inquest resumed and Major Rome was the next witness.

His mind was made up before he stepped foot into the courtroom. He would make sure the evidence he gave would have Agnes declared 'criminally suspect.' He said that he was confident of a solution to the case, because it was the work of a woman, and the act of an insane person. He further believed it was done by someone who had the time, and was in no hurry to get away. He stated that he had learned from relatives and friends that the relationship between Agnes and her daughter-in-law had not been cordial.

There was a fifteen minute recess while the doctors discussed something. Then Major Rome continued, "I don't think she planned to kill Dorothy. She just got mad at her, it started in a fit of anger. Then she saw what she'd done and she thought she'd better finish the job. Then she had another thought, to make it look like robbery. It's the work of a confused person, someone who couldn't carry an idea around the corner."

Other witnesses were mostly relatives, friends, co-workers and church-workers. They were questioned about the relationship between Dorothy Thompsen and her mother-in-law. It was difficult for them to keep their composure. They wiped their eyes took deep breaths, and were thankful when the Coroner announced, "This has been a trying day for everyone. We will convene until ten o'clock in the morning."

It was now October 11, almost four months since the murder, and during this time the animosity between Sam Rome and the other officers escalated rapidly.

Coroner Guion said, "At this time I will consider the inquest concluded. There is reasonable cause to believe that Agnes Thompsen is criminally responsible. Motive, time element, opportunity and physical evidence at the scene, all point to Agnes Thompsen. A warrant will be issued against her at the Connecticut Valley Hospital. It's just a technicality to permit her arrest, if she is ever released."

Lieut. Fussenich said to Coroner Guion, "Sam Rome is licking his chops now, but wait until the piggy bank is found, and we re-open the case, that's the day when the shit hits the fan."

Commissioner Leo J. Mulcahy announced in a press release, "We want to reassure the residents of Barkhamsted, and surrounding towns, that the killer is no longer at large." That was all he said, without elaborating.

Late afternoon on New Year's Eve, five children were playing in the wooded section of their grandparents' property located at the corner of Martin and Wedtwoods Roads near Route 179. Mrs. Cora Clark called to the children, but there was no response. She walked out to see what they were up to. At the old stone wall she saw them examining something. "Look, Granny," yelled one of the kids, "It's a piggy bank." Mrs. Clark wiped the mud off and as she brought the bank in the house and handed it to her husband, she said, "It must be the missing bank, I'll call the State Police." Mr. Clark immediately called Lieut. Fussenich, who instructed them to remain quiet about the bank. He said he would pass on the information to the Connecticut State Police, in Hartford

After the discovery of the piggy bank on New Year's Eve, the Canaan State Troopers were notified of a strange incident that happened the week following the murder. A man who lives on Westwood Road just beyond Clark's property said, "I have seen a car drive up and down the road several times at night, but, every time I started walking through the woods to get a closer look, it would take off quickly. It was a dark car: I think it was a 1959 Chevy. The car was not around here before the murder, at least I didn't see it. Since the murder, everybody's senses are a little sharper. It looked as though someone in that car was looking for something along the road."

Major Rome was notified of the finding. He and Sergeant Ragazzi drove up to the Litchfield Barracks, at which time he identified the bank. "If robbery had been the motive, stepping on the plastic bank would have been a quicker way to get at the contents, rather than using a sharp instrument to enlarge the slot," Rome said, as he handed the bank to Sergeant Ragazzi.

"How did the bank get from the Thompson house in Barkhamsted to Westwood Road in East Hartland?," Ragazzi asked. He placed the bank on the desk, and continued, "Agnes doesn't drive, she didn't own a car, and she certainly couldn't walk from route 179 in Barkhamsted to East Hartland. What do you think major?" "Oh she did it alright, she's a strong woman. It was summertime, the roads were good, she could walk it. The major's one track mind was in full gear. He said, "I'm more convinced than ever that Agnes is the murderer."

The newspapers again ran headlines about the missing bank. They said that the police were renewing the investigation, however, there were no further reports from Canaan to Major Rome in Hartford.

On the morning of March 15, 1966, nine months after the murder, Major Rome sat at his desk and picked up his copy of The Hartford Courant. The headlines read, *"Harry Solberg of East Hartland, Arrested for the Murder of Mrs. Dorothy Thompsen of East Hartland"*. Rome's anger and frustration exploded. He screamed out loud, "Why wasn't I told about this!?" "Ragazzi move your ass, we're going to Litchfield."

At the Litchfield Barracks he learned that the twenty-year-old aircraft worker was picked up on Sunday morning, and taken to the Canaan Barracks for questioning. In the afternoon he was driven to the Hartford Headquarters for a polygraph test, at which time he was accompanied by his parents. That evening he was allowed to go home with the understanding that he would return the next morning for additional testing. The second polygraph, taken the following day, resulted in his being booked for murder.

Rome listened to what the State Troopers had to say. He banged his fist on the desk, and screamed, "I don't care what you say, that fucking kid didn't do it!"

Harry A. Solberg had graduated from Gilbert High School in Winsted, the week of the murder. Seven months later, he married his high school sweetheart, Sharon Provencher of East Hartland. A month later, he was hired by Pratt and Whitney, a Division of United Aircraft, and he also worked part-time in his father's plumbing business.

As he neared the courtroom, in the arc of TV floodlights, his young girlish looking wife rushed from the nearby Law Library screaming, "Get away from him!, Get away from him!"

Harry A. Solberg walked head erect, between Detective Fred Rebillard and Sergeant Victor Keilty. His curly blond hair was rumpled. He wore a blue ski jacket, with white and brown pinstripes, black shoes and a wool shirt open at the neck. Except for his somber face, he resembled a six foot two athlete being escorted by bodyguards.

Dorothy's father, now sixty eight years old, stood in the corridor as Harry was led in. He said he had heard of the arrest over the radio. Dorothy's sister and brother-in-law, Mr. and Mrs. Robert Scully, were with him. Harry's parents and his brother and sister-in-law sat with Harry's young wife, who was clutching her fingers, and biting her nails as tears streamed down her face. She sobbed, "What will happen now, I'm going to have a baby, and Harry's going on trial for murder?"

7

| SUPERIOR COURT | LITCHFIELD, CONNECTICUT |
| LITCHFIELD COUNTY | SEPTEMBER 28, 1966 |

#4458

STATE

VS.

HARRY A. SOLBERG

Before Honorable Herbert S. MacDonald and a Jury of twelve.

Appearances;

Thomas F. Wall, Esq., Attorney for the State.

William D. Shew, Esq., Attorney for the defendant.

Arthur E. Roberts, Alfred K. Tyll, Official Reporters

On the second floor of the Court House, towards the back of the hall, is a large oak paneled high ceiling room; its dark furnishings and somber appearance instantly conveys to the onlooker, the Judicial solemnity of the Superior Court. Herbert S. MacDonald, a handsome, gray haired, middle aged judge, occupied the bench. Below him is the court reporter, noiselessly recording the proceedings. September 28, 1966 Litchfield, Connecticut. Superior Court, Litchfield County. #4458 State Vs Harry A. Solberg. Standing a few feet away, near the low railing which separated the spectators from the players in this drama, stood Attorney Thomas F. Wall. This short, blue eyed lawyer, who is from one of the most distinguished families in Torrington, is the son of a lawyer, and brother of a Superior Court Judge. He studied the expressions and body language of the prospective jurors he was interviewing.

Stanley Clark, the Sheriff, escorted Harry to the Defense table, to sit beside his Attorney, Mr. Shew. Harry looked pale, and seemed unconcerned as he toyed with his glasses. His parents were seated in the section outside the rail. Sitting next to them was his pregnant wife. These months had been a great strain for her, as evidenced by deep lines etched around her mouth.

The seventy two spectator seats were filled, and the chairs reserved for the witnesses, and news media were occupied. The selection of the jury continued until one o'clock, at which time Harry was handcuffed and returned to jail, until after the lunch break. There was confusion when his wife Sharon rushed towards her husband. Harry slipped his hand-cuffed arms over her head and held her close for a minute.

Hundreds of people resembling a mob scene, lingered outside the courthouse, all waiting to get a glimpse of the defendant. As the reporters came out, one spectator shouted, "Is it true that Rome's coming here?" "Why is Rome mixing in now?" "Canaan is here in force, what's Rome coming for?"

During the lunch break, the three nearby smoke filled restaurants were packed with news media and lawyers. The main topic of conversation centered on the defendant, the jury and Major Rome. Shew was uneasy about older people on the jury, especially those living with a son and daughter-in-law. Mr. Shew had another worry. Months ago, a close old friend of his, a man close to the inner workings of the Canaan Barracks, informed him of the friction that existed between the Troopers and Major Rome. Just after Solberg was indicted, Shew met a Litchfield County official who said to him, "They've really got this kid cold." Shew asked, "Where does this leave Sam Rome?" The official answered with relish, "Way out in left field." Another man said, "Even after the warrant for Agnes, the case wasn't closed. We knew there was more to it."

After several days of careful deliberation, the jury was finally chosen. The Judge asked, "Before the jury is sworn, I would like to just ask you twelve jurors and two alternates one question. As I have tried to make it clear to you, it is important that no outside influence enter into your consideration of the case. I realize that during these few days, perhaps you don't realize it and I hope you don't, there has been a great deal of publicity connected with certain angles of this case, some of which items have really nothing to do with the case, but are extraneous, but closely connected with the case, and I would simply like, before you start giving your attention to the case, to ask whether any of you since you were chosen, some of you were chosen as long ago as last Thursday or Friday, I want to ask you whether anything that has occurred, anything that you have unwittingly overheard, anything that has come to your attention without your deliberately trying to hear it, has in any way influenced you or has entered into your consideration, your thoughts in such a way that it might interfere with giving this defendant an absolutely fair trial, fair to him and fair, as well, to the State of Connecticut. If any of you have anything that has occurred or has entered into your consideration since you first came here and were questioned, I would appreciate it if you would let me know at this time." There was no response. "Hearing nothing, I know you all realize the importance of this, and that nothing has occurred. If that is so, Mr. Clerk, will you please administer the oath."

The twelve jurors and two alternates were immediately sworn. The Judge continued, "We are now ready to proceed, Mr. Clerk." Thomas McDermott, the clerk, read the indictment.

"Ladies and gentlemen of the jury, the indictment returned by the Grand Jury, Litchfield County, reads as follows: In the Superior Court of the State of Connecticut held at Litchfield within the County of Litchfield on June 14, A.D. 1966. The State of Connecticut VS Harry A. Solberg. The Grand Jury of the County of Litchfield accuses Harry A. Solberg of Hartland, Hartford County, Connecticut, of the crime of murder in the first degree and charge that on the 15$^{th.}$, day of June A.D. 1965 at the town of Barkhamsted in the County of Litchfield and State of Connecticut the said Harry A. Solberg did wilfully, deliberately, and with premeditation and malice aforethought, kill Dorothy B. Thompsen of Barkhamsted, Litchfield County, Connecticut, by lying in wait and stabbing, beating and strangling her, in violation of

Section 53-9 General Statutes of Connecticut, Revision of 1958. A true Bill, Signed, John H. Cassidy, Jr Foreman of the Grand Jury."

"To this indictment, Ladies and Gentlemen of the Jury, the accused has pleaded not guilty. It is your duty, therefore, to inquire whether he is guilty or not guilty, and if you find him guilty or if you find him not guilty, you will say so by your foreman and say no more. Kindly attend to the evidence."

Ranging in ages from thirty to sixty, the twelve jurors watched with interest and apprehension. After three days of screening and a minimum of instruction, this small group of citizens was now ready to tackle the gargantuan task of judging a man's guilt, or innocence. His life was virtually in their hands. "Kindly attend to the evidence," They were told, so they listened.

8

The crisp, sunny, autumn days enticed an increase in the number of visitors, on special foliage tours, all centered around the beautiful town of Litchfield.

Tension was escalating in the Court House, to the point where you could almost cut it with a knife. Wall, the State's Attorney, called Arnfin Thompsen to the stand. He requested, "Your Honor, may I stand at the other end of the jury box so as to have the witness speak loudly enough for all of us to hear?" The Judge asked Arnfin to speak loudly enough for the court reporter and jury to hear. Arnfin's face was ashen, and he spoke mechanically. You could hear a pin drop while everyone was straining to hear. For many of the jurors and the spectators as well, it was their first experience and they naturally wanted to hear every word.

Wall began with, "What's your name?"
"Arnfin Thompson."
"Where do you live?"
"Maynard, Massachusetts," was his answer
"How long have you lived there?"
"Since last November."
"What is your occupation?"
"I'm an accountant."
"In June of 1965, by whom where you employed?"
"Carpenter Brick Co., in South Windsor, Connecticut."
"At that time, where was your home?"
"In Barkhamstead."
"How far is it from your office in South Windsor, to your home?"
"Say about, not quite 30 miles."

"Is South Windsor on the other side of the Connecticut river from Barkhamstead? and to get back and forth you had to cross the river?"

"Right."

"And what bridge did you ordinarily cross between Barkhamsted and your place of business at the Carpenter Brick company?"

"Route 91."

"And were you able to go by way of Rte. 20?"

"Yes. "And then to reach the Interstate Springfield-Hartford highway, is that correct, Rte. 91 is Springfield-Hartford?"

Arnfin nodded, "Springfield-Hartford."

"And across on that bridge, and then go to your work in South Windsor?"

"Yes, that's right."

"And that is the ordinary Route. For how long a time approximately, prior to June 1965, did you work at the Carpenter Brick Company?"

"I started the first of May, 1965?"

"And before that where were you employed?"

"Westfield Woodworking Company."

"Pardon?"

"Westfield Woodworking Company."

The Judge once again instructed Mr Thompsen to speak louder. "We'll have to let everyone who is connected with the case, including, the jurors, reporters and attorneys, hear what you. have to say Mr. Thompsen."

"Was that in Westfield, Massachusetts?"

"Yes, that's right."

Wall finished the questioning concerning the employment, the commuting, the new house, the rented house and the distance between the two. Also the distance to East Hartland, which is three miles. Wall, quietly and patiently continued.

"And what was the route number of the road upon which your new house was located?"

"Route 179."

"And what was the route number of the house from which you moved in East Hartland?"

"Route 179."

"Route 179. In other words, the new house to which you moved was located on the same road but approximately two and one half miles away, is that correct?"

"Correct."

"And will you describe generally the area there where your old house was? Was it a single house all by itself?"

"It was a single house by itself."

"Was there another house near it?"

"Yes."

"And from whom did you rent the home, the older house?"

"Mr. Solberg."

"That would be the father of the accused?"

"Yes, sir."

"And where did Mr. Solberg live in relation to the house in which you lived and which you rented from Mr. Solberg?"

"In front of our house.

"In other words, one house was in the rear of the main house and you rented the house in the rear?"

"Yes."

"Right, and Mr. Solberg and his family lived in the front house, is that correct?"

"Correct."

"And the accused Harry Solberg was also living in the front house, the house which was in front of your tenant house there?"

"Yes."

"In 1963?"

"Yes."

"And did you know the Solberg family well?"

The answer in a muffled voice was, "Yes."

Shew asked, "May we have the answer please?"

Wall replied, "I think he said yes."

The witness replied, "Yes."

The judge again asked, "I hate to keep mentioning this to you Mr. Thompsen, but please try to remember and don't drop your voice. You have a tendency, after I speak to you, of answering a few questions audibly, and then dropping your voice."

Wall said, "I am standing here, Your Honor chiefly for that purpose. It may not be courteous, but I am standing this distance away."

"You knew the Solberg family then quite intimately?"

"Quite."

"And in general, will you state how well you knew the Solberg family say from 1963 to June 1965?"

"Well, I have known them a good many years. We were over there for dinner a couple of times."

The Judge again reminded Arnfin to speak up, so as to be heard.

As Arfin testified, the eyes of the jurors wandered from him to the defendant, and his family, and to the back of the court where Asa Burdick, Dorothy Thompsen's Father, sat with his head bowed.

And the young man, the accused here, did you also have occasion to see him frequently during the time between 1963 and 1965 and June of 1965?"

"Yes."

Again the Judge asked Arnfin to raise his voice as he answered questions regarding the building of his new house on Rte. 179.

"And approximately how many people at various times did you employ to assist you in building the new home?"

"Mr. Solberg helped me with some framing. and I hired Harry for a few weeks."

Once again Mr. Thompsen was told to speak up.

"You mean Harry senior?"

Arnfin answered, "Harry Solberg.

"The accused?, the young man here?, the accused here?"

"Yes."

"And what is the Fathers name?"

"Tobey."

Wall continued with questions about Harry helping his father on the Thompsen house, before and after the family had moved in, and over an extended period of time. Also helping to make an apartment for Agnes Thompsen, Arnfin's mother, who came to live with them in December of 1964. He also asked him to describe the location of the house, its sidelines and depth on the lot, the fact that it was clearly visible from Route 179, the distance to the Solberg property on Route 179 in East Hartland, his departure for work in the mornings, and his work hours.

"Calling your attention to the date of June 15, 1965, were you and your wife and daughter living in the house on that date?"

"Yes."

"And was your mother living in the apartment on the second floor?"

"Yes."

"And will you tell His Honor and the jury, just what you did between the time that you got up that morning and the time you arrived at work?"

Arnfin testified that his wife always got up before he did and made toast and coffee, and that they had breakfast together.

"And what was your wife's name?"

"Dorothy."

"For how long a time had you been married to your wife?"

"Since 1959."

"At the time that you were married to your wife, where was her home?"

"In New Hartford."

"And where was your home at that time?"

"East Hartland."

"The same general area?"

"Well, on the old Rte 20."

"At that time your child was in the house, wasn't she?"
"Yes."
"And what is her name?"
"Christa."
"And Christa, then, was how old?"
"Two and a half."

Wall, continued questioning Arnfin concerning his leaving for work, his car, his, co-workers, officers of the firm, and the plant foreman Gordon Disley with whom Arnfin ate lunch at Dells Ice Cream Bar in South Windsor. Arnfin testified that he was with fellow office employees, Pat Bayek and Gordon Disley all during the day, until he left for home at 5:30. He stopped briefly at the post office on the way home, collected his mail from the box about 6:10 and went right home. He parked his car in the driveway and entered the house through the front door, went through the hall and into the kitchen. The next series of questions related to the location of driveway, doors, front entrance, back porch, number of outside doors, the walkout basement, and the height of the rback porch from the ground.

"As you entered the kitchen was there anything that you observed?"
"Yes, a pool of blood. It was blood all over."
"All over the kitchen?"
"Yes."
"And you say All over the kitchen. Was it on the floor, or on the furniture?"
"On the floor, and on the counter."

Arnfins low, whispering tones made his answers inaudible. Jurors, reporters and court spectators were straining to hear.

"Upon seeing this pool of blood, what did you do?"
"I went upstairs and asked my mother what happened."
"Was your mother there when you went upstairs?"
"Yes."
"And what did your mother say?"
"Well, she said she thought Dottie had gone with her brother."

"And did Dottie have a brother?"
"Yes."
"What was his name?"
"Paul Burdick."
"Was that all the conversation that you had with your mother at that particular time?, and what did you do then?
"I went downstairs to call Dottie's mother."
"What was Dottie's mother's name?
"Annie Burdick. They had a regular schedule of calling three times a day. I asked her where Dottie was, and she said, she didn't know, she hadn't heard from her since morning. She was crying, and asked me to call her back when I found out something. Then I took a good look at the room and I could see a trail of blood going out to the dining room. It led out to the glass doors onto the porch."
"Yes, and you went to the edge of the porch, what did you observe?"
"I looked down and saw her lying there."
"You saw your wife, Dorothy, lying there?"
"Yes."
"And where was that, Mr. Thompsen?"
"On the ground below the porch."
"And how far off a perpendicular was it from where you observed her to the top of the porch where you were standing?"
"About eight feet."
"And approximately how far away from the edge of the porch was Dorothy at the time that you saw her?"
"Well, she was right on the edge there really."
"Just at the edge of the porch not any great distance, is that what you mean to say?"
"Well, she was right on the edge there really. Away from the porch."
"What did you then do when you saw her body there?"
"Well, I ran down to her."
"You ran down to her."
"Pardon?"

"Back out the front door."

You went out the front door. In other words, was this height such that you couldn't jump, or get down that way?"

"Well, there was a stepladder there. I was going to use that, but I was a little shaky at the time."

"And there was a stepladder, but it was not one you could depend upon, because it was shaky?"

"Well, I was shaky."

"You were?"

"Yes."

"And you went out the front door of the house and you proceeded where?, after you went outside?"

"Around the north side, and down back."

"And did you approach the body that you had seen there?"

"Yes."

"And what did you observe?"

"Well, I touched her. She was cold."

"You touched the body did you?"

"Yes."

"And was it your wife?"

"Oh yes, yes."

"And was she living or dead at that time?"

"She was dead!"

"Upon making this discovery, what did you then do?"

"Well, I realized I hadn't seen my daughter and started calling for her."

"And you called for her when you were near the body, is that correct?"

"Yes."

"And did you get any response?"

"No."

"And what did you do then?"

"Ran across the road to the neighbors'."

"On Rte. 179 where you new house stood, Mr. Thompsen, was it a well settled area, or was it far out in the country?"

"It's country."

"And were the houses far apart?"

"Yes."

"And approximately how far north was the next house on the same side of the road as yours?"

"Probably not quite a mile."

"About a mile?"

"Not quite, it would be a little less than that."

"And you said though, there was a neighbor across the road?"

"Yes."

"And who was the neighbor across the road? Who resided in the house there?"

"Robert and Carole Stadler."

"And was their home directly across the road?"

"No, it was a little bit North."

"And it was visible from the front of your house?"

"Yes."

"And did the Stadlers have children?"

"Yes."

"And approximately how old were the children in the Stadler family?"

"One was about Christa's age and the other one, I think was five."

"And did Christa, your daughter, have occasion during that period of time, to play with the child of her age in the Stadler family?"

"Yes."

"And was that sometimes on one side?, sometimes the other?, or was it in any particular place that they played?"

"I'm not too sure about that."

"Well now on this occasion then, you went over to the Stadler house?"

"Yes."

"And whom did you see, if anyone, there?"
"Bob and Carole Stadler."
"The two of them were at home, were they?"
"Yes."
"And were the children at home?"
"I didn't notice."
"What did you say at that time?"
"I told them Dottie was in the back yard dead, and I couldn't find the baby and wondered if she had seen anything."

Wall asked, "May we have that answer Mr. Tyll please?"

The Judge instructed the reporter to read back the answer. Silence fell like nightfall over the country courtroom. Tobey Solberg and his wife, Solveik sat stiff in their seats, their faces expressionless as their eyes wandered from Arnfin, on the stand, to their son at the defense table showing little emotion while Harry's wife Sharon sat with her hand to her mouth.

Wall continued," What did they say?"
"Carole said she had better call the police and I agreed and Bob came—wanted to go back to the house with me."
"And while you were going. to the house, Carole was to call the police, is that correct?
"Yes, right."
"And you and Mr. Stadler then proceeded where?"
"Back to my house."
"And where did you go then?, Did you go around to the rear of the house?"
"Bob went over to the side."
"Which side?"
"The north side."
"And you went where?"
"Went inside."
"Through the driveway?"
"Yes."

"Yes, I hollered for Christa and I got an answer from her bedroom."

Shew requested that the witness speak louder.

The witness repeated, "I hollered for Christa and got an answer from her bedroom."

"And what did she say?"

"I don't remember. I just know she answered."

"You had not previously gone to look in the bedroom had you?"

"No."

Wall handed Arnfin Thompsen a sketch, and said, "Now Mr. Thompsen, I show you this sketch which purports to be a sketch of your house roughly drawn to scale. It includes the floor plan of the first floor of your home, and the drawing of the outside of the home. Will you look that over carefully and see whether it is a fair representation of the floor plan of the first floor of your home, and a fair representation of the general appearance of the outside of the home from the front?"

"Yes."

"Have you seen this before?"

"No."

"Well, have you examined it carefully or is it necessary for you to examine it any more to know whether it is a fair representation of the floor of the house?"

"No,—it is—it is."

Wall passed the large sketch to Shew, who offered no objection. Wall then asked, "May I show it to the Jury Your Honor?" The Judge agreed.

Shew offered a suggestion to put the sketch on a board, where everyone could see it better.

Both Wall, and the Judge agreed. It was now 11:33 and a short recess was called.

At 11:53 the jurors and alternates were seated, and Arnfin resumed his testimony. Wall addressed the bench, "Your Honor, I have shown to counsel for the defendant, a United States Department of The Interior, geological survey of the New Hartford quadrangle, which includes the village of East Hartland, and Route 179. Counsel for the defendant has agreed that he has no objection to that being entered as State's Exhibit "B". The map is dated 1956, and is merely to show the general area, it doesn't show the house on it."

In the interest of saving time, it was agreed that they show and explain; the area around the East Hartland and Washington Hill section of Barkhamsted, the town lines between Hartford County and Litchfield County, the back country roads, paved town roads, and the Barkhamsted Reservoir.

"Mr. Thompsen," said Wall, "Will you please step down from the witness stand and with this pointer, indicate to His Honor and the Jury the front entrance to the house." Arnfin explained in detail, the front entrance, the hallway, the location of their bedroom and, Christa's bedroom, which was in the front of the house, and the little hall leading to the kitchen

"And when you returned home from work that evening, did you make any observations to determine whether there had been any changes that were indicated as having occurred between morning and the night?"

"Well, the blood for one."

"Well, did you make other observations about whether objects that were there in the morning, were still there at night?"

"Not at first."

"But did you at a later time?"

"Yes."

"And did you determine that anything that had been there in the morning was not there upon your return.?" Wall had at last brought to the fore, The piggy bank.

"And what did you determine was missing?"

"A piggy bank."

"A piggy bank. Would you describe that piggy bank?

"It was made of pink plastic, and about a foot long."

Arnfin was again asked to speak louder.

He repeated, "A plastic piggy bank, about a foot long and six to eight inches high."

"And when you left that morning, where was the piggy bank?"

"I think it was on a coffee table. Either one of two places, either on the coffee table or on the raised hearth fireplace."

"Did you make a search around the house for it at a later time to determine whether the piggy bank was there upon your return?"

"Yes."

"And could you find it?"

"No."

The famous piggy bank, in a cellophane wrapper, was marked as States Exhibit 'C' Wall continued, "Would you tell His Honor and the jury approximately what this piggy bank had been used for, up until the day that it disappeared?"

"I used it to give my daughter some coins, and she would put them in there."

"And did you have any knowledge as to approximately how much, if any, money was in the piggy bank at the time, the last that you saw of it that day?"

"There is no real way of knowing, but I could guess, probably about twenty to twenty five dollars."

"And was that all in coins?"

"That was all in coins."

"All in coins. I believe you said, then, that Mr. Stadler came over with you and viewed the body of your wife, is that correct?"

"No, he went over to the north side of the house."

"Did you observe what Mr. Sadler did on the outside as far as the body was concerned?"

"No, I didn't."

"Did you observe later what he had done?"

"Well, after I found Christa."

Arnfin again was asked to speak up.

"After what?"

"After I found Christa, I gave him a blanket to cover her up."
"You gave him a blanket?"
"Yes, to cover the body?"
"Now, you did find Christa?"
"Yes."
"And what was her condition when you found her?"
"She was standing up in her crib"
"Did she appear to be agitated or anything?"
"No."
"What was the usual procedure when you came home from work to your wife in the evening, so far as Christa was concerned?"
"She generally would be in the window and wave."
"And wave. And in what window was she ordinarily there to wave to you?"
"In the bow window. And then what ordinarily occurred when Christa waved at the window to you?"
"My wife would open the door."
"Your wife would open the door?"
"Yes."
"And was there any reason for your wife to open the door on all these other ordinary occasions?"
"To save me trouble of unlocking it."
"Did your wife ordinarily keep that door locked?"
"Yes."
"And in the event that your daughter did not see you, and your wife did not come to open the door, did you have a key?"
"Yes."
"Now, on this particular occasion on June 15, of 1965, did it not appear to be unusual that your daughter did not come to the window?"
"Yes."
"And when you went to the door of the house on that day, how did you find the door?, Was it locked or unlocked?"
"It was unlocked."

"After you had found Christa, what did you then do with Christa?"
"I brought her upstairs to my mother."
"To your mother? And you left her there?"
"Yes."
"What did you then do?"
"Went downstairs and got a blanket for Bob."
"Got a blanket for Bob Stadler to use to cover your wife's body?"
"I assumed he did, yes."
"Did you later see the blanket over the body?"
"No, I didn't go back there."
"What did you do after that? Had any police arrived at that time?"
"No."
"What did you then do?"
"I called Dottie's mother."
"You called Dottie's mother?"
"Yes."
"I told her she was dead. I guess I wasn't too tactful. I don't remember what I said, but I told her Dottie was dead."
"And was Bob Stadler around at that time when you made the call?"
"I think he just came in."
"He just came in from outside?"
"I think so, if I remember right."
"Did he remain with you in the house for any length of time after that?"
"Yes."
"For how long?"
"Until the police came."
"And approximately how much time elapsed between the time that you made this telephone call, or that Mrs. Stadler made the telephone call, and the time one of the police arrived?"
"About a half an hour."
"And during that time, what, if anything, did you do?"

"I poured myself a couple of good shots. We waited in the living room for the police."

"You took a shot of liquor?"

"Yes."

"Between the time that you arrived on the scene from work and the time that the police arrived, was any article that was around there, set aside or disturbed in any way? Was anything moved or was anything done by cleaning up the blood?"

"No"

"Anything done about moving the body or moving any articles that were in a particular place?"

"No"

"Then, did the situation so far as the various articles and the body and so forth were concerned remain the same?"

"Yes."

"Did you have occasion to observe any other articles that were—that appeared to be out of place, or to have been disturbed between the time that you left in the morning and the time you returned at night?"

"No."

"Now, when you came home at night, did you have occasion to observe an ironing board?"

"Yes."

"And where was that located?"

"In the dining room."

"And did you observe what, if anything was on the ironing board?"

"There was an iron, and one of my white shirts."

"And did you observe whether or not the iron was connected with the electrical outlet?"

"I didn't observe it."

"You did not observe it. And did you observe whether nor not the shirt had been completely ironed or not ironed at all?"

"Might have been partially ironed, but it was bloody, too."

"It was bloody, too?"

"Yes."

"Now, I believe you said that the house was still in the process of construction on or about June 15, of 1965, is that so?"

"That's right."

"And in general, what more remained to be done to complete the house?"

"Oh, kitchen cabinets, they were just partially done. The walls, needed a lot of trim, and two closets hadn't been done."

"Two that hadn't been done?"

"Yes, and the porch was still incomplete, under construction."

"Was there any rail around the porch or anything of that sort?"

"No"

"When you left in the morning, had there been a ladder in any particular location?"

"Yes"

"And where had the ladder been?"

"Under the porch."

"And was it lying on its side or was it upright?"

"Upright, and under the porch?"

"Under the porch."

"Was it a stepladder?"

"Yes."

"How high a stepladder was it, approximately?"

"Probably five feet."

"And when you returned at night, where was that stepladder?"

"It was off the edge of the porch."

"At the edge of the porch?"

"I had been using it to get down to the ground."

"Was it in such a position that one could use it for ascending from the ground on the outside?"

"Yes."

"And are you certain, then, that the ladder had been previously there in the in the morning when you left it under the porch?"

"Yes."

"Approximately how far under the porch was it?"

"Three or four feet."

"Now, had there been tools left in various places that you recalled, that had been there in the morning?

"Yes."

"And was there a carpenters hammer?"

"Yes."

"And do you recall that tool as belongings, to you?"

"Might have belonged to my wife's Father."

"It might have belonged to your wife's father, but you remember the particular hammer do you?"

"Yes."

"And was such a hammer on the back porch of the house that morning,?"

"Yes, sir."

"Now, was there another type of hammer. Was there a four pound hammer also?"

"Yes."

"And where had that four-pound hammer been left in the morning?"

"It was on the porch also."

"That was on the porch. Now, I show you this hammer and wish to have you examine it very carefully, so as to make sure of what your answer will be—what you mean to say."

"Yes."

"Do you recognize that hammer?"

"Yes."

"That is the one."

"When you returned at night, and after you had an opportunity to look around, did you again see this four-pound hammer?"

"I didn't see it, no."

"Did you at a later time see this hammer?"

"Yes, at the Grand Jury hearing."

"And what else, if anything, do you recall as having been left on the porch in the way of tools, on the morning of the fifteenth?"

"There was one or two saws probably, and a ruler, and a nail apron."

"And was there a "nailset"?"

"Yes."

"And of what did the "nailset" consist? Was it just one "nailset"?"

"Well, there might have been two."

"And did you find one of those, or did you find a "nailset" that had been on the porch in any position that was different at the time that you returned, or after your return?"

"Well, I found out later it was a "nailset". I didn't really look that close to see what it was."

"And did you actually at some time see this "nailset" in some different position?"

"Yes."

"And where did you see the "nailset"?"

"It was hammered in, on the edge of the porch, hammered into the wood of the porch."

"Now, I show you this board and ask you whether or not you can recognize it?"

Yes. It is part of my porch floor."

Wall said, "I offer it." Shew replied, "No objection."

"The Judge said, "I understand there is no objection by counsel and so this may be marked as State's exhibit "D"."

Wall requested permission to pass all exhibits at one time, in order to save time.

The Judge agreed, after which Wall asked, "May I pass these exhibits to the jury Your Honor?" The judge nodded, yes.

The jury examined all the exhibits, including the piggy bank. Wall then continued his questioning of Arnfin Thompsen regarding; the piggy bank, the board from the porch, with the "nailset" in it, the hammer, the letter he received on June 19th, all other items exhibited, plus Arnfin's relationship with Harry Solberg.

Judge MacDonald suggested a noon recess. He urged the jury to be careful about talking to anybody during lunch hour. He also emphasized. "Don't listen to any conversation about the case, and don't talk among yourselves about the case."

The Court reconvened at 2:01 and Arnfin Thompsen was back on the witness stand. Wall requested permission to read the letter to the Jury. Before doing so, he indicated that the envelope had two addresses on it. These read: Mr. A Thompsen, Winsted, Connecticut, postmarked June 17, with East Hartland printed underneath the Winsted address. The back of the envelope bore a New Hartford postmark, dated June 18

Wall passed the envelope to the Jury, each member scrutinized it carefully, and passed it back to Wall. He then read the body of the letter, spelling out each misspelled word: I killed your wife, she worked with me at the bank, etc. When Wall had finished reading the letter, he resumed the questioning. He asked about the state of construction of the house in Barkhamsted, and the finding of the body. Then he dropped the bombshell with, "Are you married now?"

"Yes, sir."

"And is your daughter living with you and your wife?"

"Yes."

"And how long have you been married?"

"Ten months."

At that point Shew began the cross-examination.

"What month were you married in, Mr. Thompsen?"

"November.

Shew repeated, "November, almost a year."

Arnfin answered, "Ten months."

"And could you give us the name of the girl you married?"

"Jean."

"Jean what?"

"Jean Griffin."

"And how long had you known that girl?"

"Oh, possibly four years."

Shew again instructed Arnfin to speak up, "If the jury can't hear you, or if I can't hear you—." At that point the Judge told Arnfin to speak up.

"And did she work with you?"

"Yes, sir."

"Whereabouts?"

"At Rural Gas Service, and she helped me with some part time bookkeeping."

"And you say she did extra work for you?"

"Yes."

"Whereabouts?"

"At her home."

"And would you explain a little more about the bookkeeping she did?"

"Well, she'd write up journals and things like that."

"Well, you had no business of your own did you?"

"I had a few part time jobs."

"And how long had she been helping you in your business?"

Wall interrupted: "Your Honor, I object to this line of questioning. I don't see any relevancy to it."

Shew protested. "I am certainly going to—excuse me, Your honor." The Judge consented, "I think that Mr. Shew should have an opportunity to tie it in. I don't think it's entirely out of line." Attorney Shew said, "I was very liberal with Mr. Wall, with leading questions, all along the line, and I made no objection, whatever." Judge MacDonald replied, "He wasn't objecting to that. He was objecting to the irrelevancy."

Attorney Wall agreed. At that point Shew said, "He opened the door." The Judge's reply was." Anyway, I'll permit it, go ahead."

Shew established the length of time that Jean had been working for Arnfin. Then he asked. "And besides working for you, you saw her socially, did you not?"

"It developed as such. Yes, sir."

"When did it develop that way?"

"In 1963."

"And can you tell us a little more about these developments? How did it develop—what do you mean by develop?" Withdraw the first question."What do you mean by developed?

"Well, I saw her socially."

"And when you saw her socially, what did you do?" "Tell us about it."

"Probably have a drink or two, or so."

The Judge again reminded the witness to speak up, and to speak clearly.

Shew requested that the answer be read, then he continued. "When, and how often?"

"Oh, it started out possibly once a week."

"Couldn't it have been more than once a week Mr. Thompsen?"

"Yes, after awhile."

"And did it get more frequent after 1963?"

"No, stayed about the same."

"Was your wife aware of this social situation?"

"No. She was living with her mother at the time."

"Please explain?"

"She ate and slept there."

"When did your wife live with her mother?"

"Right after the baby was born."

"For how long?"

"About eleven months."

"And then where did she live?"

"Barkhamsted."

"Well, during this transfer of her residence, was there any change in the social situation?"

"Not too much, I guess."

"Why did you make the remark that you made, that she was living with her mother?"

"It's a fact, that's all."

Shew requested that the answer be read by the stenographer.

Judge MacDonald said," I am not sure the witness understands that question as to which remark. I am not sure that I would know which remark, you are referring to."

Shew replied with," Well, as I understand it, Your Honor, he said that while the social situation was going on, she lived with her mother. What I am trying to find out from the witness is when his wife changed residence from her mother's residence, to Barkhamsted, what change took place in the social situation, and that's the question."

Arnfin answered," There wasn't much change."

Shew asked, "There wasn't any change? As a matter of fact, Mr. Thompsen sometime previous to her death, you discussed divorce with your wife, did you not?"

"No, I haven't.".

"You hadn't?"

"No sir."

"Did she know about the social situation?"

"I don't believe so."

"Isn't it a fact, Mr. Thompsen, that she found at one time, a piece of evidence that made her aware of this situation?"

"Not that I know of."

"And did she ever discuss it with you?"

"No."

"Do you realize you are under oath, Mr. Thompsen?"

"Yes."

"And the social situation was in existence at the time of your wife's death, was it not?"

"Yes."
"When did it exist before that date?"
"I saw her the night before."
"Where?
"In Westfield."

And did your daughter meet you at the house when you came home, or at the window when you came home that night. I'm talking of the night previous?"

"I didn't get home until probably eleven o'clock."
"So that was one night she wasn't waiting at the window?"
"Not at that hour."

Shew now began his questioning concerning the morning of the murder. Arnfin again told of having toast and coffee in the living room, shaving, getting dressed, going to work, and about the tools on the back porch. Yes, he saw the piggy bank. It was either on the hearth or on the coffee table. He said he didn't go out and check the tools that morning but they were all there the night before."

"Mr. Thompsen, you are a C.P.A., are you not?"
"I passed the exam, I haven't got my certificate yet."

"The questioning now focused on Agnes Thompsen She had been living in the upstairs apartment, and until recently had been employed as a domestic. She had worked for a family in West Hartford, and one in Granby. Arnfin said his Brother would take his mother to West Hartford, and the woman in Granby picked her up.

"Was she doing housework on the day of June 15th?"
"No, she was home."

Shew asked a number of questions concerning Agnes Thompsen's health. Arnfin was quite nervous and was showing evidence of considerable strain. He once again began to mumble, "I don't really know what was the matter with her. It has been described about five different ways to me and I don't think they knew themselves." The Judge was getting a little fed up with Arnfin's low tone of voice and mumbling and once again requested him to speak up. "This is an important trial and your testimony is an important part of it. I can't help but think that you can speak more clearly and more loudly if you try, and I don't think you are trying. Now, speak up please. I know it is disturbing to you, and I sympathize with you, but your testimony has got to be heard. It is no harder for you to speak up clearly than it is to speak indistinctly. Please try from now on to answer the questions so Mr. Shew and all of the jurors can hear them."

Shew interjected, "I'd rather have the jury hear them, and I know they are not hearing them."

Judge MacDonald said, "I can't hear half the words myself."

Upon request the stenographer read back the last answer. The questioning continued about Agnes losing the few jobs and about her failing health. Then Shew got back to the location of the ladder, and Arnfin's actions on the night of the murder. Arnfin repeated, almost word for word, the answers he had previously given to Wall. The condition of the house, Dottie's calls to her mother every day, etc. He, however, was reluctant to admit that Dottie had been afraid of his mother, especially Dottie's objection to his mother coming to live with them.

Arnfin's voice again faded to an inaudible mumble. Judge MacDonald again reprimanded him, "I don't know what we can do about this situation. I don't like to keep speaking to you Mr. Thompsen but it is simply impossible. We don't have a microphone system do we?" Wall replied," Not that I know of Your Honor." The Judge reiterated, "I am going to have to ask you once again to speak up, and just remember. Don't drop your voice. It's very difficult, and not only difficult, but extremely irritating."

The witness was called from the stand and ordered to sit directly in front of the jury box.

Shew asked. "When you lived in back of the Solberg house, your mother lived in her own house didn't she?"

"Yes."

"And did you and your brother sell that house?"

"I did."

"And did you use the money to build your present house, or the house that you lived in, in 1965?"

"Used it to build her apartment upstairs."

"And what did you use to build the rest of the house?"

"Mortgage."

"And so that the money you took from your mother's house, you built the top part, is that right?"

"Yes."

"And the mortgage money built the bottom part, is that right?"

"Yes."

Arnfin said, 'Well, the house she was living in was not doing her any good. Even if she got well enough to get out of the hospital, the authorities wouldn't permit her to go home to live alone. I sold the house, and she got better, and lived in the apartment upstairs."

"And how did you arrange to give your mother the top part of the house she had spent money for? How did you do that?" Whose name was the house in?"

"Mine."

"But I understood you to say that her money was used to build the top part of the house that she lived in?"

"The money I got from selling her house."

"But she had nothing on paper to show, is that correct?"

"True."

The next questions pertained to the building of the house, Mr. Solberg and his son, Harry, helping with the project, Arnfin's habits, his coming home to dinner only two evenings a week, about the baby watching for him out the window, his admission that the baby watched out the window only when he came home to supper, and his "drag out fights" with his wife, concerning his staying out all hours of the night.

Judge MacDonald instructed the jury to retire, but the witness and counsel to remain. In a calm voice the Judge continued, "Mr. Thompsen, this is a very serious problem. Now I don't like to, in the presence of the jury, continue to reprimand you, but you can speak more clearly than you are. You are probably emotionally upset, I realize that, but you keep your hand up beside your face, and you are mumbling. You have a normal voice, and I don't like to keep creating a scene out of it, and I have so refrained. Ordinarily I would have spoken ten times as frequently. I can hear practically nothing of what you say. I don't see how the Court Reporter can get it, and I'm sure the jury can't get it, and I am sure both the lawyers are having difficulty. Is there anything wrong with your speech?"

"It's the way I talk."

"But you drop your voice. It isn't so much the volume, it's the fact that you are mumbling.

You start to answer the question, and you say two or three words, and then you drop your voice. Now, I know it's embarrassing to you. It's embarrassing to me, and I don't want to hold you in contempt for failing to answer questions, but it's gotten to the point now where it's becoming a very acute situation. This is a murder trial. A man's life is at stake. You are a witness. You were called by the State, and you have simply got to do something about it. You have got to keep your voice up, and speak up, and answer questions. The reason, I think, that you can control it, is that it is not so much the volume, it's the fact that you mumble.

Now, is there anything that you—any explanation that you want to make to me about this aside from the fact that I assume that you are upset?"

Arnfin replied:" I have been talking this way all my whole life. I don't know."

The Judge said: "I don't see how you can hold a job down if that's the way you talk all the time. I want you during this recess—I want you to sort of pull yourself together, and I want you to get out here determined to speak slowly and distinctly. Now, I know you can do better than you are doing. If either of you have any suggestions, I am sorry for anybody who is in the position Mr. Thompsen is in, but we have got to get a record of this trial, and it is impossible."

At 3:35 the court was reconvened. The judge instructed Mr. Shew to continue with the questioning. With Arfin back on the stand, the questions concerned the attire and appearance of Agnes Thompsen, the pools of blood, the smears on the drapes, ironing board, doors and the telephone, and the little conversation he had with his mother. With that Shew said, "That's all."

Wall then started his redirect examination of Arnfin Thompsen.

"Was there any occasion Mr. Thompsen for anyone moving the hammer, or either of the hammers, or any their tools, or the ladder between Sunday and Tuesday?"

"No."

"And was there any reason for you to believe that there would be any change in the position of any of these articles in that period of time?"

"No."

"And when you first went upstairs to see your mother, did you then know that your wife had been murdered?"

"No."

"And did you have any knowledge of anything other than the pool of blood at that time?"

"No.

"And did you make any inquiry of your mother, relating to that pool of blood at that time."

"No."

"And did you talk to your mother about what had happened?"

"When I brought the baby up."

"And what did you say to her then?"

"I told her Dottie was dead and to please take care of the baby, you know."

"And did you have any conversation with your mother at that time, or did you then go right out?"

"I went right out."

Wall said, "I have no further questions, and Shew nodded, "That's all."

The Judge excused Arnfin with the understanding that he would be notified if it was necessary to bring him back.

9

Sitting in the kitchen of an old farm house, set back from the road, on two hundred acres of uncultivated land, Margaret Campbell said, to her friend Kay Prowse, "I'm glad you could get away for a week. It's nice to have you here even for a short visit. We're supposed to be safe now that Harry is in jail, but I'm still nervous at night listening for every sound. When a fox starts his mating call in the middle of the night, it sounds like a woman screaming."

"Oh well," Kay sighed, "Everything has its good, and its bad. The city is vibrant, exciting, alive, with lots of things to do. We get dressed up for the opera, concerts and dances and people are out on the streets at all hours of the night. But, there is no privacy, we live in apartments. Out here it is quiet, almost silent, the air smells sweet from the pine trees, the well water is better than anything you can buy in bottles, but there is nothing to do. Nowhere to go, unless you drive twenty eight miles to Hartford. It is a long, dark, drive back." Kay poured herself another cup of tea, and said, "I remember something funny about this town. I think it's the name."

Margaret laughed, "Satan's Kingdom. It is a funny name for such a quiet place, but that's not as bad as Louse Hill, the other section of town. There is a beautiful estate up there."

Kay put everything away. When the place was tidy, she said, "Let's go in to the city. We can stop off at Lord and Taylor in West Hartford and look at the new fall fashions, I want to buy a new fur hat. There's nothing to keep us home. This is a farm, without crops, not even a farmer, or a dog to feed."

Down the country road to Rte. 44 and all the way to Hartford, the conversation never deviated from the murder, or the trial. Margaret said, "I bet Arnfin Thompsen is glad the questioning is over for awhile, he really looked scared. It must be awful to sit there with everybody looking at you. while you are answering those questions about Dorothy, and looking at those gruesome pictures. The defense lawyer, the prosecuting attorney and the judge all telling him to speak up. Those lawyers act like they hate each other."

"Do they?," Kay asked, "I wonder how much Dorothy knew about her husband's affair with Jean. How did Jean feel about taking a man away from his family? How could Arnfin justify his actions? How could he sell his mother's house without her knowing about it? He must have had her sign a quit claim deed. And what about the piggy bank?"

Margaret said, "I suppose there will be some answers to the mystery. Reading about this murder, and being at the trial, makes me feel guilty. It makes me feel almost as bad as Jean. Being in love with a married man is awkward, difficult, and painful not to mention the impropriety of it. Always being in the background, taking the crumbs of love, telling yourself his wife and children have everything money can buy. They don't come up here. They have their boat on Long Island Sound. He takes the children to horse shows, and he takes her to the opera and concerts, and any other event she wants to see. I don't think I'm taking anything away from them."

Kay patted her on the arm and said, "Don't be too hard on yourself, the only one hurting is you. You're too young to be up in the woods alone, just waiting for him to visit. Especially this year with the stress of the murder." Margaret sighed. "I spent some time in London, don't you remember? He made arrangements for me to stay at the company's flat on Tottingham Court Road, and he visited as often as he could. I saw all the new plays, and some of the old ones including 'The Mouse Trap'. Believe it or not, it's still running after thirty years. Just think, Agatha Christie gave the rights to that play to her nephew, so now he's the one collecting the royalties."

Kay said," My situation is different. Charlie isn't married, and has never been married. His mother won't do anything for herself. He has to drive her everywhere. Even on Sunday mornings he has to get up early to take her to church. Then go back and pick her up. He even takes her for drives in the afternoon, and he feels guilty if he stays out at night. He claims he can't get married as long as his mother is still alive. She knows about us, but isn't happy over the situation. I have to be content with things as they are, and take each day as it comes."

They went shopping at the Lord and Taylor department store in West Hartford, then to Hartford for lunch at the Bond Hotel dining room. They walked around window shopping for an hour, then over to Witkower's book store, on Asylum Street. By the time they returned to the parking lot it was dusk. The drive back to the country was pleasant due to most of the traffic traveling east, towards the city.

When they returned home, Margaret left the headlights on until Kay opened the front door and turned the house lights on. Margaret walked into the kitchen and saw Kay standing there looking at the table. "Didn't we clean up this place before we went out?" Margaret was just as surprised. "There wasn't a speck on that table when we went out. How did that get there? It looks like soup, or gravy. How can that be?"

Kay said, "The doors were locked, how could anybody get in? Let's look around and see if anything is missing." In the dining room every piece of silver was in place, even the small serving dishes, that could easily be carried away. In the den the silver candlesticks were on the mantle. Nothing was disturbed upstairs. The women wondered why someone would go into a person's house, eat something, lie on the sofa, and then leave.

Margaret said, "Let's look in the attic and closets."

Kay didn't agree. She said, "Let's call somebody, but who? The Trooper will ask lots of questions. Do you think the little store is still open?" Margaret dialed the store number, the clerk answered the phone immediately, and said he was just closing. When he listened to the story, he told the women.

"That's nothing unusual. Someone got into a house in Canton Center last week, ate and slept, and nothing was stolen. It apparently was some homeless person walking around, looking for a place to have a nap." He asked. "How could he get in? Were all the doors locked?, Did you check the bulkhead? Don't worry, whoever it was is way up the road by now."

She thanked him, and then they went down to check the bulkhead., and found it wasn't bolted. They assumed that's how the intruder got in. That evening they shared the same bedroom, but couldn't sleep. They were both wondering if the correct person was in jail.

10

The next person to take the stand was Mr. Robert Stadler. Called by Wall as a witness for the State, and was duly sworn.

The direct examination by Wall began with the first question. "You live on Rte. 179, do you Mr. Stadler?"

"Yes."

"And directly across from Arnfin and Dorothy Thompson's home. And how long have you lived at that location?"

"A year and a half."

"And had you moved there rather recently when this incident occurred in June of 1965?"

"It was a year and a half."

"Was it a year and a half before June of 1965, that you moved there?"

"No, I moved there in April of 1965".

"However you are quite well acquainted with the neighborhood because your father lives next door?"

"Yes."

"And he had lived there sometime previous, had he?"

"Yes."

"And approximately how far down Rte. 179 does your father live from your house?"

"Three hundred yards."

"And approximately how far away is the Arnfin Thompsen residence from your home?"

"Fifty yards."

"And would you say almost directly across the street?"

"Almost, yes."

"And you have how many children?"

"Two."

"And how old are they?"

"Six and four."

"And between April and June of 1965 had your younger child become acquainted with Christa, the child of the Thompsens?"

"Yes."

"And they played together?"

"Yes."

"And in your yard, and in Thompsen's yard also?"

"Yes, but I think mostly in Thompsen's yard."

"And on the 15$^{th.}$, of June, were you working?"

"Yes, In Avon."

"And what was the name of the concern with which you are connected?"

"John Swift Chemical."

Wall asked several routine questions including; what time of the day Mr. Stadler finished work, if he went directly home, how long it took to drive home, and if he noticed anything out of the ordinary about Thompsen's place, or in the neighborhood, and what he did when he got home.

He said, "I read the paper until it's time to sit down to eat, about six."

"And as you were seated at dinner, did something occur?"

"Yes, that's when Mr. Thompsen came over."

Then Wall asked about finding the body, and, about Christa being missing. He also asked about Arnfin's appearance, waiting for the State Trooper to arrive, seeing Dorothy dead in the back yard, and the condition of the house. He also touched on the subject of the big pool of blood on the kitchen floor, and the path of blood, as if something had been dragged across the kitchen floor, through the dining room across to the porch.

"Will you please describe to His Honor and the jury, the condition of the kitchen floor as far as the blood is concerned, that you observed when you first looked into the kitchen?"

Mr. Stadler was articulate. He again described the kitchen, the blood, the forks, and the electrical cord. Every chilling detail was becoming familiar. They listened. Mr. Stadler didn't have to be told to "speak up." He told of covering the body with the red blanket that Arnfin had given him, and he identified the State's Exhibit "D", the photographs of the board on the porch, with the cord attached to what appeared to be a "nailset".

He explained that when Officer Soliani arrived he went with him to the scene of the murder. He lifted the red blanket and looked at the body. Up to this time Mr. Sadler had not seen Christa, so the two men went back into the house. The officer said, "Everybody out." Mr. Thompsen said, "The baby is upstairs with her grandmother." Officer Soliani went upstairs and escorted Agnes and Christa down, with Christa still in her grandmother's arms.

Shew, the defense attorney, asked, "Did the Mother make any remark?"

"Yes," she said to me, "Is she dead yet?"

On Re-direct, Wall asked, "Where was Christa during all this time."

"I cannot say, because up to this time I had not seen her."

On re-cross, Shew asked, "Did you say the grandmother, Agnes, said, is she dead yet?"

"Yes, she volunteered that information, right out of the blue sky."

The third prosecution witness identified himself as, Lieutenant Cleveland Fuessenich of the Connecticut State Police.

Direct examination by Wall began with. "You are a member of the State Police, are you, sir.?"

"Yes, sir."

"And you have been for how many years?"

"Nineteen and a half."

"And presently, what are your duties?"

"I am Commanding Officer of the Canaan Barracks."

Wall asked about the area covered by the Canaan Barracks.

The lieutenant told him, "All of North West Connecticut, fourteen towns in all."

Wall then asked, "In connection with your duties with the State Police on June 15, 1965 specifically, you were called to the home of Arnfin Thompsen?"

"Yes, sir."

"And what was the occasion of your being called there?"

"It was in connection of the death of Dorothy Thompsen."

"And how did you receive word?"

"Over the Police telephone. It was 6:40 P M, and I arrived at the Thompsen house about 7:17 P.M. I came in from Thomaston."

"Trooper Soliani, Arnfin Thompsen, Sergeant Joseph Riley, Agnes Thompsen, Christa Thompsen, and several other people I didn't know."

"And did you have occasion, then, to observe the condition of the house and look it over and examine it closely?"

"Yes. sir."

"During the time you were there, did you have photographs taken, that is under your direction?"

"The photographs were taken from about 7:30 to 8:30 or 9:00."

Wall was now ready for the shocking dramatics. Knowing that the jury was composed of "Country Folk", not accustomed to being involved with murders in any fashion, he passed the first of fifteen photos to the defense table, and then to the jury box. He knew what the reaction would be. They had seen the pictures before, but that didn't lessen the shock, and the feeling of helplessness, that some sadistic person could come into your home, and so brutality murder you. The most frightening pictures naturally were of the mutilated body. The jurors glances lingered, as though they couldn't believe what they were seeing. They wiped their eyes, and tried to compose themselves. Some of the jurors began to shake from fright.

Wall said, "There are a few more exhibits coming, Your Honor, but they would take a little time I—"

The Judge interrupted. "I wonder if any of the jurors have problems with transportation that requires leaving promptly at five?, or do any of you have commitments immediately at five o'clock? If so, I'll try to adjourn a little bit before five. Is this a good stopping point?"

Wall replied, "Very Good."

The Judge then said, "Court recessed until ten a.m. tomorrow."

The jurors were instructed by the judge, not to discuss the case with anyone, not to listen to anything on the radio concerning the case, and not to read anything about the case in the news papers.

Shew did not go directly to his office after court. He walked across to the jail to talk to Harry. However, it was a waste of time. Harry was sulky. He said, "Good day Harry, don't you think?" Harry replied, "Why did you have to bring out all that fringing dirt about Arnfin?" Shew pretended he didn't hear Harry, and said, "Goodbye. Harry." As he walked to his car he remembered what Major Rome said about Arnfin, "Knowing her condition, he moved her in upstairs and then he never came home. He also knew she was resentful because he sold her house, and yet he left her with Dottie, without even a door that Dottie could lock between them." "Could Rome, be right on this one?"

The next morning the accused and counsel were present in the Courtroom at which time the Deputy Sheriff took the roll call. The Judge asked, "And are all the Jurors who are supposed to be here, present"

Cleveland Fuessenich, having been previously sworn, was then recalled to the stand.

Wall said, "I believe that, at the close of the session yesterday, there were certain exhibits that were being made "full exhibits," that had been exhibits for identification only." The Judge said, "I think the last one, exhibit "J", was made a "full exhibit".", to which Wall agreed.

The Judge asked, "And have we gone through "Z" as full Exhibits?"

Wall asked the lieutenant to point out certain items which show in the photographs, which are in evidence, "Beginning with the photographs of the kitchen, please point out any articles that appear on the floor." Lieutenant Fuessenich named the blood and many of the other items. Then he said, "Here are footprints of a man's shoe." Shew sprang to his feet, "I object to that Your Honor and move, that go out."

"Sustained, the characterization of the footprints should go out." Shew was so angry he couldn't help himself, he shouted, "I think the jury should absolutely disregard that. The lieutenant knows better than to say it!"

Wall, in a thunderous, angry tone said, "I think the lieutenant can" Shew, angry as hell, replied in an harsh tone, "I don't care whether you do or don't. I think he has enough experience to know better than that." The Judge instructed the jurors to disregard the characterization, to simply note that there were footprints visible. The lieutenant unruffled by the disturbance between the lawyers, continued his description of the kitchen, and all the bloody details. "Blood everywhere from the refrigerator to the telephone." Wall walked to the table and picked up the rock. The judge noticed that Wall was straining under the weight, and asked, "Would you like somebody to carry it for you?"

"I think so, your Honor."

Shew said, "I don't think it's that heavy." "Well, maybe you'll carry it," replied Wall. Shew carried the rock around the room, then in a sarcastic tone, "If you have to move it again Mr. Wall, I'll gladly do it for you. I wouldn't want you to hurt yourself." The lieutenant pointed out the bloodstain on the rock. Wall said, "I'll show it to the jurors later." Shew replied once again in a sarcastic tone, "I'll hold it for you."

Wall got back to the photographs, and Lieutenant Fuessenich identified the pieces of Dorothy's clothing, the ladder, and the "nailset" with the cord attached. He was now finished with the photographs, and started the questioning about the police investigation. "Were any items of clothing taken to be examined?

"Yes, sir, Arnfin Thompsen's shoes were taken to be examined for blood, plus some of Agnes Thompsen's clothing"

Wall asked, "The four-pound hammer, was that located on the night of the fifteenth?"

"No, sir it was not, it was located the following day, in the bushes, to the southeast of the porch, about eighty feet from the porch."

Fortunately for the jurors, Lieutenant Fuessenich remained alert and professional as he repeated the information about the items found in the house: the hammer, the search of the area where the hammer was located, and everything about the outside.

Wall asked, "During the evening were you with Agnes Thompsen at any time."

"Yes, Sir. I talked with her briefly as she was leaving the house to go to the Connecticut Valley Hospital in Middletown."

"What was her condition at the time?"

"I met her at the foot of the stairs as she came down. We spoke briefly, she seemed composed, and was dressed neatly. There was nothing unusual about her that I noticed." "Composed?, Nothing unusual? Then why was she being taken to the mental hospital?" At that point Wall suggested, a break for lunch.

Spectators, reporters, and the lawyers, all hurried to the small restaurants nearby. The topics of conversation among the reporters were: the rock, the sarcasm of the lawyers, and the constant bickering, with each side fighting to win. One man said, "Wall struggled with the nineteen-pound rock, and Shew carried it around the room. Do you think Agnes could lift it?"

After lunch Shew began his Cross-examination. He asked Lieutenant Fuessenich to name the officers who were on the scene when he arrived.

"Don't remember everybody's name, Sir, there were Trooper Soliani, Sergeant Riley, Detective Rebillard and Trooper Pennington, either were there or came shortly after."

"Were you in charge of the investigation?"

"I was under the direct supervision of my field Captain, Thomas O'Brien who happened to be at the scene."

"Was little Christa there when you arrived?, or was she across the street?

I am not sure, I didn't see her at all that night."

The next questions were, did he inspect Christa's bed?, or bedroom?, did he inspect Agnes Thompsen's apartment?, did any officer inspect it that night?, and if it had been inspected, would he have known about it?"

"I might not have known, they were pretty busy there. It is possible that somebody did.

Yes, Sir, it's possible."

"When they did search Agnes's apartment, did they take any articles for examination?"

There were many things taken that day, and three weeks after that. They were taken to Hartford where a list was made, and that list is in Court today."

Shew asked to see the list.

Wall said, "I have something here, Your Honor," He handed the list to the lieutenant, who upon examination agreed it refreshed his memory, however, it was not a complete list, and some of the things were picked up under his supervision and some were not.

The Judge agreed, "We will accept what the lieutenant knows, from his own knowledge."

Shew said, "That's all I want, Your Honor."

The Judge said, "As long as it is simply refreshing your recollection, as to something else that you yourself know about, of your own knowledge, and that you recall, proceed down the list."

The lieutenant replied, "There were two white shoe laces found in the driveway."

"Can you describe the white shoe laces? Was there anything that characterized them that will help us out on this at all?"

"Now, as I remember it, they were short laces, more or less a child's size."

"And as far as you know, you attached no significance to those?"

"All right—let's have the next one please."

"Wall said, "I object to this—the next one, Your Honor?"

"Shew asked, "Is there another one?"

At this point the Judge was getting fed up with the juvenile behavior of the two lawyers with their petty bickering, and was beginning to lose his patience, "The next item on the list, which refreshes your recollection, to the extent that you that you recall it having been removed at the time you were there, or under your supervision."

The lieutenant answered, "Arnfin Thompsen's shoes."

"What did you do with those—Arnfin Thompsen's shoes?"

"They were checked for blood on the soles."

After a short recess the Cross Examination of Lieutenant Fuessenich resumed. More questions were asked about Arnfin's shoes, the hair found in Dorothy's hand, if the blood on the floors were dried, how large a mass of blood was on the kitchen floor, about the photographs, and how long would it take someone to commit this crime.

After lunch, Dr. Owen Murphy arrived, and the lieutenant's testimony was interrupted to permit the doctor to testify. The doctor answered the questions quickly and crisply. His answers to his qualifications included: Practicing physician and surgeon since 1921 in Hartford and Simsbury, Officer on the Board of Health, Coroner and Medical Examiner. He stated he was called to the Thompsen house about seven o'clock in the evening, at which time there were several people, other than the state troopers, standing around.

Doctor Murphy read from his report, and checked his notes.

The jury and spectators wiped their eyes, as they listened again to the chilling account of the brutal and horrific murder. The doctor was asked to relate to the judge and the jury, what findings he made upon arriving at the scene.

He described in detail every step from his first look at the body to the autopsy, from what Dorothy was wearing, to the state of mutilation. He was asked about Agnes Thompsen. His testimony was almost verbatim to that given at the inquest. Wall, was getting furious as he jumped to his feet, "I protest!, Your Honor. Dr. Murphy is going too far a field." Shew skillfully turned the questioning back to the night of the murder, "What was the mental condition of Agnes?"

"I think she was in a grandiose state of mind. She was glad to see me."

"And had you seen her before?"

"I had seen her about three years before, in her home in East Hartland when I was called to examine her. We sent her to the Hartford Hospital to the Psychiatric department, and from there they transferred her to the State Hospital in Middletown."

"And what was she doing three years ago?"

"At that time she had a lot of neurothentic ideas. She had a large bottle of medicine she got from some doctor down in Brooklyn, and she seemed to be quite intelligent along the use of herbs and all that, and then suddenly she would say, "Do you hear that?" Well, I'd go along with her and say, "Yes, I do." And she'd say, "No one hears that but me." One day she said, "You know, last night I killed the devil with a butcher knife."

"And you say she was in a joyful mood?"

"Yes"

Wall objected. Your Honor, "It's all been stated, but I don't see any point in belaboring it. It's not part of the direct examination, that I can see."

The Judge agreed, "Well, just the doctor's observations at the time he arrived at the scene, that would cover it."

Shew again asked about the physical condition of Agnes, and the Doctor's qualifying, as to her mental condition. Dr. Murphy listed his qualifications including: Columbia, two years at the Rhode Island Hospital psychiatric department, and under MacDonald Farren at

Harvard. Although he didn't like the work and didn't pursue it, 'I found psychiatry interesting, but depressing." The doctor reiterated everything that happened from the time he arrived on the scene.

Then Shew asked, "Doctor, in your opinion, is Agnes Thompsen strong enough to lift up the body of the deceased?"

"Yes."

"Was she strong enough to lift up the rock?

"I don't know anything about a rock."

"Well, there is a rock here, let me withdraw that question. Would you know whether or not this is the rock you saw lying beside the body—was it this rock or something similar to that?

"It could be similar to it."

"It could be similar to it, and Lieutenant Fuessenich has testified that the rock weighs nineteen pounds."

"Yes."

"She could lift it all right, she was an outdoor woman."

"Would it be in your opinion, doctor, that having a woman like Agnes Thompsen locked in a house with the decease, would it, in your opinion create a dangerous situation?"

Wall objected, "None of this is part of the direct, Your Honor."

There were more questions about items found at the murder scene. Then Shew said, "I think that's all, Doctor, thank you."

Wall then said, "No further questions, Your Honor." The Judge added, "That's all, Dr. Murphy, Thank you."

The doctor was dismissed, and Lieutenant Fuessenich returned to the stand. He answered the same questions. About the rock, the clothes in the washer and dryer, the photographs, and the blood on the kitchen floor. After a brief redirect, Lieutenant Fuessenich was excused.

11

Another weekend ahead. It was a relief for jurors as well as the spectators to get a break from the constant discussions of the gruesome details.

Kay said, "I'm so excited, I can't wait to get all the details. I don't know of any other case where three people have been suspect."

Margaret gladly related all the dirt, and gory details of the court proceedings of the previous week.

After breakfast, they drove to the Hayes' store to buy meat. A small group of women were waiting in the corner next to the Post Office for the mail truck, which usually arrived at about ten o'clock. The women nodded a polite good morning to Margaret and Kay, then continued their conversation. One said to the others in a hushed voice, "City folk. They move out here, and the next thing you know, they want indoor plumbing. No wonder our taxes went up to twenty-three dollars this year. That's a lot of taxes for way out here in the country." Her friend agreed.

As a farmer delivered a bushel of apples from an orchard in Simsbury, one of the women helped herself to one, took a bite, then held it up to show Mr. Hayes that she intended to pay for it. They continued gossiping, "Doctor Murphy's testimony sure pointed a finger at Agnes." Another thought Arnfin did it, "He was married, but screwing another woman."

Another said, "No, Harry did it. He has a bad temper problem, ask anyone who knows him."

The mail truck finally arrived and, and everyone dispersed to get their mail. Margaret and Kay drove straight back to the house with the food. When everything was put away, they took a ride to Torrington to view the foliage.

Kay said, "I can't help thinking about Dorothy's mother and father, sitting there in Court, day after day, listening to the gruesome details of their daughter's murder."

Margaret agreed, "Yes, and it must be hard on Harry's family, also. I understand his wife is expecting."

Kay noticed that her friend seemed preoccupied. She asked her, "Is the trial getting to you? Do you think it wise to go up there every day?"

Margaret sighed, "No, it's not going up and listening to the testimony every day, it's John, he hasn't been up for three weeks. He calls every day, or so, and he told me he has to spend more time with the children these days. She laughed, "He'll have to go on a business trip soon"

Kay suggested that they start for home. Then she said, "I haven't seen Charlie much either. He wishes his mother would go to Boston for a few weeks. No such luck."

The next witness was Mrs. Carole Stadler. Wall began his Direct Examination. Mrs. Stadler was well-organized; she responded precisely, and quickly to every question. She even spelled her last name for the court stenographer. She acknowledged that she's a housewife, lives almost across the road from the Thompsens, has two children age, four, and six, and that, she knew Christa, Thompsen's baby. She said the children played together, usually at Thompsen's house or yard, and that they played together on the day Dorothy was murdered.

Her son, Randy went over to play with Christa from 9:30 to 11:45, he then came home for a few minutes before going to my mother-in-law's, Dr. Stadler's house. She worked outside planting, and cleaning out flower beds until 1:05. At 1:25 she walked to Dr. Stadler's house. From 1:30 to 2:30 she was inside the house, then at 2:30 she walked back to her own place to start preparing dinner. At 2:45 she walked back to Dr. Stadler's house to use the vegetable grinder. From 2:45 until 3:00 she was inside Dr. Stadler's house, and at 3:00 she went back home, where she worked outside until her husband came home.

Wall went over the timing, from 9:30 in the morning until 5:00 when her husband came home.

"And you had the Arnfin Thompsen property in your view?"

"Yes."

"And since you had the Thompsen property in view, you could have seen anyone going in, or coming out? And during that time, you did not observe anyone at any time?"

"No"

Do you know Arnfin Thompsen?

"Yes."

"And you knew other members of the family?"

"Yes."

"Did you know the defendant, Solberg?"

"Not personally."

"Did you know who he was?"

"Yes."

Wall asked many more questions about the Solberg family. She answered, "The Solberg family lives about two miles north, and in the country, two miles is no distance at all, so she knew of the family."

Harry Solberg looked up occasionally from the table, where he was sitting next to Shew. He certainly didn't look like a suspect in a murder trial. He more closely resembled a school boy in class.

"On that particular evening, did something occur in your home?"

"Yes."

Wall then questioned Mrs. Stadler about the night of the murder. She told of Arnfin coming over—he was in a state of shock—he said, "Dottie's dead in the back yard, and I can't find the baby." Step by step, she accounted for every minute and every detail, from the time they went across to the Thompsen house, until the State Trooper asked everyone to leave. Then Wall asked about Christa who was upstairs with her grandmother. Mrs. Stadler replied, "The officer asked me to go upstairs and get her and I said no, so he went up and knocked on the door, and then came down with the little girl."

"And did you have any conversation with Christa as she came down?"

"Well, Christa did say something, yes,"

"And what did Christa say?"

She said, "She killed. She killed."

"And did you know from familiarity with her manner of speech, what she intended to convey?"

"Objection, she cannot know what was in the child's mind."

"Sustained, she can only testify as to what she heard."

Wall asked, "Did Christa talk as an adult?"

"No. She spoke clearly, but not in sentences."

Then questioning about Christa's understanding. "Would she know the difference between a passive voice and an active voice? What did Christa mean by, 'she killed, she killed. Did she mean that Dorothy was killed, or that Agnes had killed Dorothy? Would a two year old child know what the word killed meant?"

Mrs. Stadler said, "Christa did not want to leave her grandmother, she hung on to her. She didn't want to go with Mrs. Stadler but, after a few minutes she did go, and stayed there until her aunt came for her."

Shew began his Cross Examination of Mrs. Stadler by asking almost the same questions; about Christa's speech, "If she talked like an adult?, Why didn't she want to leave her grandmother?, and how long was she with Mrs. Stadler.?"

"The deceased girl, Dottie, have you ever talked with her about Christa's relationship with her grandmother?

"I may have."

"You don't remember particularly?"

"No."

"Now Mr. Wall asked you if you went upstairs to get Christa, Correct?"

"Right."

"And you stated I believe, that one of the police officers asked you to go up and get her, is that correct?"

"Yes."

And I believe you answered, no you wouldn't go up?"

"Yes."

"And why wouldn't you go up?"

"Well, I knew Mrs. Thompsen wasn't mentally balanced and I certainly didn't want to try to take the baby from her."

Shew continued the questions about Mrs. Stadler not wanting to go upstairs; about Dorothy's feelings towards her mother-in-law, and if Dorothy was afraid of her?

Mrs. Stadler said, "Well, the first time she came over for coffee, after we moved there, she told me her mother-in-law lived upstairs, and that she was mentally ill. She also told me that the mother-in-law had been in the Middletown Mental Hospital. I asked her if she was afraid to have her living upstairs and she said, "I am, I'm petrified."

Shew continued his Cross Examination. More questions about Dorothy and her mother-in-law. About the time when Dorothy said she was afraid about Christa being well cared for on the afternoon of the murder.

Mrs. Stadler testified that the baby wasn't hungry, and that her pants were dry. She then had to describe the training pants a two year old wears, and how long a time a child that age could go without wetting. Shew thanked Mrs. Stadler, and said that was all.

Wall started his redirect. He asked Mrs. Stadler if she knew the accused, Harry Solberg. What kind of car was he driving during June of 1965?, if she remembered the age of the car, and if she saw Harry's car at Thompsen's house that day. All of which were answered, "No."

Wall began his direct examination, of the next witness, Doctor Lincoln Opper. He asked the Doctor if he was a physician, and if he had a specialty. The answer to both questions was, "Yes." He then asked the doctor to state his educational background, to the judge and jury.

The doctor listed his qualifications: Graduated from Yale University, received his M.D. from the University of Munich, Germany, returned to Yale New Haven Hospital for four years residency, then assistant Professor of biochemistry at the University of Arkansas, and subsequently, was pathologist for the William W. Backus Hospital in Norwich, Connecticut and the Norwich State Hospital. "Then, in 1946"—.Shew interrupted, "You don't need to qualify him as far as I am concerned. I'll agree to his qualifications."

Wall said," Suits me, also. I think the Jury is interested in the background of Dr. Opper, and we are nearly through."

"Then you were on the staff of at least one hospital in June of 1965?"

"Right."

Dr. Opper answered nine more questions about his qualifications, before the gruesome details of the autopsy began, with direct examination by Wall.

"And will you please state to His Honor and to the Jury what you observed in connection with—or, first of all your procedures in the performance of the autopsy, and then your observations, then your conclusions. First, as to the procedures."

"Well, in attendance at the autopsy were two officers of the State Police Department, namely, Sergeant Chapman and Officer Yudnick of the Canaan State Police Barracks. The usual procedure in such an autopsy is the external examination of the body. This is prior to the making of any incisions, Would you have me tell you what I found?"

"Yes, would you please tell what you observed from the external observations?"

"Well, it was evident, almost at once that the wounds were the result of several different types of instruments. Firstly, there was a torn electrical cord tightly wound around the neck and knotted on the right lateral aspect of the neck just below the jaw bone."

The Doctor was on the stand almost the entire day. He described every detail of the autopsy, every bruise and wound, every type of instrument used, he identified the wounds and condition of the body from the photographs. His testimony was almost verbatim with that of

Doctor Murphy. He also agreed that the murder must have been committed about noon, because the food had not as yet been digested.

The next witness was William L. Flagg, with direct examination by Wall.

Mr. Flagg testified that has been employed by the Metropolitan Water bureau for sixteen years that he lives in the village of East Hartland, Connecticut, and he knows Arnfin Thompsen, and the Thompsen family in general. He didn't know Harry Solberg. He moved out of town before Harry had really grown up, however, he did know the other members of the Solberg family.

On June 15, 1965, about 1:30, or 1:45 in the afternoon, he drove by Arnfin Thompsen's house, at which time he noticed that a shiny, 1959 Ford pulled up there as he heading south. "I noticed this car pull up and stop. As I drove by, I looked in the rear view mirror and noticed the driver getting out, and walking around to the front, then I lost contact with him."

"Will you relate to His Honor and the Jury your experience with automobiles—just about how much you have handled them and what?"

"Well, I have dealt in used cars, and primarily worked on old cars, restoring them and reselling them.

"And by reason of that experience are you any more conversant than the ordinary individual with the appearance of automobiles?"

"I-would certainly say I was, yes."

Shew began his cross examination of this witness.

"Mr. Flagg, you are very definite about the kind of car, aren't you?"

"Yes, I am."

The questions continued about the car. Then he asked, "How long had you known Mrs. Thompsen?"

"I had known Mrs. Thompsen probably since 1955"

"Did you ever keep company with her?"

"Yes, I had been out with her."

"How many times?"

"Probably three or four."

"And when did this take place?"

"Back in 1955."

"And you had never stopped in to see her in her home?"

"No, I hadn't."

"And you knew she lived there?"

"Yes that's right, because my wife had stopped in to see her. My wife used to work with her at the bank in New Hartford."

"And, the man you saw get out of this car, you would not have any idea of whether or not that is the gentleman sitting beside me, to my left, would you?"

"Not positively."

And what do you mean, "Not positively? You don't know, do you?"

"No, I don't," that's why I said, not positively, that's what I mean."

"Mr. Flagg was then excused.

12

The next witness sworn in, Mr. Frederick P. Richards, presented a welcome respite from the bizarre. He is the jeweler who sold Harry Solberg the engagement and wedding ring. He explained that he lived in Winsted, Connecticut since 1929, and his store is located at 572 Main Street, Winsted. He has been in business at the same location since 1945, selling, silverware, glassware, china and all kinds of jewelry.

Wall asked, "Does that also include watches, rings and other articles of personal adornment?"

"Yes."

"Do you know this young man, Harry Solberg, here?"

"Very little, I know who he is."

"Did he ever come to your establishment that you know of?"

"Yes he did."

"And when was it that he came to your establishment?"

"Well, I don't remember the exact date right now, but I have it on slips of paper, sales slips."

"I show you this slip and I ask you whether you can recognize that as the sales slip to which you refer as being applicable to Harry Solberg?"

"Yes it is, the date is on it, 17, of June 1965."

"The 17, of June 1965. Having recollected the date of this visit, would you please state to His Honor and the Jury just what occurred when Mr. Solberg came into your place of business that day?"

"He came in to purchase an engagement ring and a wedding, ring, which he did. The price is on here. He made arrangements to pay for it by time payments. At that time I asked him if he was 21 years old and he said he wasn't. I said, "You will have to have your mother or father sign for you." He said he would do it, which he did. He didn't take the ring at that time, he returned later to get it.

"And did he make a payment on that day to you?"

"No, I guess he didn't. He agreed to pay ten dollars a week. He paid twenty-five dollars when he first took the ring."

"He did pay you twenty-five dollars?"

"The first payment was twenty-five dollars and he agreed to pay ten dollars a week after that."

Wall handed Mr. Richards the anonymous letter saying, "I ask you whether that date is the same date as the one on which he came to make this payment to you?"

"Yes, the date on the envelope is June 17, It don't say 1965, but it's June 17.

"I call your attention to the upper flap showing there, New Hartford post mark, and what is the date on that?

"June 18, 1965"

Wall then concluded his questioning of this witness. Shew had no questions, the witness was, therefore, excused.

Mr. Robert Slattery was the next witness. He stated that he lived in Northampton, Massachusetts, and was employed at the East Hartford Division of Pratt & Whitney Aircraft, as a personnel investigator. He said he first met Harry Solberg when he applied for work there in February 1955. Wall asked, "In the course of your interviewing him, did he write anything that you observed as unusual?"

"Yes, sir."

"When you observed him, what did he write?

"His signature."

"And were there other items that you saw him write besides his signature?"

"I am not sure of that, sir."

"I show you this paper, and I ask you to examine it carefully, so that you may give an answer relating to the handwriting. Is any portion of it, in your handwriting?"

"Yes, sir."

"And whose is the other portion?, that is not your handwriting?"

"Mr. Solberg."

"And can you distinguish and point out, what is Mr. Solberg's writing on this paper and what is your writing?"

"Yes, sir."

Wall offered the Judge the sample of Solberg's handwriting.

Shew objected, "It hasn't been established." Then he asked, "Did you see Mr. Solberg write this so-called writing?"

"No, Sir."

The attorneys argued and objected about the signature. Now the preliminary examination of Mr. Slattery began. Shew asked all the same questions, about the signature and handwriting. Were people allowed to take an application blank home, or outside the building to fill it out, and did they sign it in the presence of a personnel officer. More objections.

With all the evidence building against him, Harry sat in his regular place making notes on a pad, not paying any particular attention to what was going on around him. Perhaps he was thinking about his wife, Sharon, who was in St. Francis Hospital, where she had given birth to a baby girl, and he wasn't allowed to visit either Sharon, or the baby.

The questions continued about the signature, the employment questionnaire and application.

Both Attorneys said, "No further questions."

Detective Frederick Keller was the next witness. He testified that he resided in Lakeville, has been with the Connecticut Police Department for over twelve Years, and that he had been assigned to investigate the handwriting of the accused Harry Solberg. On Friday, March 11, 1966 he went to the Pratt & Whitney, Corp., in East Hartford, to have Harry write a paragraph, the context of which had been prepared by the handwriting and fingerprint expert, Mr. Anthony Liberi.

Mr. Anthony Liberi was called to the stand. Wall asked the usual questions, such as, place of residence, employment, qualifications, experience, and the particular type of work assigned to him during his nineteen years with the State Police Department.

"Well, I am the supervisor of the Fingerprint Division. In addition, I do document review, involving examination of handwriting, typewriting, and related problems."

"And would you amplify a little, some of the particular training courses that you had with the State Police Department, Mr. Liberi?

"Well, we were given the history of handwriting systems, and the evaluation of various factors which are used in the comparison of handwriting. Such as ratio, relative dimensions, writing skill, and finger dexterity. As with fingerprinting, handwriting cannot be duplicated"

Mr. Liberi displayed the photographic enlargements of the handwriting, to the jury. An easel was placed in front of the jury box, and Mr. Liberi was asked by the judge to step down from the stand and explain to the court, and to the jury, what this display showed.

Mr. Liber explained the individual inconspicuous characteristics of each letter, in every word.

"Mr. Liberi, are there any dissimilarities there at all."

"No, there are no fundamental dissimilarities."

"And is there any question in your mind as to your conclusion that these were written by the same person."

"There is no question, whatever, in my mind that they were written by one and the same person."

13

Another weekend passed, and as usual, the spectators formed into small groups while waiting outside for the doors to open, and talked about the trial. They naturally formed their own conclusions, and in effect, finding a premature verdict of guilty, and/or not guilty in their own minds.

Every scenario imaginable was discussed, such as: Arnfin had married his girl friend just a few months after Dorothy was murdered. Was he the murderer? Or, was it Agnes? The baby said, "She killed, she killed." What did the two-year-old Christa see? Mrs. Stadler testified that Dorothy was afraid of her mother-in-law. Harry buying the rings the day after the murder. Mr. Flagg testified that he saw a shiny black "59" Ford parked in front of Thompsen's house. Harry is supposed to own a black "59" Ford. The piggy bank was found in East Hartland. It was established that Harry sent the anonymous letter. The more they discussed the various testimony, the more confused they became.

The door was finally opened, and the spectators went in quietly to their seats. Many were sent away, because of the "No Standing Allowed" ruling.

An air of anticipation enveloped the environment as everybody wondered, what will happen today. "This trial," they said, "was more exciting than anything they ever watched on TV." The first two witnesses were employees of the Carpenter Brick and Clay Company, Patricia Bourez and Mr. Gordon Disley. They both testified that Arnfin Thompsen was at the office all day, that they had coffee together about three times every morning, and Arnfin went to lunch with Mr. Disley about 12:30 every day, and they returned together. He then he left the office at five o'clock.

Mrs. Clara E.Clark, the third witness, whose house is about two miles from the Thompsen's residence, told about the children finding the piggy bank on December 31st, and where it was found. She also stated that she was well acquainted with the location, because she has lived there all her life.

Next was the redirect examination of Lieutenant Fuessenich by Wall.

Now lieutenant, on March 15, 1966 did you have occasion to see Harry Solberg?

"Yes, sir, I did."

"And was he then in custody?"

"Yes, sir."

"And had he been arrested?"

"Yes, sir."

"And when had he been arrested?"

"Just prior to midnight, about—well, it would be a little before that—would be about 9:30 at night."

"And who made the arrest of Solberg?"

"I did."

"And what and where was Solberg at the time he was placed under arrest?"

"At the Hartford Barracks."

"And had he come voluntarily to the Hartford Barracks on that day?

"Yes, sir, he had."

Shew interrupted, "If your Honor pleases." The judge answered, "If we get to a certain point, I will stop for possible objections."

Wall said," I can see what counsel is having in mind."

"What were the circumstances of his coming to Hartford Barracks on the 14th?"

Shew again objected to this line of questioning. "I think it should be done without the presence of the jury and I think if we go any further, it might be highly prejudicial."

The Judge agreed, "I know it is approaching that point, and I didn't know whether we had gotten quite that far. Is there anything other than the controversial subject Mr. Wall, which will be, or is preliminary?"

"I wish to be very careful along with Mr. Shew, that we take no chances."

Shew suggested, "I don't see why it couldn't be gone into without the presence of the jury, and then we can determine it."

The Judge said, "Well, when it reaches that point, and it hasn't reached a point, the fact that he was there."

Shew said, "I want to see to it that it doesn't reach that point."

Wall said, "There are certain matters—"

The Judge said, "As long as it has appeared that he came to the Barracks voluntarily, there is certainly nothing prejudicial about that, and if Mr. Wall will just give enough opportunity after asking the questions for you to object, I think we can—"

Shew replied, "That very characterization, Your Honor, I object to, and that is why I am objecting at this time."

The Judge asked, "The word 'volunteer?'"

Shew answered, "And I certainly—"

Wall said, "That's why I asked the further question, what the circumstances were of his going to the Barracks, to meet the objection that I felt counsel was making. I asked the circumstances under which he came. It's one way or the other, Your Honor."

The Judge said, "If the witness can describe the circumstances under which he came, and nothing which transpired after he came, or none of the questions or answers, then I think that would give more opportunity for the Court to decide whether the stopping point has been reached or not."

Shew agreed, "All right, Your Honor." To which the Judge replied, "I will allow it to go carefully."

Shew, "I object, however, to the word 'voluntarily,' as a characterization at this particular time."

The Judge said, "Well, perhaps that can be clarified by indicating that—whether or not he was brought there—"

Shew replied, "Well, it's already been testified he was under arrest. From there on, nothing is very voluntary. Your Honor, it has already been stated that he was under arrest."

Wall said, "It's not been stated he was under arrest in the Hartford Barracks. He was—"

Shew explained, "Perhaps I misunderstood."

Wall interjected, "The testimony is, he was under arrest at Canaan."

The Judge then said, "Well, let's just proceed with a description at this point without the use of the characterizing of the word "voluntarily," the circumstances under which he came to the Barracks in Hartford.

Wall then asked, "Do you know the circumstances under which Solberg came to the Hartford Barracks on March 14, 1966?, and will you relate to His Honor and the jury, what those circumstances were, and how he happened to go there."

"On March 13 he had been at the Hartford Barracks, and he said that he would return on the 14 after he was through work."

"And did he?"

"Yes, sir."

"And at that time, on the 14 in consequence of what occurred there, was he placed under arrest?

"Yes, sir, not immediately."

"And when was he placed under arrest?"

"About nine thirty."

"And at that time, who placed him under arrest?"

"I did."

"And where did you bring him?"

"To East Hartland."

"And what was the occasion of your going to East Hartland?"

"Harry had requested that he be allowed to speak to his wife and parents."

"And did he state at that time what he wanted to talk to them about?

"He said he had a lot of things to tell."

Shew interrupted, "Just a minute Your Honor. I object to it from now on—anything he said. He was obviously under police custody. I think we are going to get into it.

The Judge agreed, "I don't think we can take any chances."

Wall said, "I claim this is a matter of which he wanted to talk to his mother and father about, and the circumstances of his getting to Canaan."

Shew interrupted, "If your Honor pleases, that, obviously, is inadmissible as it could possibly be."

The lawyers argued back and forth, as they have done all during the trial. The point of contention this time was what is admissible.

The Judge stated, "I think we have reached a point, if we are going to get into what he said after he was arrested, we have reached a point where Mr. Shew should have an opportunity to find out where we are going in the absence of the Jury. "Wall accepted that. He said, "Well, as a matter of fact, I can skip that and come to another question, Your Honor." The Judge agreed.

The questioning continued. "After then, you—when you went to Hartland—East Hartland with Solberg, did you go into the home with him? And did you advise the family that he was under arrest?"

"Yes, sir."

"And will you relate what conversation, took place between the accused and his father and his mother?"

Shew strongly objected.

The Judge said, "These are statements made by the accused, even to somebody else, in the presence of the officer, the same possible objection exists."

Shew again objected, "I will again make it very specific why I object to it, Your Honor. Clearly on the ruling just made by the Supreme Court of the United States."

The Judge asked, "Miranda?"

Shew said, "Recently referred to."

Wall then said, "Miranda has nothing to do with a conversation between parent and child Your Honor. It is between the officer and the individual. It has nothing, whatever, to do with a conversation between a father and mother on the one hand, and the son on the other. Miranda is absolutely not any authority with relation to that, at all."

The Judge said, "I think that, perhaps, if we are getting to a point of having the Court have to rule on any question as to whether statements made—whether addressed to the officer or addressed to somebody else in his presence are covered by The Miranda decision, the arguments had better be in the absence of the jury."

Shew asked, "Would Your Honor note an exception to the remark just made by Mr. Wall in the presence of the Jury?"

The Judge answered, "All right. Note an exception. I am not sure of the basis, but I will note an exception."

Shew asked, "On the basis of the ruling of the Supreme Court."

Wall said, "I resent any implication that there is anything improper as to anything I said."

Shew remarked, "Mr. Wall, I can't help if I resent your trying to bring this in—"

The Judge interrupted, "Just a minute, gentlemen. I don't believe Mr. Wall has said anything improper. I don't believe anything has been said which is prejudicial, and the jury may be excused."

The reporters remained, but were cautioned by Judge not to write anything they heard in the absence of the jury.

The Judge continued, "I might say at this point that perhaps Mr. Shew is being very quick to anticipate the objectionable statements at this moment. Perhaps the Court is also, but I think we should lean over backwards here in taking care that nothing happens which could, in any way give rise to a mistrial or grounds for reversible error. For that reason, at this point, although I am not expressing a ruling, however, based upon what I think about this, I would like to hear what the arguments are in order to have an opportunity to compare the situation which we have here with the specific situation ruled upon by the Supreme Court, what the nature of the statements were."

The Judge said, "Mr. Shew, I'll hear your objections, specifically to the line of questioning, as to what the witness—what the accused said, in the presence of the witness, to his parents or to his family."

Shew said, "If your Honor please, I think I am—I think it is very clear that under the cases that we have just been referring to, the burden is on the State to prove that anything took place so far as conversation, including this young man who was with his parents or anybody after he was in police custody. It's a very unusual situation in the sense of the word, that it is true that in the Miranda case and the other three of them, there were no parents there, and so forth, and that doesn't have to be. The intent of the Supreme Court is very clear on the matter and the intention of the Supreme Court is to prevent unfair advantage being taken of someone that's in police custody without being warned of their rights. Now, the fact that he admittedly was under police custody at this time, the State's witness so admitted. So we have that element in there. Mr. Wall has not established anything else in that connection, and that is his burden to do it, and he has not done it at this time, and he is now asking questions that have to do with certain statements made by the accused in the presence of the police officer."

The Judge said, "In other words, as I understand your position with respect to the Supreme Court decisions, we all know of course, that if Mr. Wall was seeking to admit admissions made directly by the accused to the officer, that the State would shoulder the burden of establishing that he had previously been warned of his rights. I don't think there is any argument about that. The Supreme Court has made that abundantly clear. Your contention, then, is that the Miranda case goes so far as to establish that no statements made by the accused whether directly to the officer, or to somebody else in his presence, is subject to the same burden of proving, that he had previously been warned of his rights."

Shew agreeing said, "That is absolutely correct, Your Honor."

The Judge turned to Wall and asked, "Do you wish to oppose that interpretation?

His response was, "I vehemently oppose it, Your Honor. I challenge counsel to show anything in Miranda that has anything to do, whatsoever, with anything other than interrogation by police officers. In fact, my question was directed to the fact of their—of the talk with the—the parents in order to show the circumstances under which the confession was later made."

Shew said, "I object to that word, "confession", Your Honor. I am not aware of any confession."

Judge MacDonald listened to the arguments and protests of the attorneys. He said, "Now it seems to me in this situation we have remarks made which are not in any sense an admission of confession. If those words were used during the course of the argument, I can assure counsel that I understand thoroughly that there is no such statement involved here. Nothing has been introduced pertaining to any confession or any admission. The only statements that are being discussed here are statements made by the accused, not the police officer, under interrogation, but apparently voluntarily made when he saw his parents and said, "I'm sorry." They were not made incommunicado. They were made to his mother and father, and I can see nothing in the Miranda case, or any of the cases, the facts of which are stated here, which involve a situation even comparable to this, although I won't say that I agree with everything that the majority of the Supreme Court has said in these recent cases. I can say that I do agree with the specific findings in the Miranda case, based upon the facts that were involved there, and readily see how an individuals rights could be violated. But, until the Supreme Court of the United States goes a step further and says that voluntary statements made by an accused to persons other than his interrogator not at the police station, not during question, not under compulsion of any kind, but which happen to be, or intentionally are made in the presence of police officers, or anybody else who cares to be injected into the case, and to testify as to what he saw or heard under the circumstances. I will rule that such statements are admissible and on the particular facts of this case, and I will expressly overrule the objection to the testimony and permit the interrogation of the officer along the lines indicated, to continue in the presence of the jury."

Shew asked, "May I have an exception Your Honor?"

The Judge responded with," An exception of course may be noted. Call the Jury."

Further Redirect examination of Lieutenant Fuessenich began.

Wall asked the lieutenant, "I believe that you did testify that you and the accused went to the home of the accused's father and mother in East Hartland, on the evening of the 14th of March, was it?"

"Yes, sir."

Wall then asked several questions which the lieutenant answered, "Yes, he took Harry to his home in East Hartland about 10:15 to let him talk to his parents and his wife. Harry made a telephone call from the Hartford Barracks to notify the family of the intended visit and Sergeant Keilty went with them to Solberg seniors house. Harry spoke to his parents for a few minutes, then he went into one of the downstairs bedrooms to talk to his wife. The lieutenant told Mr. and Mrs. Solberg that he was taking Harry to the Canaan Barracks, and that they could visit him in the morning at 11:30."

"And what happened when you arrived at Canaan?"

"Well, Harry went into the kitchen, where he ate with some of the officers, who happened to be there, and then we went upstairs."

"Alone or in the company of someone else?"

"The County Detective Holden, was there at the time."

"And had any arrangements been made previous to that to have anybody else present?"

"Yes, sir there had been."

"And who made the arrangements?"

"Detective Rebillard."

"And in response to those arrangements, who then arrived?"

"Mr. Arthur Roberts, the Superior Court stenographer."

"And now when you and County Detective Holden and Solberg went upstairs, did Mr. Roberts accompany you also?"

"Yes, sir, but not at the moment."

"And then did you have a talk with Solberg before you asked him any questions?"

"Yes, sir."

"And will you please relate to His Honor and the jury just what you said to Solberg at that time?

Shew said, "Well, if Your Honor pleases I object to that because, we are now coming to a situation in which I think will require the jury to be excused again."

The Judge replied, "Well, the questions that are being asked now are not pertaining to anything that—"

Shew interrupting asked, "I would like, if Your Honor is going to admit that, I would like an exception to this particular question. The last question."

The Judge answered, "In other words, in order to be ultraconservative, I gather that you feel that the asking of the question, the preliminary questions themselves might in some way—"

Shew interrupting again asked, "In front of the jury Your Honor."

The Judge said, "Might in some way be prejudicial." To which, Shew concurred.

The Judge said, "Well, I don't think it has gotten to the point yet where we are in any immediate danger, but here again, in order to be extremely careful, I will excuse the jury and then we can have arguments on this particular question while they are absent. I will excuse the jury."

With the jury out, the lawyers argued, objected and protested. The main topic of discussion was Miranda. Did the officers read Harry Solberg his rights? Lieutenant Fuessenich repeated his testimony. Yes, the officers did allow Harry to talk to his parents in the living room, and to his wife in the bedroom. Yes, they did take Harry to the Canaan Barracks that night. Yes, Harry was read his rights.

Shew asked, "You were aware of the fact, were you not lieutenant, that this boy was a minor?"

"Yes, sir."

The Judge said, "The burden as I understand it is on the State to prove that a man was advised of his rights to remain silent, and to have counsel before he makes an incriminating statement, or something which might be construed as self-incrimination. Now, Mr. Wall has introduced some evidence to that point, and as I understand it, your purpose in cross examining this witness is to show that there were circumstances surrounding this. I think the State has made the necessary preliminary proof that the man was advised, and now you have certain reasons that you wish to give, to indicate that you don't think this was a voluntary choice on his part, and so think that cross examination is the proper way to establish it. I will therefore permit it."

Shew commenced cross-examining Lieutenant Fuessenich from about the time Harry came to the Hartford barracks, to having something to eat in the Canaan Barracks. Detective Rebillard said he talked to Harry for about forty-five minutes while they ate. The lieutenant also said that he then talked with Harry and suggested to Harry to clear the air. I asked him if he would consider taking a polygraph examination. It was at this time that Harry admitted writing the letter.

Judge MacDonald asked the lieutenant, "During the conversation about the letter, and the polygraph, was anyone else present?"

"Yes, sir, the court stenographer, Mr. Roberts."

Judge MacDonald attempted to clarify the facts: "By having testimony to the effect that the boy was advised of his rights to counsel, and to remain silent before the interrogation, that we are concerned with at this time, and on the question of custody, and the length of time he had been in custody, that you have introduced evidence upon which you have cross examined the witness, to the effect that he was free to come and go. Whether it came out during your cross examination or direct examination, I don't think is a matter of importance. That he was allowed to speak to his parents, that he was allowed to eat, that he was allowed to talk to his wife, and the fact that he was an emancipated minor, at least he was a boy who was working, he was twenty years old and married. It does seem to me that the State Police, under these circumstances might very well have been following the book, that we now realize they must follow at the time of interrogation. I don't see that they did anything wrong."

Shew protested, "Your Honor, you have only the version of Lieutenant Fuessenich. Your Honor has no evidence before him as to what Mr. Solberg went through. What his parents knew about the situation, what they were warned of."

The Judge replied, "This would imply that we have to have, practically, a trial of this whole portion of the case in the absence of the jury, with the defendant or others called to testify in his own behalf, as to what happened. Mr. Wall has put on what I would call roughly a prima facie case, that the accused was warned of his rights. Now what suggestion do you have as to how the court can be more fully advised as to what happened, except from the prima facie case that's been presented and subjected to cross examination?"

Shew continued his argument at which time Judge MacDonald said, "we'll will take a short recess."

14

The next two witnesses were Mr. and Mrs. Solberg, Harry's parents. Mr. Solberg showed severe emotional strain as he nervously spelled his name, and Judge MacDonald had to instructed him to speak up. He repeated everything he had previously told the attorneys and the Judge. Mrs. Solberg seemed, calmer than her husband, while she basically repeated everything to which her husband had previously testified.

Lieutenant Fuessenich resumed the witness stand for additional redirect examination by Wall.

"Now lieutenant, the time that you were there in the presence of all these people, did you make any statement preliminarily to the defendant Solberg?"

"Yes, sir, I did."

"And will you state to his Honor and the jury what you told him at that time."

"I told him that he had a constitutional right to remain silent, that he had the right to an attorney, and that anything he might say might be used against him in Court."

"And after that, did you proceed to ask questions relating to the circumstances of this case of the defendant Solberg?"

"Yes, sir, I did."

"And were those taken down by a stenographer?"

"Yes, sir they were."

"And was that by, Mr. Roberts, the stenographer here at the Superior Court?"

"Yes, sir."

"And has he transcribed those questions and answers?"

"Yes, sir he has."

Wall said, "You may inquire."

Shew then began his re-cross of Lieutenant Fuessnich, with, "Did Harry tell you he was very tired that night?"

"Some time after this incident he did, yes?"

"And did he tell you that he'd rather have you wait until morning, before you proceeded any further with questioning?"

"No sir he did not."

"But he did tell you he was tired."

"Yes."

"And did you make any reply when he told you he was tired, or did you keep right on questioning?"

"No, the questioning—"

Before he could finish, Wall interrupted, "I object to that."

The Judge replied, "Let him answer."

The questioning continued about Harry being too tired, and how many people were present? The lieutenant wasn't sure if County Detective Holden or Detective Rebillard were present. He thought the conversation took place on the way down the stairs.

Wall said, "No further questions."

Arthur E. Roberts was the next witness to testify. He stated that he has been official court stenographer for eighteen years. He further testified that on March 15, Lieutenant Fuessenich requested that he go to the Canaan barracks and take down questions and answers of Harry Solberg.

"And did you on March 15, at the request of Lieutenant Fuessenich, go to Canaan to take down certain questions and answers of one Harry Solberg?"

"Yes, sir."

"And did you transcribe your notes as to what occurred on that morning?"

"Yes, sir."

"And I show you this document and I ask you whether or not this is a transcript of what occurred on that morning?

"Yes, sir."

"Would you please proceed to relate exactly what occurred during the time that you were there with Lieutenant Fuessenich, Harry Solberg and County Detective Holden?

Well, when I arrived—"

Shew interrupted, "Wait a minute Mr. Roberts please. I certainly object to this and ask that we proceed along on the same basis."

Judge Macdonald stated, "I would assume that any evidence which follows, which pertains to that, with which you have made an objection, will be subject to a continuing objection, and exception."

Shew replied, "Thank you, Your Honor."

The court stenographer, Mr. Roberts said, "When I arrived at the State Police Barracks in Canaan on that evening, I was escorted to a room which contained a desk and a couple of chairs. I went to another room and got a chair for myself and proceeded to set up my stenographic equipment, just as you see it there on the floor. Shortly thereafter Lieutenant Fuessenich came in accompanied by Harry Solberg and they sat down in front of me. Lieutenant Fuessenich introduced me to Harry Solberg and proceeded with the interrogation, exactly as it is here in this transcript. I just sat there and took it down just as I would here in Court, just exactly as it is here in this transcript. Everything that was said, by the lieutenant, and everything that was said by Mr. Solberg, is contained here, and when you get to the last page and the lieutenant's last comment, the two of them walked out of the room. That was the end of it, as far as I was concerned.

Wall asked, "Might I ask the Court Your Honor, whether the Court might consider it more proper to have this introduced into evidence, or to have the questions and answers stated by the stenographer, as he transcribed them?

The Judge replied, "Well, I think that probably for the sake of the record, it should be offered as an exhibit, to give an opportunity to counsel to object to it and then have the reporter read it."

Shew said, "Obviously it would take a while to read it. I don't know how many pages there are here. I suppose we could have a recess, and while I am reading it.—I don't care, but I certainly want to see it before I agree to its admission. I suppose it could be read."

Wall stated, "I wonder, Your Honor if perhaps it is going to take that length of time that we might proceed with the questions as such and if anything appears objectionable, as we go along, counsel would no doubt notice it."

The Judge replied, "All right. Let's do it that way then before it is marked in evidence as a State's Exhibit."

Wall questioned, "Before it is marked?"

The Judge aid, "It can be marked for identification at this time if you wish, just so that there will be no doubt. I don't think that's necessary. Then Mr. Shew can object to it as it goes along with the notation of course, that this is all subject to the same exception that has been taken at the outset."

Wall started his direct examination of Mr. Roberts by having him read from his transcript. The following occurred on 12:13 a.m. March 15, 1966, By Lieutenant Fuessenich."

You know that I am Lieutenant Fuessenich, Commanding Officer of the Canaan Barracks?

"Yes."

"What is your full name?"

"Harry Albert Solberg."

"When were you born?"

"January third, 1946."

"And where do you live?"

"East Hartland, Connecticut."

"It is my duty to inform you that you have a constitutional right to remain silent. You have a right to an attorney, and I also want to warn you that anything you say may be used against you.

Do you understand that?"

"Yes."

"Do you remember June 15, 1965?"

"Yes."

"What did you do in the morning?"

"I went to school."

"Where?"

"In Gilbert High School in Winsted."

"What time did you return home?"

"I don't know, I get out eleven-forty-five, and the bus usually gets me home around forty-five minutes afterwards.

"What did you do after you got home?"

"I guess I ate, and then went to Granby to see if the lawn mower was ready."

"How did you go to Granby?"

"I went through—I don't know what you call it."

"Route 20?"

"Yes, Route 20. Then we took the cut off, that took us right down past the Lincoln Dairy, directly across from the lawn mower shop down there, the boathouse. Then I went—was going to go home. I needed some information from Arnfin Thompsen, so I went down College Highway and took another road home. I don't know what the number of that road is or anything. I know, but I can't think, and I stopped in front of their house."

"In whose car were you?"

"In my car. My father's, but it was my car."

"What kind of a car was it?"

"59 Ford, black, two door coupe."

"What happened after you stopped in front of Arnfin Thompsen's house?"

"Went in, I knocked on the door, and Mrs. Thompsen came and answered the door, I don't remember much after that except that I went in, and I can remember climbing the ladder on the back porch and running out. That's all I can remember."

"Do you remember anything about a bank?"

"Yes. I must have taken a piggy bank with change in it."

"What kind of a piggy bank was this?"

"A red plastic bank about a foot and a half long and ten inches high or something."

"What was in the bank?"

"About sixteen dollars in change."

"Do you remember anything else that happened in the house?"

"No, I don't. Part of it came back after I had been reading the papers, but that's all I can remember, just part of it.

"Do you remember anything about a hammer?"

"Very little, I can remember seeing one and picking it up. That's about all."

"What kind of a hammer was it?"

"A sledge hammer."

"Approximately how big was this sledge hammer?"

"I don't know—must have been a heavy one. I don't remember how big it was."

"What did you do with it?"

"All I can remember is throwing it. That's all I can remember doing with it."

"Where were you standing when you threw it?"

"On the porch."

"Where abouts on the porch were you standing?"

"In the part by the living room, facing Washington Hill."

"And in which direction did the hammer go when you threw it?"

"Just back, I guess."

"Do you remember anything else about the back porch?"

"No, except just climbing up to it."

"Do you remember anything about the inside of the house?"

"No, I don't remember anything about the house inside."

"Do you remember anything about a fork?"

"Just the meat fork, that's all. That's all I remember about. I must have used it on her, but that's all I can remember about that, too."

"Where was this fork when you found it?"

"Must have been on the counter."

"Where did you leave it?"

"I don't remember." "I don't remember where I left it—I don't remember."

"When you climbed back up on the porch, how did you get there?"

"A ladder."

"What kind of a ladder was this?"

"Aluminum ladder."

"And what type of a ladder was it?" "Was it a straight ladder or something else?"

"What would you call it?"

"Is it the type of ladder that stands by itself?"

"Yes, it is."

"A stepladder?"

"Yes, maybe yes."

"When you got onto the porch where did you go?"

"I guess I went out to the car, took off."

"Towards where?"

"Towards my home."

"What happened after that?"

"I stopped on the way to wipe off some of the blood on my shoes and a little bit on my pants.

"Where did you stop?"

Right down the road where there used to be either snack shop or a food stand, I can't remember which it was."

"Is this on the road from Arnfin Thompsen's house to your house?"

"Yes, it's right between, more or less."

"Then where did you go?"

"I went home, I went home."

"What did you do when you got home?"

"Ummm I must have wiped off a little bit more of the blood on my pants with a wet rag or something. After that, I can't remember too much, I don't remember too much as it is."

"Where was the piggy bank at this time?"

"In my car."

"Did you do anything at all to the bank that day?"

"No, I was scared of it."

"Where in your car was the bank?"

"In the trunk."

"When did you put it in the trunk?"

"That day when I came out."

"When you—?"

"When I came out of the house."

"Out of Arnfin's house?"

"Yes."

"In other words, before you went anywhere, you opened the trunk of your car and put the bank in?"

"Either that or I had it with me till I was going to wipe the blood off down the road, and then put it in. I don't remember. It was either one of them. I can't remember." "What did you do after you went home?"

"I went to work with my father. He was working at a home in West Granby."

"How many hours did you work over there, do you have any idea?"

"No, I don't keep track of my hours when I work with him."

"Did you do anything else that day?"

Yes, I unloaded a plumbing truck. I'm sure of that. I'm sure I went after the lawn mower. I know that because it wasn't ready. I went to school, that's all."

"But these other things were before you went to Arnfin's house?"

"Yes, I come—"

"The piggy bank, when was the next time that you did anything with the piggy bank?"

"It was a few days after that, I don't know—a couple of days, maybe a week. I don't know."

"What did you do then?"

"I cut it open and took the change out, and threw the bank away."

"How did you cut open the bank?

"I don't remember—it was a knife or scissors, one or the other."
"What portion of the bank did you cut?"
"Top."
"And what type of cutting did you do. Did you slit the bank open—or?"
"I cut a hole, I guess."
"Do you have any idea how big the hole was?"
"No, I don't remember."
"What did you do with the money?"
"I spent it, here and there."
"Do you have any idea where you spent the money?"
"No, I don't, just gone."
"What did you do with the bank?"
"I threw it out the window of the car when I was riding."
"On what road?"
"Route 20, Granby, East Hartland line. Some of the kids must have picked it up or something. I don't know."
"Which direction were you heading when you threw the bank out?"
"Home."
"From where?"
"Granby, Granby direction, anyhow."
"Which side of the car did you throw it out of?"
"On the right side."
"Did you stop the car?"
"No, I don't believe so."
"You threw the bank out, while you were driving?"
"Yes."
"What kind of shoes were you wearing that day?"
"I don't remember if I had my working clothes on, or my school clothes on. seems to me as if I would have my working clothes on because I—I was going to go after the lawn mower, got to pick it up and everything else. I can't actually say."
"Do you remember anything about a letter?"

"Yes, part of it."

"Will you tell me about this letter?"

"I wrote it to divert suspicion."

"What was in the letter?"

"Telling how I knew her for quite a while, and I had worked at the bank with her, and that I had killed her. This is the only part I can remember."

"Did you mention anything about a car?"

"Something about borrowing a neighbor's car, something like that, borrowing a neighbor's car."

"Who did you send the letter to?"

"Arnfin."

"Where did you get the paper on which you wrote the letter?"

"I must have gotten it in school."

"Gilbert?"

"Yes."

"How about the envelope?"

"Just a regular envelope, I guess. I don't remember exactly what it was. I saw copies of it—a printed envelope, something with a stamp printed on it, or something."

"Why did you send the letter to Arnfin?"

"To divert suspicion, that's the only reason."

"What was the reason that you felt you had to divert suspicion?"

"The same reason I am here."

"Why did you feel that people might be suspicious of you?"

"Just because my car was black, that's all, and I had the same kind of car. That's the only reason. I was scared, I guess.

"Did you have any idea that police were looking for a certain type of car?"

"Yes."

"Where did you get this idea?"

"Well, off the radio—not—yes, in the paper, somebody said they saw black 59 Ford in that area at that time. It was stopped, and requesting all about that, and my mother was saying that all the time too, and I got scared."

"Why are you here, Harry?"

"Because I'm accused of killing Dottie Thompsen."

"Did you?"

"Do I have to answer that right now?"

"Don't you want to answer it, right now?"

"No. I killed her, that's what you want."

"Is that the truth?"

"I can only give you my answer."

"What is your answer?"

The silence of the courtroom was broken with gasps, as he shouted, ***"I KILLED HER!"***

At this point Lieutenant Fuessenich left the room and County Detective Samuel Holden came into the room, sat down and started to interrogate the young Mr. Solberg.

"Harry, why don't you just face up to this, now? The lieutenant is trying to get you to tell him what happened up there that day. Now, you walked up to the door, and you are claiming to draw a blank until you are walking up the stairs or throwing a hammer out. Why don't you just—if you are going to tell the truth, let's tell the whole truth? Tell him, step by step, what happened, what she said to you, what you said to her, and what happened in the kitchen, and what happened in the rest of the house?"

"I don't remember."

"Is it you don't remember because it's convenient not to remember, or you don't want to remember?

"I don't know. I just can't remember what actually took place. I don't actually remember what happened."

Lieutenant Fuessenich chimed in, "What started it all?"

"I don't know. I know I didn't have those intentions when I went there. I couldn't have. That's why I don't know what happened.

And then County Detective Holden put his 'two cents in'," "You know you killed her, right?" "You know that, don't you?"

"Yes."

"And you know how you killed her, don't you?"

"I guess I know."

"How did you kill her?"

"I guess I stabbed her, and beat her."

"What did you beat her with?"

"I don't know."

"What did you stab her with?"

"Guess it was that meat fork."

"Was there any other forks?"

"No."

"Or just the one?"

"I can't remember any other forks."

"Did you strangle her?"

"Yes, with an electric cord."

"Was the cord still attached to the toaster?"

"I don't remember."

"What did you do with the cord after you strangled her with it?"

"I don't remember that either."

"But you remember using the cord?"

"Yes."

"Do you remember dragging her out to the deck?"

"No."

"Did you carry her?"

"No, I don't remember."

"You knew she was outside, didn't you?"

"What is that?"

"You knew she was outside afterwards?"

"Yes."

"Didn't you tell the lieutenant that you were outside and you thought she was still alive. Didn't you also tell him that she had grabbed your hair?"

With that question, Harry simply sat there mute, and nodded his head up and down.

"Where did that happen?" "Was that in the kitchen or on the floor, or was it outside?"

"I don't—"

"Where was that, inside or outside?"

"I don't—"

"Why don't you describe what happened in the kitchen, first?"

"I can't.

"You remember what happened, don't you?"

"No."

"You know you stabbed her and you beat her?"

Harry once again, didn't answer, he simply nodded his head up and down.

"And you used the cord on her?"

"Because I remember parts when I read them, but don't remember what happened."

"Well, this is a pretty important happening in your life, and you certainly must remember some of the details."

"No."

Did you have an argument with her?"

"No, I don't think so."

"Something had to provoke it. Were you friendly with Dottie?"

"Not, just a friend, that's all."

"How long had you known her?"

"Just since she moved into the house that we rented to her."

"And all you knew her as a friend, nothing more?"

"That's all."

"What happened when you arrived at the house that day?"

"All I can remember, is going in."

"What happened after you got in?"
"I don't know."
"You're going in—?"
"No, I don't remember."
"Where was she when you got in the house?"
"I don't know. She came to the door."
"She let you in?"
"Yes."
"Where did the two of you go after that?"
"I don't remember."
"How long were you at the house?"
"I don't remember that either."
"Which way did you leave the house?"
"I can remember climbing up the ladder."
"What kind of a state was Dottie in at that time.?"
"Where was she when you left?"
"I guess she was outside."
"Now, before, you said you stabbed her and beat her, and you used the electric cord on her.

What else did you hit her with?"
"I guess I used a rock."
"Do you remember using the rock?"
"No."
"Why do you say you guess you used a rock?"
"Because that's what I read, and I just recalled something."
"Didn't you write that in a letter, that you sent to Arnfin, that you hit her with a rock?
"Yes."
"You didn't read that somewhere, you wrote it yourself, didn't you?"
"Ummm."

"Do you suppose, if the lieutenant let you read that letter that you wrote to Arnfin, it might refresh your recollection, about what happened that day?"

"No."

"It wouldn't refresh it?"

"No—started to read it before, and I couldn't."

"Why couldn't you?"

"Because it made me sick."

"Did it refresh your recollection? Made you remember, didn't it?

"Not too much."

At this time, Lieutenant Fuessenich, resumed the questioning.

"Harry, in your letter you said that you wanted her to go away with you?"

"Yes."

"Was that true?"

"No, that was just somebody that worked with her before. Somebody who had supposedly sent her that letter, just somebody else who had known her for some years before, had worked with her, that was all?"

"In your letter you said something about the baby. Do you remember that?"

"No."

"Do you remember saying that you would kill the baby also?"

"I don't remember, no. I don't remember that part of it."

"Do you remember saying something about killing your wife?"

"Yes, I think that was the first sentence."

"Look—I didn't hear that?"

"I think it was my first sentence."

"Do you remember saying anything in the letter about killing your own wife?"

"No."

"You don't remember that?"

"No."

"What was your purpose in using the rock?"
"I don't know."
"How big a rock was it?"
"I don't know, it must have been a big one because I wanted it for some reason. To do a job I guess. I don't know how big it was."
"Why did you want to do a job?"
"Why did I want to do the rest of it? I don't know."
At this point the questioning shifted to Holden.
"Must have some reason, Harry, right?"
"I must have, but I don't know."
"Can't you think of any reason why?"
"No."
"Did you have an argument with her?"
"I don't remember. I am sure, about what?"
"About?"
"About what?"
"I don't know about what."
"Me, neither."
"She ended up dead"
"Yes."
"You must have been mad about something. How many other times have you been at the house when Mr. Thompsen wasn't home, when Arnfin wasn't home?"
"I don't know if I have ever been there without my girl friend, or my wife now."
"How long have you been married?"
"Two months, January 15."
"You weren't married at that time, then?"
"No."
"What did Dorothy have to say to you when you arrived there?"
"I don't remember."
"Didn't you have any conversation with her, at all?"
"I can't remember."

"You went there for a specific purpose, you say, but you don't remember what you asked her about?"

"I must have asked her, but I can't say I did, I can't say I didn't."

"Don't you remember any conversation that you had?"

"No."

"You don't remember how she was dressed?"

"No."

"What was she doing when you arrived, do you know?"

"No, I don't know."

"Was she doing housework?"

"I don't know."

Questioning now shifts back to Lieutenant Fuessenich.

"Did you make a phone call while you were there?"

"Yes. I don't remember! I don't remember! I don't remember much of what happened that whole day there."

"The lieutenant said, "All right, Harry, we'll go downstairs."

The Court reporter Roberts, finished the reading, and Wall offered it in evidence.

Shew said, "I object to it for the same reason."

The Judge stated, "For the same reason as previously stated, the objections overruled, and an exception may be noted, that may be marked State's Exhibit double "M"."

Cross Examination of Mr. Roberts by Shew.

"You naturally had a chance to observe Mr. Solberg during this examination Mr. Roberts?"

"Well, I saw his back mostly. He was sitting just ahead of me with his back to me."

"Did he sound confused?"

"In some of those places where he said repetitiously, "I don't remember," at that point, he seemed as though he might have been a little confused."

"There were quite a few of those places weren't there? You are in the habit of taking testimony, and have been taking testimony all your life?"

"Yes, sir."

"And not a great many of his answers sounded confused to you?"

"Well, I'm afraid I couldn't be too expert on that for the simple reason that taking an interrogation like that, or even here in the courtroom, you are in a sort of a trance and you are working by reflex action without any conscious thought process. If you think or try to follow the theme of what's going on, that conscious thought reflex slows you down so much, you could lose a hundred words a minute; so that you are not much of an observer."

"I can appreciate that Mr. Roberts. I assume you read this over afterwards?"

"I Transcribed that."

"Did you have a chance to think then, or observe it?"

"Not too carefully. They're just words."

Harry's father appeared near collapse as he slowly approached the stand. He sat slumped over, tears streaming down his face, as Wall said, "Mr. Thorbjorn Solberg you have been previously sworn." Mr. Solberg nodded acknowledgment.

Wall began his redirect examination, and Mr. Solberg again answered the questions about the car. He acknowledged buying a black two door 1959 Ford for Harry, however, the registration and title were in Mr. Solberg's name. He said he drove it once in a while but, he sobbed as he repeated, "But I bought it for Harry."

Mr. Solberg was excused. He left the courtroom a heart-broken man. His brother-in-law Bob Hansen, and his wife were beside him. Mrs. Solberg sat silently and motionless in the car. She apparently was still in a state of shock and couldn't utter a word. As they approached the house she began to sob profusely, and her husband put his arm around her to comfort her.

Lieutenant Fuessenich was recalled and questioned about Harry's economic status. He said he knew Harry was employed at Pratt and Whitney Aircraft Corp., and that his wife worked there also. He knew Harry had the means to employ counsel. That then ended the most heart-wrenching day, of all days.

15

Representatives of the media, townspeople and spectators have all expected the confession; still there were ambiguous feelings. Did he have an accomplice, or did he commit the murder alone? Agnes admitted to being home all day. Did she have anything to do with it, or have any knowledge of it? Everyone felt sorry for Dorothy's family, and little Christa, with no mother. Harry's parents were naturally grief-stricken—their son a murderer.

In the surrounding towns, reporters greeted each other, not with a good morning, or hi there, but with," What will Rome say now?"

The Hartford Courant headlines read: *Judge allows Solberg Story. He Was the Murderer.* The story was quite lengthy and it quoted every detail of the confession. The Waterbury Republican ran the full confession under the caption: *Solberg Admission Read Into Record, "I killed Her."*

At the Courthouse in Litchfield, Wall said, "He had brought his case to a close. Shew was surprised, and asked permission to call some witnesses. Wall agreed, and at that juncture, court was adjourned until the afternoon.

The recess gave members of the news media the opportunity to sit in the coffee chop and discuss the case. The reporters from The Hartford Courant especially liked Shew, and they often lunched with him. On this day, Major Rome was the topic of discussion, and not many good words were said about Rome. Someone summed it up by remarking, "The major's in deep shit."

Someone asked, "Has that SOB, Rome seen the confession?" The answer to that was, "Why would he see it? He wasn't on the case, he must have read the confession in the Hartford Courant like everyone else."

When court resumed, Shew Cross-examined Lieutenant Fuessenich about the confession.

"At no time lieutenant, did Harry describe to you how this homicide had been done, did he?"

"From start to finish, no sir, he did not."

"And you tried to get him to tell, did you not?"

"Yes, sir, I did."

"And you were also present when County Detective Holden was questioning him along the same lines?"

"Yes, sir."

"And he couldn't tell—couldn't or didn't tell him?"

"No, sir, he didn't."

"Is there anything in these statements, that Harry Solberg made to you, that hadn't already appeared in the papers?

"What was it?"

"About hitting the victim with a rock."

"Are you sure, lieutenant that you have seen all the papers? In other words, let's put it this way, to be fair to you. If that had appeared in the papers, you hadn't seen it. Is that correct?"

"Yes, that's right."

"Is there anything else that you can remember?"

"Not that I can remember, sir."

"And was there any reason why you didn't question any further about the difference in location of the piggy bank?

"No—no reason except that this interrogation was going along and there seemed to be no reason to pursue that part further than we did."

""Did you have any—didn't you give consideration to the fact that there was a statement in regard to the piggy bank which couldn't have been true?"

"Yes, sir, we did."

"And didn't you think he should be questioned about it?"

"We did question him sir."

"Further than you did? You made one statement about it, correct?"

"We questioned him, and he gave us his answers."

"What answer was that?"

"That he had thrown the bank out on Route 20."

"But you knew the piggy bank hadn't been found anywhere near that location?"

"Yes, sir, we did."

"Didn't you think it was necessary to clear that matter up?

"We had tried to clear it up by asking him."

His answer was, "Some kid must have changed it?"

"Yes, sir, I believe he said that."

"Did you think the location of the piggy bank had been changed?"

"No sir, I did not."

"So that you thought as far as that particular statement of Harry Solberg is concerned, you thought that was not true?"

"I did sir."

"What other statements in this exhibit "MM" did you consider not truthful?"

"Most of his statement where he said, I don't remember."

"You thought he did remember."

"Yes, sir."

"Can you give us any reason why he would give you a wrong location of the piggy bank?"

"I can only give you my opinion."

"What was that?"

"That in this type of case, it's quite unusual that a person will withhold something for some reason, best known to himself."

"Can you think of any reason why he would withhold the location on an item, such as the piggy bank, that everybody that had any connection with the case, knew where it had been found at that time?

"Perhaps that's his reason."

"Did you ever question Donald Paulsen in connection with this case?"

"No sir, I did not."

"Did you know what members of the department did, to save some time?"

Wall objected to this, "This is no part of the direct Your Honor."

The Judge said, "I would say that it is not. This is bringing in something extraneous. I sustain the objection."

"I think in this exhibit, on page six lieutenant, Harry said that the piggy bank stayed in his car for three days, is that correct?"

"I'm sorry sir?"

"On page seven, lieutenant."

"I don't see anything here sir about three days."

"Well, a few days."

"Yes, sir."

"Did you or any member of your department check this car very shortly after the murder?"

"No sir we did not."

"When did you first check it?"

"It was in March of this year."

"Did it seem reasonable to you, that it should be left in there for a few days?

"Yes, sir, it could very well be."

"Have you in the police brief or whatever you call it, have you a written statement, that you, or any other member of the force, obtained from Harry Solberg at this particular time, referring to March 13, to the 15th?"

"Yes, sir we do."

"And where is it?"

"I believe the State's Attorney has it."

Shew asked Wall for it.

Wall replied, "It's not in evidence as yet."

Shew answered, "I'm not going to necessarily put it in evidence, I'm just asking you to let me take it."

Wall replied, "Well, it is part of the State's Attorney's file isn't it."

Shew said," That's right, now the State's Attorney's files."

Wall conceded, "I have no objection if he wants to put it in evidence, I have no objection."

The Judge became confused: "This doesn't involve prior inconsistent statements. I'm trying to think on what particular basis?"

Shew relented, "I just wanted to know where it was, let it go."

Judge MacDonald agreed.

Continued re-cross examination of Lieutenant Fuessenich by Shew.

"Do you recall whether or not that statement was inconsistent with this statement, that is now in evidence lieutenant?"

"Yes, sir."

"And did you take that other one—or did someone else—or under what circumstances was that taken?

"This was taken under the—"

Wall interjected, "This could be, Your Honor, objectionable on the part of the defendant. This is no protection that I want, but it might be harmful to the defendant."

Shew stated, "I don't care, I'll take a chance. I think that's all."

Further Redirect Examination of Lieutenant Fuessenich by Wall.

"Lieutenant, I show you this paper and I ask you, whether or not this is the statement signed by Harry Solberg, to which you refer in answer to Mr. Shew's question?"

"Yes, sir it is."

"It is?, Was it voluntarily given by him, do you know?"

"It was sir."

Wall handed the statement to Shew for his perusal.

Shew asked, "You offer this Mr. Wall?"

Wall replied, "Yes."

Shew offered no objection.

The Judge ruled, "Without objection, it may be marked State's Exhibit double "O."

Wall read the statement dated, March 14th, 1966.

8:27 p.m. Voluntary statement of Harry Solberg; On my ride back from Granby, I stopped into their house to see if my report information he had gotten for me was there. I went inside because the front door was open, and the baby was crying. I was going to leave a note but I decided not to. I kept calling for someone home, but no one answered. I then went into the kitchen and saw blood on the floor, and I saw it in the living room too. Then I saw her, Dottie, out on the ground because the blood went that way. I tried to help her but she was too full of fight so I grabbed the ladder (spelled latter) and ran through the house and got out. I was going to call the police but I was too scared, so I went to work with my father. That is all I can remember except for the letter. Harry Solberg, witnessed by Lieutenant Robert E. Reamer.

Continued further redirect examination of Lieutenant Fuessenich, by Wall.

"In whose handwriting is that exhibit?"

"Harry Solberg's."

"Entirely in his own handwriting?"

"Yes, sir, except for Lieutenant Reamer's signature."

"And he wrote that entirely in his own handwriting?"

"Yes, sir."

"And the misspelling and so forth, are some of the words—are—as is, is it."

"Yes."

Wall said, "That's all."

Further Re-cross Examination of Lieutenant Fuessenich by Shew.

"Lieutenant, that was written at eight o'clock Monday night."

"8:27, Monday night, Yes, sir."

"Monday night. This was after he had.—withdraw that question. When had Harry Solberg first—when had you first started to question Harry Solberg?"

"It was around five o'clock."

"On Monday?"

"On Monday, Yes, sir."

"But how about the previous day?"

"It was, I would say, about 4:30—are you talking about the—?"

"I'm talking about the previous day."

About the questioning at what place, sir—Hartford Barracks or—?"

"When you first started to question Harry Solberg, in any barracks?"

"At the Canaan Barracks, sir. It was about ten minutes to eleven in the morning."

"Sunday morning?"

"Yes, sir."

"And how was Harry Solberg gotten to the Canaan Barracks?"

"He rode in Detective Rebillard's police car from East Hartland."

"Your records show when he was picked up by Detective Rebillard?"

"Yes, sir."

Lieutenant Fuessenich was showing signs of fatigue and irritation from the long days of examining, and from the repetitious questioning, and boring answers. The questioning of Harry, at East Hartland, and the telephone calls to his parents, what they talked about, and why he called his parents, only exacerbated his weariness. The parents were told that Harry had admitted writing the letter. The most important question was, however, what had happened that Sunday and Monday, concerning Harry at the Canaan Barracks.

Wall said he had no objection.

The Judge asked, "You wish to answer? All right."

Shew asked, "You want the polygraph tests?"

The reply was, "Yes"

Following this round of questioning, came a question that demanded an explicit answer, "Was anything ever said that didn't appear in the newspapers?"

The answer was, "The rock."

"Well, you are certain, lieutenant, that there was nothing in the newspapers about the use of the rock, in this killing, prior to the delivery of the letter, State's Exhibit "K"?"

The answer, convincingly was, "Yes, sir I am quite positive of that."

Wall then declared, "The State rests, Your Honor."

It was now time for the defense to present their case.

The first witness for the defense, Fred Rebillard, was sworn, in at which time he spelled his name for the court stenographer. Then Shew began his direct examination.

"When did you first go to the Thompsen house?"

"That would be June 15, 1965."

"What time?"

"7:13 p.m."

"And who was there when you got there?"

"I believe Trooper Pennington was there. Also Trooper Soliani, Arnfin thompsen, Sergeant Joseph Riley and Lieutenant Fuessenich arrived, I believe shortly after that. That's all I can recall at this time."

"Did you know who was the officer that took a dress out of the washing machine, a dress that was referred to by Lieutenant Fuessenich?"

"I believe it was Captain O'Brien."

"Did you take any articles out of the house?"

"I took several hairs from the hand of the victim and gave them to—I didn't actually take them out of the house, but I turned them over to a C.S.B.I. man."

"And where are those hairs, if you know, now?"

"I believe they are in our evidence room."

"Where did you take them?"

"They were turned over to Trooper Yuknat from C.S.B.I., and he took charge of them." "And then they left your possession?"

"That's right sir."

"And Detective, were there any other articles that you took from the scene, or had in your possession, that you gave to some other officer?"

"I don't recall any others that night, no."

"Do you recall whether or not any hairs were found on the sliding doors?"

"Yes, there was a hair found on the sliding door."

"Did you find it?"

"No sir."

"Did you know who did, of your own knowledge?"

"Not positively, no."

"Did you know whether or not it was some member of the State Police Force?"

"Yes."

"Can you tell us who would know about that, if you know?"

"To the best of my recollection, Sergeant Chapman spotted it, and I believe Sergeant Ragazzi had something to do with it, however, I'm not positive about that."

"Do you remember anything else?"

"About what sir?"

"That you took from the premises?"

"I didn't take anything else that I can recall from the premises, no."

The questioning now turned to Sunday, March 13, the date Detective Rebillard went to East Hartland Center. Harry lived in the house next to the church, and at about 9:30 a.m..

Harry came out of the house carrying a snow shovel to clear the snow away from his car. The Detective said he called to Harry. "I'm Detective Rebillard Harry, do you remember me?" Harry replied, "Yes." He remembered me. They had talked before, on June 18, at Harry's home, three days after the homicide, June 1965. Trooper Pennington, and Detective Rebillard was there as well as Harry's mother, brother or sister. Harry was not married then, and was still living with his parents.

The officers glanced at Harry's car as they walked in the yard, but didn't go inside it. They were there for only about fifteen minutes. We were checking for black cars and any possible witness that would be of help in this investigation.

The Judge asked, "Did you find his black car there?"

"Yes it was."

"At that time were you in possession of the information from Mr. Flagg?"

"Yes."

"Why didn't you look in the car?"

"If we had found anything, it would have been thrown out anyway."

"There is no rule against looking around is there?"

"No sir, I don't believe there is—yet."

Continued Direct Examination of Detective Rebillard by Shew.

"Well, if you had any reason to look in the car, you could have asked to do it, couldn't you?"

"Yes, we could have asked."

"Now, when you accosted Harry with a snow shovel Sunday morning, what did you say to him?"

"Well, first I introduced myself and made sure that he recognized me and remembered me, which he did. I then advised Harry that I wanted to talk to him about a very confidential matter, and that I would like him to accompany me to Troop "B" Canaan, to do this. I also advised him he was not under arrest. Harry asked me how long it would be, and I told him, due to the bad road conditions, that it had snowed quite heavily during the night, it would take at least an hour at the Troop. Then Harry mentioned that he was going to church that morning and that it would interfere with going to church, but he would go in and talk with his wife about it. So I said, "All right," and he went back through the snow and into his house and stayed there for approximately five minutes or so, I would say."

"And he came out and got in your car?"

"Yes, he did."

"And when you got to the Barracks at Canaan, who started to question Harry then?"

"Well, he hadn't had his breakfast, so we stopped and had coffee and doughnuts in the kitchen, and at approximately 10:45 Harry and I went upstairs to a private room.

"And will you give us the conversation that took place in that private room?"

"Well, when we were—made ourselves comfortable in this room, I advised Harry of his rights before I questioned him on any further matter."

"What did you say to him?"

"I told him he did not have to make, or write, or sign any statements also, he didn't have to talk to me, he was entitled to counsel, and I believe, I also added anything he said could be used against him."

"And at the time you said that, did you indicate why you were questioning him?"

"No sir, I hadn't questioned him up till then."

"Or why you were about to question him?"

"I don't quite understand."

"Did you tell him you were going to question him?"

"Yes, I was going to question him."

"About what?"

"About the letter."

"Well, what did you say about the letter? You talked about the letter before you talked with him about—made the statement to him—how did he know about any letter?"

Wall objecting said, "Well, I object to that Your Honor, unless it's a two-headed question, one at a time."

Shew replied, "All right. How did Harry Solberg know about any letter?"

"After I advised him of his rights, I asked him about the letter."

"Was the room bugged?"

"Yes, it was."

"And in what form is that recording?"

"On tape."

"And you think that you were in the room with Harry for about an hour and a half, is that a fair statement?"

"Be close to that, yes."

"And after that, what happened after you left the room? Who took over after you left?"

"Lieutenant Fuessenich.
"Were you present when Lieutenant Fuessenich questioned him?"
"No, sir."
"When you questioned him, were you all alone in the room with him?"
Yes, sir."
"And then Lieutenant Fuessenich took a turn, he was all alone, correct?"
"That's right, sir."
"When did you next see Harry Solberg—we have got him being questioned by Lieutenant Fuessenich, right?"
"That's right."
"You weren't present?"
"That's correct."
"Were you listening in a side room?"
"Yes."
"Who was listening, besides you?"
"I believe Sergeant Keilty was listening."
"Did you have that rigged up so that you can listen without the person being questioned, knowing he's being listened to?"
"That's correct."
"Besides that you had a taped recorder turned on?"
"That's correct."
"Did you tell him that you had a tape recorder on?"
"No, I didn't."
"So you knew exactly what was taking place when Lieutenant Fuessenich was questioning him, yes or no?"
The Judge interrupted, "Excuse me, I want—"
Shew then asked, "You knew what was taking place when Lieutenant Fuessenich was questioning him, right?"
"Yes."
"How long did that take place?"
"A short time, I would say—possibly twenty or, thirty minutes."

"About thirty minutes. And who took over after Lieutenant Fuessenich got through?"

"No one."

"What happened then?"

"We had coffee, sandwiches, and milk."

"And when you got through with the coffee, sandwiches and milk?"

"Harry went with the lieutenant to Hartford, and Sergeant Keilty and I followed in our car."

The questioning now turned to the phone calls between Harry and his family and, what took place at the Hartford barracks when Harry was met there by his mother, father and wife. He had been advised by his parents to tell the detective about the letter. Then more questions regarding Lieutenant Reamer's talk with Harry, in the room that was bugged and taped. That took about half an hour, during which time, Lieutenant Fuessenich and Sergeant Keilty also listened. Harry was returned to Canaan that night.

Shew said, "I think that's all."

The Judge said,"Your witness Mr. Wall."

Wall commenced his cross examination of Detective Rebilard.

"Now Mr. Rebillard, I believe you stated that, in answer to a question from defense counsel, that three days after the death of Mrs. Thompsen, you went to the Solberg home, is that correct?"

"That is correct sir."

"And was that on the 18th., of June?"

"That is correct sir."

"When was that—with reference to the postmark on the letter that was sent to Arnfin?"

"That was the day after the letter was postmarked."

"At that time, had you knowledge of that letter?"

"No sir."

"At that time had you any knowledge relating to Solberg other than that he owned a black car?"

"No sir."

"Was this in the daytime or in the evening that you went to the Solberg home?"

"I believe it was the afternoon."

"Did you have a conversation with Harry that afternoon?"

"Yes I did."

"Will you please relate to His Honor and to the Jury what your conversation with Harry Solberg was on June 18 three days after the death of Mrs. Thompsen?"

"At this particular time we advised Harry and his mother that we were checking on black 1959 Fords and possible witnesses. We asked Harry if he had been using his car that day and he said yes. He then stated that he arrived home from school at approximately 12:30 p.m., after which he had dinner. He then changed his clothes, and left, in his black 1959 Ford, to work with his father all day, that day. It was at a person's home in North Granby, whose name I believe was, Howard Zimmer."

"Was that the extent of his conversation with you?"

"I believe there was some discussion as to whether or not he had picked up a mower or something that day too."

Did he state to you what time that he finished working that day at the Zimmer place?"

"He stated he worked there all day and got home around six or 6:15 for supper, and his mother agreed with him.

The questioning about the conversation with Harry continued, and then it turned to the visit with Sharon Provancher, Harry's girl friend.

"And after having talked with Sharon Provancher, you then on the 23rd. of June, talked again with Solberg?"

"Yes, sir."

"And will you relate to his Honor and the jury, what your conversation was with him at that time?"

Shew interjected, "If Your Honor pleases, I don't think this is proper cross because, I didn't bring anything out—however, I don't object."

The Judge then stated, "Well, I think it is time for recess anyhow, after which we will continue this. I'm not going to sustain an objection and rule on it at this time. If counsel wants to think about it, I will rule on it after the recess." After the recess, Rebillard was recalled to the stand.

Wall began the questioning, "Mr. Rebilliard, I believe, before the recess, I was asking you about an interview that you had with Solberg, the defendant, on the 23rd. I believe at that point, objection was interposed.

Shew withdrew his objection, to which the Judge stated, "It was withdrawn."

Wall asked similar questions. Concerning the interview with Solberg, and about the previous interview with Sharon Provancher, now Mrs. Harry Solberg He asked if Harry's Harry's black Ford was on Rte. 179 on the day of June 15, and if Sharon said anything in his presence as to what time he had been there?"

The answers, like the question were routine and repetitive.

Redirect by Shew.

Shew raised a question as to whether Sharon Provancher said anything in his presence, as to the time of day he had been there?

"She thought it was about 2:00 p.m.."

And are these times referring to a particular day of the year?"

"June 15."

"So that Sharon—the present Mrs. Solberg, thought you were there at 2:00, right?"

"That's correct, Yes, sir."

"Were you alone with her?"

"No. Trooper Pennington was there."

"And when did Harry appear on the scene?"

"Oh, maybe fifteen minutes later."

"And then you asked him whether he was on Rte. 179 that day?"

"Yes, sir."

"Just what were the words that you asked him then, as near as you can remember?"

"As near as I can recall, we had asked him if he had used Route 179 that day, other than going from his home on Rte. 20."

"And then you talked with Sharon about whether or not he had seen her that day, referring to June 15."

"Well, she thought it was around 2:00 p.m., and at first Harry said he hadn't been there. Between the two of them, Harry finally remembered he had been there, but said it was about five. We never did resolve the time between the two of them."

"It hasn't yet been resolved, but he thought he was there at five and she thought he was there at two, is that correct?"

"That's correct."

"But, as a mater of fact, he didn't try to pretend he was there at two o'clock, either, did he? He told you he was there at five."

"Yes, that's what he said, around five, yes."

"And it was she, who thought he was there around two?"

"That's correct."

"And you came away without any definite conclusion?"

"That's correct."

Shew then asked Wall if he was through.

Wall replied, "I am."

Shew then said, "That's all."

16

The trial was now well underway, and was still the main topic of conversation everywhere, from the country store to offices in the cities, and especially in the living rooms of the locals.

But, today, in the house on Louse Hill, Kay and Margaret were more interested in their personal problems than what was happening in the Court House in Litchfield.

Margaret said, "I don't know if I should say I'm sorry that Charlie's mother has died. I don't like to see or hear of anyone dying, but now, you and Charlie can get married."

Kay sighed, "I'm afraid not. Now he says his brother, Jim, has heart trouble, and he's going to move in with Charlie. There are just the two of them now, and Charlie will take care of him, as he did their mother."

Margaret asked, "Couldn't you get married and have him live with you two."

Kay shrugged, "A bachelor who was dominated by his mother, now takes on the care of his brother, forget it, it just won't work. I would end up as the housekeeper for both of them. We'll get married and live by ourselves, or not at all."

"That's too bad," said Margaret, "You two have spent over twenty years together. It's hard to start over. We become so accustomed to one man, his peculiarities, moods, both good and bad, he almost becomes part of you. You even know what he's thinking."

"That's life," Kay replied.

Margaret continued, "I can't see any hope for John and me either. I think about him day, and night, but we're drifting apart, I can feel it. The children need him, the business needs him, he has less vim and vigor than he once had, let's face it, he's simply too busy to be concerned about me. The excitement and romance has petered out. I just don't know to do about it. There'll never be anyone else for me, and if I don't do something this year, I'll end up an old maid. I can't spend the rest of my life up here in the "sticks" alone. He wants to deed it to me, and I don't want it. Up here in the country, we'll always be considered "city folk"."

Kay got up from the chair and said, "Well, let's go for a ride, we can view the countryside. As they drove along West Road, they had to stop the car and wait as a dairy herd crossed the road from a pasture to the barn. While the cows slowly lingered single file, the farmer walked to the car and talked to the women. They asked him why the cows were across the road, and not in the barn.

He replied, "They have to go from one pasture to another. When they chew it up on one side, they go across to the other side."

The women watched as the cows filed slowly into the barn, it was then that Margaret inquired, "Why are they going in the barn so early?," "It isn't dark yet."

The farmer laughed, "Because they have to be, or I should say need to be milked twice a day, at five in the morning and five in the afternoon. Daylight saving, or standard time, it makes no difference to the cows. They're ready every twelve hours."

Kay then asked, "What about weekends? What happens to their milk then?"

He laughed again, "We dairy farmers work seven days a week, no holidays, not even Christmas. The cows don't know when it's a holiday. If we have to be away for a day, for a funeral or wedding, a neighbor or a friend comes and takes over. We all know what to do, and where everything is."

He invited the women in, and talked to them as he put on his white coat and boots. They were amazed at the cleanliness of the barn. He washed the cow's udders and attached the milking machines. He then removed a package of paper cups and a jug of cider from a cupboard and offered them a drink. When the women finished the cider, they thanked the farmer for the milking indoctrination and started back home.

"What a way to make a living," said Margaret, "working with cows every day of the year, growing hay to feed them, taking them from field to field and then milking them twice a day. What a boring existence." We go to the store, buy a quart of milk, period. We don't give a second thought as to where it came from, or how much labor was involved in getting it from the cow to the milk bottle."

"Yes," replied Kay, "But he lives in a farmhouse on his own property, and he's with his family every day. I wonder what it would be like to have a husband home all the time.

"Yes," said Margaret, but imagine what it must be like to be tied down, not even going away for a weekend."

Kay's response was, "These country wives were born and raised out here. It's their way of life and they're happy. It's all they know. Besides, they probably get more loving, and better sex, than we do."

Back at the house they put some logs on the fire, and started supper. The farmer and his family had now taken a step back in their minds. The conversation turned to their own problems and the uncertainty of the future.

Margaret suggested that Kay stay overnight and leave early in the morning, to which Kay agreed.

would be here, either at a certain hour later this afternoon or tomorrow morning. That's—"

Shew answered, "Yes, Your Honor, I am expecting to do that." Shew further stated, "And you know the dress I am referring to, I think lieutenant, the one that was found in the washer?"

This started another barrage of petty accusations, with both lawyers, behaving like spoiled children.

Wall said, "This is his witness, Your Honor."

Shew replied. "I know it is, that's correct."

Wall said, "He's leading."

The Judge answered, "Well, I don't think that there was any harm done.

Shew said, "He led all last week, and I haven't criticized."

The Judge finally interceded, "Let's forget the exchange. Just proceed and tell the witness what you want, I think he understands."

Shew asked, "Is there any question in your mind of the dress I'm referring to, lieutenant?

All I know of the dress, sir, is that it is listed on one of our reports. I don't remember having seen it, but I am sure that we can locate it."

Now it seems to me that there has been reference here to some hair found in the hands of Mrs.—the deceased Mrs. Thompson, is that correct?"

"Yes, sir."

"Do you know where that hair is?"

I believe that would also be in our evidence room in Canaan.

"Do you know who found that hair lieutenant?"

"Yes, sir, I believe that was detective Rebillard."

"And do you know what happened to it after he took it?"

"It was turned over for examination, either to the State Department of Health, through Officer Yuchnakor directly, I don't know, from my own knowledge."

"What is Officer Yuchnakor's position, is he connected with the State Department of Health?

17

On Monday morning Cleveland Fuessenich was again on the stand for Direct Examination by Mr. Shew.

"Are you in charge of the Canaan Barracks now?"

"Yes, sir."

"And you have in your possession over there certain items—quite a few items connected with this case?"

"Yes, sir."

"And have you got any of them over there, that you are not perfectly willing to display in court?"

"No, sir, not a one."

"Let's start with the dress that was referred to when you testified as Mr. Wall's witness. Is that in this courtroom?"

"I will have to do a little research to determine where it is. Sergeant Raggazzi is here. I think, perhaps, he could answer that question."

"Well, I'm not trying to confuse anything, lieutenant. I am merely trying to find out where these various items are, and it's—"

Wall interrupted, "May I state for the record, Your Honor, that the—if sufficient notice is given to the State, the State will at all times produce anything that counsel wishes for exhibits here where required in Court."

Shew asked, "Do you think you can locate it?"

"Yes, sir."

"And how soon could you reasonably produce that dress?"

"Probably an hour and a half."

Judge Macdonald interrupted, "Might I suggest that, perhaps, if it can be certain during the course of questioning of this witness or other witnesses, just what items are wanted, a time can be fixed when they

"No sir, he is a State Policeman attached to the Bureau of Identification, in Hartford."

The Judged remarked, "Mr. Shew, excuse me, but I understand that you will make it clear, which of these items you wish produced."

Shew replied, "I do."

"Can you bring that in—get it here?"

"The hair found in the hand of the victim?, Yes, sir."

"And reference has also been made, too, I think, some hair being found in the sliding door separating the kitchen from the rest of the house?"

"This would be the sliding glass door from the dining room, to the rear porch."

"Do you know, yourself, whether or not such hair has been found?"

"I know from reading reports that such hair was found."

"And do you happen to know what was done with it?"

"It was examined—I don't know—by the Department of health. I don't know what happened to it after that."

Department of Health, presumably in your possession, have you not?"

"Yes, sir, we do."

"Do you, off hand, remember what they are?"

"There are many dealing with blood known on numerous articles and, examination of several samples of hair. I believe that is all. I can't remember anything else."

"Referring to the articles, that had blood on them, do you know anything about any samples being taken from the sink upstairs in Mrs. Agnes Thompsen's apartment, lieutenant?"

"I know that samples of water were taken from the traps, under the kitchen sink, and bathroom washbowl."

"Do you know when that was done, approximately?"

"I believe it was on the 16, of June, the day after this incident we're talking about."

"And do you know what was done with the samples after they were taken?"

"Yes, sir, they were turned over to the Department of Health."

"And is a Department, of the State Department of Health, frequently used by the State Police for analysis, and so forth?"

"Yes, sir, it is. It's done under the supervision of Dr. Stolman."

The questioning continued about the reports on the samples.

"They're available right now in the Court room. The State's Attorney has a copy."

Wall said, "Your Honor, I am glad to produce these, however, I intend to object to any examination with reference to them, because Dr. Stolman is not here and. If Dr. Stolman were here, he might very well tell me what these reports do state."

Judge MacDonald remarked, "I take it that at the present time they are offered to help the witness refresh his memory."

Shew said, "That's right Your Honor."

The Judge replied, "For that purpose, I assume there is no objection."

Shew asked, "Will you have Dr. Stolman here Mr. Wall?"

Wall replied, "He's not in the Courtroom, but I am sure he's on call. He can be here on a short notice."

Shew commented, "What do you call a short time?, three weeks?"

The Judge stated, "Because of his schedule, he usually can make himself available on a half-day's notice. At least that has been my experience with him. I would think if he were notified today that he is wanted tomorrow, he could make it. I think it might be pushing it a little bit, to say that he could get here this afternoon."

Wall said, "I will see that a call is made. If it's at all possible, we'll have him here."

Shew said, "I would appreciate that. Now, would you read my last question Mr. Tyll, please, I think I know what it is."

The Direct Examination of Lieutenant Fuessenich continued by Shew.

The questions were primarily about reports. "Were all the reports sent to the State Toxicologist?And for the purpose of the record, are those reports numbered? Are they in consecutive order?, and how many are there? I will ask you to give us specimen numbers."

Wall commented, "Your Honor, I don't see the relevancy of this. It would seem a waste of time to go into numbers. When Dr. Stolman appears, he will be available to testify relating to these. What numbers this witness has in hand at the moment, is of no significance. It's irrelevant."

Judge MacDonald said, "I assume that Mr. Shew's purpose is just to be certain that he has, all of the samples that were sent to him."

Shew commented, "Correct your Honor, I want to get everything in here. I want to make sure, because there is a lot of stuff apparently that would have never gotten in, unless we get it this way."

The Judge answered, "I don't think it would do any harm to have the lieutenant simply give the numbers of the specimens he has, and answer the questions as to whether to his knowledge, there are any more."

Wall then asked, "I ask that the last remark of counsel, which, to the effect, indicating that the State's Attorney is trying to prevent certain evidence from going in—"

To which Shew replied, "I didn't say anything about the State's Attorney. Don't be so sensitive, I didn't mention your name."

Judge Macdonald once again had to make a ruling, "I am assuming that there was no implication of any kind made. Now, let's have the numbers!"

The lieutenant read the numbers on the items listed; Clothing, tools, plumbing parts, water samples, household articles taken from Agnes's apartment, hair taken from Dorothy's right hand, hair mixed with dirt and twigs taken from her left hand, blood scrapings from all over the house, a cow manure bag, cuticle and nail cuttings taken from Agnes, and blood samples from members of the family.

Wall stated, "If your honor pleases, these are not in evidence, and they are not—"

Shew replied, "Well, they are getting in, if I can get them in Your Honor.

Judge MacDonald asked in his usual loquacious manner, "I wonder, and this is simply a query on my part having to do with saving of time. I wonder if it is going to be repetitious to go through this once today and again when Dr. Stolman is here. That's just an inquiry. Now, counsel may have something else in mind, but if we are going to have a report on what each item is, and then an analysis or report by the doctor, I wonder if that isn't just going to be an awful lot of repetition. Now, I can understand why you wanted to get the numbers in, so that you'd be sure that you had everything when you questioned Dr. Stolman. If there is some reason why it is necessary to go through it twice, why certainly you can do it."

Shew said, "Well, I thought it was important to get the items listed, and there may be some when I won't need Doctor Stolman. Apparently, as I understand it, these reports, some of them at least, have quite a few items in them."

The Judge responded, "Right."

Shew replied,"And they may be of no interest whatsoever, unless I hear from Mr. Wall."

Wall answered, "They are of interest and they are relevant Your Honor. I withdraw my objection. If he feels it's not a waste of time."

The Judge said, "It may be the only way to shorten the proceeding that will take place with Dr. Stolman, so, perhaps it's the best way to do it."

Continued Direct Examination of Lieutenant Fuessenich by Mr. Shew.

Once again the questions, and answers were wearisome. Each item was carefully numbered for identification purposes. The most important items seemed to be the hair found in Dorothy's hands, the water taken from the trap under the upstairs sink, and a stained woman's white dress, with blue trim, from the dryer in Dorothy Thompsen's kitchen.

Wall commented, "Your Honor, rather than go into—there is a great deal of evidence connected with this, and these titles include evidence for identification. I don't think it's necessary to go into anything more than the particular articles involved, rather than the characterization of what was claimed to be on them. I think that would be confusing."

The Judge replied, "I wonder if this—this is an inquiry only. I wonder if the same result would be accomplished, that Mr. Shew is seeking to obtain and to which he is entitled, by given him an opportunity to look over the list, so he can determine what is on the list. This will then give him an opportunity to indicate what he would like to have produced, and to examine Dr. Stolman on."

Shew answered, "I would be very glad to bore myself, and not the others here, if I could do it that way."

Wall said, "I would be very happy to have one of the officers be ready for private examination by him, so as he can give him the titles of these various things. I think that there is other information on them, that is not in evidence in them now. When they are in evidence, I presume he would have the right."

The Judge replied, "Just so Mr. Shew would be able to obtain a list with sufficient identification, so that he would know which samples of hair it was, or which dress it was, as has been going on so far. I think it would save an awful lot of time, if that could be done at the conclusion of today's testimony. We have only covered four, of something like twenty or twenty-five items here, so far."

Shew said, Well, I have had a feeling that maybe some of them, when Lieutenant Fuessenich described what they were, could be skipped, but I have been interested in—"

The Judge asked, "All of them?"

Shew replied, "All of them, so far."

The remainder of the day was spent with Lieutenant Fuessenich reading numbers and identifying articles, in order that everything would be ready for Dr. Stolman.

Gerald Pennington, the next witness was sworn in, for direct examination by Shew.

He stated, he has been a State Police Trooper for eight and a half years. On the night of June 15, 1965 he was at home, when he was called to go to the Thompsen house. He arrived at the house about five minutes after seven, and present at that time were, Mr. Thompsen his mother Agnes Thompsen, as well as Sergeant Joseph Riley and Trooper Soliani. Upon his arrival Arnfin Thompsen and Agnes Thompsen were sitting on the front steps. He stated that Sergeant Riley took him inside to get a brief look at the interior of the house, and then to the rear of the house where the victim was located. At about 7:15 he took Mrs. Thompsen upstairs with him went upstairs into Agnes Thompsen's apartment. They sat on the couch, and he asked Agnes what had transpired.

After about fifteen or twenty minutes of conversation, he was sent out to check the neighborhood, to the south of the Thompsen home. He then returned to the house and stayed there until one thirty, in the morning. He explained that he didn't take anything with him that night, but the next day Captain O'Brien showed him a white dress with blue trim, that was taken from the dryer. Arnfin identified the dress as belonging to Dorothy.

Cross Examination by Wall.

"Do you know whether the door of the clothes dryer was open or closed at the time that you arrived at the kitchen of the Arnfin Thompsen residence?"

"I believe it was closed."

Wall said, "That's all."

To which Shew asked, "I didn't get that—the door what?"

Wall answered, "Was opened or closed, believe it was closed."

Shew replied, "Oh, the dryer—That's all."

The next witness was Orlando P. Ragazzi, with Direct Examination by Shew.

"And what is your occupation, Mr. Ragazzi?"

"Connecticut State Policeman."

"And how long have you been with the Connecticut State Police?

"Fourteen and a half years."

"And you were requested to bring certain records and so forth with you? Have you arranged them so that we can find out just what you have there, Sergeant?"

"Well, if you will tell me what you want, I will find it for you."

I want to know what you have."

Wall once again objecting said, "Well, I object to that, Your Honor."

At that time, the Judge said, "That might be a long list."

Shew replied, "Well, did you bring what I asked you to bring under subpoena, Sergeant?"

"The subpoena requested all reports and records that were available to me at Hartford and Canaan. I have everything from Hartford here."

"And can you tell me why some records were in Hartford and some in Canaan?"

"Well, all I can testify to there, Mr. Shew, is what was kept in Hartford, which had to do with Agnes Thompsen. Subsequent to that, I was transferred out of that Division. I don't know whether any of their files should be in this jacket or not, or what the arrangement was from that point on."

"You mean that everything you have there, has to do with the investigation concerning Agnes Thompsen, is that correct?"

"Not exclusively of her, but everything up to a point."

"When did you first have knowledge of this homicide?"

"On June 15, 1965."

"And how did you get that knowledge?

"I was at my home and was assigned by the Executive Officer to proceed to Route 179 to Barkhamsted, and there to be of whatever assistance possible, to Captain Thomas O'Brien."

"And what did you do when you got there, Sergeant?"

"I asked Trooper Soliani where the lieutenant was. The lieutenant had been across the road at Mrs. Stadler's. I waited until he came out. About that time, we had a brief conversation. Captain O'Brien then arrived on the scene, and I reported to the Captain. He assigned me to keep people away, that were congregating at the scene, and also to interview Ted Thompsen."

"So that, for the moment, you were occupied in keeping the house cleared.?"

"Keeping persons away."

"And how long did you do that?"

"Until some other troopers arrived and took over this job, and then I interviewed Ted Thompsen for a while. He is the brother-in-law of the deceased."

"Then what did you do?"

"I was assigned to assist in the search of the Agnes Thompsen apartment. One section of her room, that would be up on the second floor, in the living room area, and in the attic area. We didn't go in her bedroom at the time, because she was in there with one of our policewomen.

"What policewoman was she in there with?"

"I believe it was Virginia Butler."

"And will you tell us how you went about it?"

"As systematically as we possibly could. It was Trooper Pennington, myself and Trooper Bonolo. We started over—underneath the eaves which was a storage space in the Agnes Thompsen apartment, and there was quite a bit of material there, and we went through everything as minutely as possible."

"And, what do you remember, or have you a list of what you took from her apartment?"

"As I recall, we took cow manure bags and their contents, a waste paper basket which had hair clippings, a pair of blue dungarees, a nightgown, two handkerchiefs, a pair of shoes and, a pair of sneakers. All of these were packed in cellophane bags and turned over to Trooper Yuknat of CSB-1. As it is our standard procedure, if there is a CSB-1 man on the premises, he assumes custody of all evidence at that particular time.

"And what did you do after you got through searching the apartment, did you have any conversation with Agnes Thompsen at that time?"

"I had no conversation with her, as I recall. I believe Captain O'Brien and the Policewoman were conversing with her."

"What was the Policewoman's name?

"Virginia Butler."

"Do you know when they left?"

"They left at about the same time we did, which would be roughly, 1:00 or 1:30 a.m."

"With Agnes Thompsen?"

"Yes, sir. We returned the next morning at about 9:00 a.m., for a meeting with Members of the Bureau of Identification. Namely, Captain O'Brien, several members of Troop "B", and several members from the Detective Division."

"What did you do then?"

"My assignment at this particular point was to check out an individual by the name of Martel, and his assistant, a Mr. MacDonald, as to their whereabouts on the day in question."

"The whereabouts of who?"

"Of Mr. Martel, I believe it is, and a Mr. MacDonald. Mr. Martel is a contractor and, as I recall, he had done some work on the premises for the Thompsens, and because Agnes Thompsen had stated that she had seen a vehicle parked in her yard, one resembling one owned by Martel, I was then assigned to determine the whereabouts of Mr. Martel's vehicle, Mr. Martel, and Mr. MacDonald.

"Had she described the vehicle that she had seen there?"

"She said, as I recall the information given to me, the vehicle was larger than an automobile, and it green. This information was given to me by Captain O'Brien, as I recall."

"And as a result of that, you did go and interview a Mr. Martel?"

"Yes, and a Mr. MacDonald."

The witness then gave the location of their houses. Mr. Martel lived about a mile up the road from the Thompsen's. Mr. MacDonald also lived in Barkhamsted, to the south of the Thompsen's. Then, he said, he had to go check with Metropolitan Water District policeman William Flagg about the black 1959 Ford he said was parked in front of Thompsen's house the day of the murder. The following day he was detailed to search the grounds of the Thompsen house, run down certain leads, and taking into possession certain evidence and transporting it to the State Laboratory.

"And I believe you named certain articles that you brought downtown, that you remember?"

"Most of the items that we seized, or took into our possession, I should say, were turned over to Trooper Yuknat."

"And is there anything else you did, Sergeant?"

Wall said, "Your Honor, I don't see the relevancy of this. I object to it."

To which Shew replied, "I will show it to you before we get through Mr. Wall."

Wall asked, "Is there a distinct promise to connect it up with something? If there is a distinct promise, I don't object. If there is no promise, I object to it."

Shew replied, "I certainly think it is admissible. I'm not doing this just for fun."

The Judge asked, "Is this in connection with the identification of objects taken?"

"No sir, it is not."

The Judge stated, "Well, on the assurance that it will be tied in with something."

Shew answered, "I will put it this way Your Honor, I will, unless Mr. Wall stops me. I will do my best, that's all."

"I intend to stop him," replied Wall.

The questioning continued about what items were taken, where, and by whom, and about the digging around the Thompsen's property. The attorneys argued, and finally the Judge said, "Let's straighten out one thing at a time. We could possibly straighten out the custody of the items which have to do with the pending examination by Dr. Stolman. If other matters which you think might give rise to some argument or extensive cross examination and objections, or if you are suggesting, as I gather you are, that we get together, that is you and Mr. Wall can get together on the items concerning Dr. Stolman at this time. You may suspend at this time, so that you could possibly agree, and don't start any other items until tomorrow. I am perfectly open to that suggestion unless there is an objection. Will you gentlemen please get together with the list, at this time? This witness may be excused, subject to being recalled."

The attorneys agreed.

18

Dr.Abraham Stallman's return to the stand created a stir of excitement from the spectators gallery. The big question in everyone's mind, was, would there be new evidence revealed today?

The Doctor reiterated, almost verbatim, the testimony sworn to during his previous examination. He also repeated his experience, qualifications and background. Shew asked about the items and exhibits taken from the Thompsen house and grounds.

The Doctor replied, "And also one pair of ladies white sneakers found in the attic at 11:30, in the apartment of Mrs. Agnes Thompsen."

I ask you Doctor, whether or not you found anything of any significance in connection with that pair of white sneakers, in your opinion?,"asked Shew.

"No, I examined it for blood and found none there."

He also stated that he didn't find any blood on the woman's dungarees, or on the pair of blue socks. He did, however, find a trace of blood in the water taken from the traps of the bathroom and kitchen sinks in Agnes Thompsen's living area."

"You found blood in each trap?"

"Yes, I found blood in the water in each trap."

Wall stated, "Your Honor, the exhibit should speak for itself. The exhibit says, A trace of blood."

To which the Judge replied, "The Doctor is testifying that he found blood. He can characterize it any way that he sees fit."

Shew asked, "Water from the upstairs kitchen sink trap?"

"Yes, sir. It's not sufficient blood to do an actual group typing. I simply indicated that it was human."

The next important item was the hair found on the inner edge of the patio door, which had the same characteristics as that of the victim. Shew showed Dr. Stolman a small plastic container, labeled, "hairs found in right hand of victim."

Wall commented, "I think that's important for the Jury to hear, Your Honor."

To which Shew replied, "I want them to hear it, too, because—"

Dr. Stolman described the hairs as being from one and one quarter inches to three inches in length. The microscopic examination showed that it had pigmentation evenly distributed throughout the length of the hair. The Doctor said, "There was no core, as we refer to it as medulla, and it had scale formation which is generally characteristic of human hair."

"The next item was the lady's white sleeveless dress with blue trim. The dress had type "O" blood stains on the bottom side of it. Other things examined were a pair of shoes Arnfin was wearing the night of the murder. There was a small amount of human blood on the edge of the right shoe, however, not sufficient for typing, a man's shirt taken from the ironing board, blood scrapings from the kitchen, dining room and porch, several hairs found on the toaster, some of Agnes Thompsen's clothing, which was taken from her at the Connecticut Valley Mental Hospital. Also, several small boxes containing scrapings from the fingernails of Agnes Thompsen. From Dorothy's left hand were, sand, dirt, fragments of twigs and plants and several hairs. There was a trace of blood on the scrapings from Agnes's fingernails, however, in an insufficient amount to type it."

"What is the date of those scrapings, Doctor?"

"The date given was taken on June 30, 1965 at Connecticut Valley Hospital."

Wall replied, "I don't mean to have him go into each one of them. Just the dates taken, where they were taken, and the names of the items."

The Doctor named several items taken from the apartment of Agnes Thompsen, including: towels, a blue bathrobe, an apron, one pair black shoes, a dishcloth, and a yellow dish drainer. All were tested for blood, however, the doctor had found none.

Items taken from Dorothy's house included: an electric cord, ice pick, "nailset", and a dress belonging to Christa. There was no blood found on any of the items, with the exception of the ice pick, which contained a trace of blood on the tip. The blood was human, but once again in an insufficient quantity for to typing. Dr. Stolman repeated his testimony about the three trips to the Thompsen house. He was concerned about the brown stain on the staircase on the third step from the bottom, which he had removed and brought to the laboratory. He didn't know what the brown stain was, but it was determined that it was not blood.

"Doctor, did you attach any significance to the quantity of blood that was found on any of the articles that came from the Agnes Thompsen apartment?"

"No sir, I did not."

"Would you please explain that to, His Honor, and the Jury?"

"Whatever blood was there, that I could detect, was in very small quantities and I really had to work hard to even detect that quantity. We spent too much time for it to be any significant amount"

"And would you explain the bodily secretions that might possibly account for slight quantities of blood?

"Well—with respect to what particular item?"

"Well, with respect to a female living in a household. Would you expect normally to find any small amounts of blood to be found in the household?"

"Yes, I would expect it. In any household, you expect to find blood in traps and sinks, in bathrooms, and so on, because even brushing your teeth, occasionally you find you spit a little blood out, or clearing your throat, sometimes in the morning, and female secretions, at certain times produce blood, or secretions which give you similar reactions to blood typing."

"And does that happen to females, even after their menstrual period has passed?"

"Well, yes, I would think so."

Wall stated, "No further questions Your Honor."

Redirect Examination of Dr. Stolman by Shew

"Did you find such secretions in the kitchen sink?"

"Well, you find blood—I have found other secretions also. Individuals may spit in the kitchen sink."

"Did you find female secretions in the kitchen sink?"

"You wouldn't find them in the kitchen sink."

"All told Doctor, there was a number of items in Mrs. Agnes Thompsen's apartment, neat as it was, which had blood on them, were there not?"

"Yes, sir."

"And in the sum aggregate of all those items that blood were found on, do you want to go on record as saying that they have no significance in this matter?"

"Well, the quantity, I would say I can't put too much significance in it. If it is a normal kitchen where normal individuals work, and using sharp instruments, a blood stain is not always easy to wash out. It has to take a good thorough washing to remove blood stains."

"Let's put it in reverse Doctor, these stains could have all been made the previous day, could they not?"

"Yes, sir, I don't know how long they were there. I can't tell."

"That's right. Now, the scrapings from Agnes Thompsen's cuticles and hands. In one of the exhibits, do you attach significance to that—taken from her hands at, 2:30, or 2:20 as I recall it, on June 16th?"

"Well I can't explain what the blood stains were doing in the fingernails of her hands."

"So it's a fact that they would have some significance in this case?"

"They might have some significance, yes."

"And maybe you have so testified before Doctor, before any other authorities, in this connection?"

"I don't know whether it was brought up in the Grand Jury or not. That was the only time I testified in this case."

"So that your recollection is, you don't know?"

"I don't know sir."

Shew said, "That's all."

Recross examination of Dr.Stolman by Wall.

"Doctor, did you know of the situation with regard to Mrs. Thompsen—about her having crocheted that day?"

"No Sir, I didn't even know she crocheted."

"I see. Would it be a possibility that a scraping of that sort would indicate that there had been some slight wound in the area?"

"Why, anything with a sharp point or sharp edge can produce a scratch of the skin and bleeding."

"And was there any—will you please refer to your notes, and determine what quantity was found in these scrapings?"

"Oh, it is just an extremely small quantity, just particles. That was all I had, was just had a small amount. I had to look under the microscope to detect it, first of all. And it certainly was in an insufficient amount to make any blood type."

"Doctor, again in connection with that, did you know whether or not the State Police examined Agnes Thompsen in the Middletown Hospital to find out whether she had cut her hand, or pricked her hand crocheting?"

"No sir, I don't know that."

"You don't. But if it was found out that she hadn't, that would have been significant, would it not Doctor?

Yes it would."

The Doctor was excused, and Orlando Ragazzi was recalled to the stand.

Sergeant, were you in the court room this morning, just before recess closed?"

"Yes, sir, I was."

"And a remark was made by Mr. Wall concerning a possible injury to Agnes Thompsen with knitting needles, did you hear that?"

"Yes, I did."

"And do you know whether you or any member of your department examined Agnes Thompsen for any possible injuries that she may have had with a knitting needle, at the time that these items were found?"

"Well, I don't know this of my own knowledge, other than the fact that I do know that there was a report come through Mr. Wall."

"I object to a "report", Your Honor."

The Judge sustained the objection. "If the witness can testify of his own knowledge—otherwise, he would have to have the best evidence."

Shew asked, "Do you know whether or not some member of your Department, male or female, had examined Mrs. Thompsen in that connection?"

"I think there was a general examination of her upon her admittance. On either that day, or that evening, or the following day, I don't recall which."

"And did you have a report showing whether anything was found indicating—?"

Wall screamed, "I object to "report", Your Honor."

The Judge commented, "I think that the best evidence would be the introduction of either the report, or the witness who prepared the report, probably the person who prepared the report."

Shew continued, "Upon another hearing, Sergeant, you made the statement, did you not, that there were no injuries on her body at that time."

Wall started to say something, "Your Honor, I—"

Shew spoke out, "I'm going to claim it, Your Honor."

Wall in his usual manner said, "I object to it. It's leading, and counsel knows that it's objectionable, and he should never make a statement of that sort."

The Judge, in an attempt to straighten out the matter said, "It's the wrong way to get it in, certainly. You can't ask him to testify whether or not he made a statement and read the statement, unless you can ask him to testify, as to certain things, and then introduce evidence of prior inconsistent statements, if you wish to do it that way. This statement—the answer—the question that was asked, I think, should be stricken."

Wall answered with a question, "And may the jury be informed, Your Honor?"

The Judge instructed the Jury to disregard any significance connected with the question.

The attorneys continued their annoying habit of arguing back and forth, and it was becoming a distraction. Judge MacDonald was well aware of the friction that existed between the two lawyers, especially when Shaw stated, "I will ask this witness be declared a hostile witness from here on. He's a member of the State Police."

Judge Macdonald, acting as a buffer said, "I don't believe that the witness has yet—I would like you to clarify the question which is being called hostile, or if you are going to call it inconsistent, by asking the witness a direct question which might be indicative of being contradictory to something which he has said previously. I don't believe that he has definitely made any statement yet which fits that category, in my opinion."

Shew then asked in a roundabout manner, "Sergeant, do you do remember testifying before Coroner Guion?"

Yes, sir."

"In July?, and do you remember being questioned by him concerning this same subject that I am questioning you about now?"

"Yes."

Shew continued the questions concerning the scrapings taken from Agnes Thompsen, then he asked the Sergeant, "And when you got through there, did you do any more?"

"I assisted Major Rome on, I believe, two or three occasions when he interviewed Agnes Thompsen. The dates June 21, July 16, July 25, and August 5." The Sergeant answered additional questions, "Yes, I did make notes, yes, someone else was with them, Lieutenant Fuessenich, and either Arnfin or Ted Thompsen."

"And what did you do when you got to the Connecticut Valley Hospital?"

"Major Rome requested to see Agnes Thompsen. He talked with, I believe, it was the Superintendent of the Hospital, Mr. Lowney, and Mr. Miller, Chief of Professional Services, who made the arrangements that she be interviewed."

"And who was present?"

"Major Rome and Lieutenant Cleve Fuessenich, myself, and one of the Doctors from the hospital, I believe, was seated in the conference room. I think one of the nurses was also present."

"And what time of day was this?"

"I believe it would be early afternoon."

"And did you see Agnes Thompsen at this time?"

"Yes, sir."

"And in the presence of yourself and Major Rome and Lieutenant Fuessenich and, who else?"

"I believe it was Arnfin Thompsen, or Ted Thompsen, one of the sons?"

Sergeant Orlando Ragazzi then reiterated the conversations that had transpired during the Hospital visit.

Major Rome asked Agnes, "Why did you clean the stairs?, there was blood on the sandpaper."

Agnes replied, "Didn't notice that."

"Do you remember the argument you had with Dorothy?"

Agnes denied an argument.

Major Rome said, "You ought to tell the truth." Then he asked her, "When was the last time you saw Dorothy?"

She answered, "A week ago today."

"You changed the baby?"

"No. The baby messed her pants, I didn't do it!, maybe Dorothy did it. I thought it was funny because it was so quiet downstairs. Maybe she went out."

The next question asked was, "Was the baby in your apartment?"

"No, you are putting lies on me."

Then Major Rome asked, "How come there was blood on the staircase?"

She answered, "Next to the last step, blood on the staircase, there was a spot there."

There were some spots on the staircase. "What did you do with the sandpaper?"

"I put it in the trash bag upstairs."

"How can you explain the blood on the sandpaper?, How did you get blood on the towel?"

Obviously very upset, she answered, "I don't know, I don't know."

"The major then asked, "The dungarees, you washed them?, they were damp."

She answered, "Could the cat have been on them?"

"Before you go home, tell the truth."

"I am telling the truth."

"Your son tells me you want to be truthful. There was blood on the towel."

Agnes repeated, "Blood on the towel?"

"Now, when was the baby's diaper changed?"

"She was in the crib from 12:45 to 6:15 p.m. I didn't have her upstairs. She messed her pants. I didn't clean her. Maybe it was the woman that did it."

"You had an argument?"

"I did not. I didn't see her all day Tuesday."

"Remember the piggy bank. It was always in the living room."

"I didn't see Dottie all day Tuesday. I didn't touch the baby."

"Could you have forgotten that day?"

"No, I was crocheting all that day."

"Sometime before, did you have trouble with Dorothy?"

"When they got married, she wanted Ted to stand up for them."

"You had an argument."

"No argument."

"What about the cloth that was used? The one with blood that we found in the kitchen."

"Where in the kitchen? Somebody must have been there. Somebody did a trick on me."

"Did you wash it out?"

"No, I am completely innocent."

"I am asking you to remember how the blood got on the yellow wash towel?"

"Someone must have done a trick on me."

"It was found right away"

"I am innocent. Isn't it bad enough that Dorothy is dead without putting this on me?"

"A few minutes ago you didn't remember the yellow washcloth. Now you remember."

"You had no idea there was blood on the sandpaper or on the yellow wash cloth?"

"I washed off my finger, which I pricked with the crochet needle. I heard something downstairs. Heard somebody, or something, but saw no one."

"Only two people could have changed the baby, you or Dot."

"Dot must have."

"No. She was dead at 1:30 p.m."

"I didn't see the body before Arnfin came home. When Arnfin came home, he said that Dot was dead. I didn't know Dot was dead until Arnfin came home."

"She was dead long before he came home. You had the baby upstairs before Arnfin came home.

"That's a big lie."

"Who cleaned the baby? Whoever cleaned the baby tracked blood on the stairs."

"I cleaned the stairs because company was coming."

"How much?"

"Just a couple spots."

"What time?"

"About two o'clock."

"Did the baby cry?"

"Not at all that day."

"She was alone."

"How did you know she was alone? You took care of her."

Agnes didn't answer that.

"Can you remember now, the dungarees? They had just been washed?"

"I didn't wash them."

"We found blood in the drain, and in the kitchen drain."

"That's a lie, I want to leave."

"Then she got down on her knees and she prayed, and then another question was asked."

"Have you been bleeding lately?"

There was no answer to that, and she was escorted from the room.

Continued direct examination of Sergeant Ragazzi, by Shew.

"Sergeant, to the best of your ability, could you describe Agnes Thompsen's attitude and physical condition at the time this interview started, and at the time it got through?"

"She appeared, as I recall it, every contact that I had with her, appeared to be extremely nervous. She wouldn't sit still in any one position too long. At certain questions being asked, her eyes would open up extremely wide and then she'd settle down. This is about the best explanation I can give you, Mr. Shew, of my observation."

"I don't quite understand what you said about her eyes opening?"

"It appeared her eyes would open wide at certain questions, and at certain times."

"Could you describe, and tell us, in what manner these questions were put to her? Were they put to her in a harsh fashion? In other words, tell us just how they were expressed to her?"

"These questions were given to her in a normal fashion. She was questioned along the lines pretty much as I read them here."

"Did she seem at any time to you to be in distress or suffering?"

"Well, there was also a doctor or a nurse present. And, I don't know what you mean by distress, Mr. Shew."

"Well, it's a general term, and I just want—want to have you express to the best of your ability, how Mrs. Thompsen was treated during this—could it have been done in a nicer fashion, that you know of, Sergeant?"

"No, sir."

"And whether or not she seemed to understand the questions that were asked of her?"

"I would say, for the most part, she did. There appeared to be times when she didn't fully understand the question, and the question was repeated. There also were times when she didn't answer."

"And can you point out any particular question which you felt she didn't understand, and she—and that she answered?"

"Well, this would be hard for me to say at this time, Mr. Shew. I really don't know. I really don't know which one of these questions she answered, what I do know, there were several of them that she didn't answer."

Sergeant Ragazzi kept his composure as he answered, and at times repeated answers to the questions. He said, the next time he saw Agnes Thompsen was July 16th after the Coroner's inquest, and subsequent to that, at the Headquarters Detective Division in Hartford. Agnes was accompanied by nurse Butterfield, from the Connecticut Valley Hospital. No, he didn't talk to her, the interviews were all done by Major Rome.

"And how long was she in Major Rome's office?"

"I would say approximately an hour, or so. This is an estimate, I don't know for sure."

"And have you got the questions that were given to Agnes Thompsen at that time?"

"Yes sir."

"Will you read them?"

Wall objected

The Judge replied, "State the grounds. I mean—this is—this was the prior, came in the same way and I just wondered if you wished to state—"

Wall responded, "Your Honor, as far as the prior one was concerned, there were certain safeguards involved, and I feel that although it was hearsay, I didn't object. I can see that many collateral issues will arise out of this situation, and I believe it is definitely hearsay, and inadmissible. It would definitely be unfortunate if we injected new issues into this case, that have nothing to do with it."

Judge Macdonald responded, "Well, let me hear if Mr. Shew claims some particular part of this as an exception to the hearsay rule."

To which Shew replied, "I certainly do, Your Honor. I was hoping we could proceed, but I can be more specific, if I have to be."

Judge MacDdonald replied, "In other words, we are coming soon to a ruling on a point of law, is that correct?"

Both lawyers responded in the affirmative.

The Judge said, "I would imagine we might just as well face that now, before we get on to extraneous grounds and something slips out. So that, at this point, I will excuse the Jury." The Judge further added," I assume that what we are getting down to, are the answers made by Agnes Thompsen during the course of an interview. Ordinarily, that would be objected to as heresy. And I assume that Mr. Shew has some arguments and exception."

Shew commented, "I have, Your Honor. As a matter of fact, I have asked Attorney Frank MacGregor from the Welfare Department, who has charge of this situation as far as Agnes Thompsen is concerned, to be here at 2:00, and he promised to be here, and I am at a loss—"

Before the Judge could get the words out, Wall said, "He's here."

Shew then remarked, "Oh, he is? I didn't see him. I have been looking for him. I think we could argue this thing—I was going to put Mr. MacGregor on to establish the fact that Agnes Thompsen was unable to be here, and can't be here unless Mr. Wall—I have reason to believe Mr. Wall knows she can't be here I don't want to create an embarrassment, if that could be agreed upon, I could proceed."

Wall commented, "I would like to consult with Mr. MacGregor, myself. I think we can agree, Your Honor, that Mrs. Thompsen is in the infirmary, and neither physically or mentally able to be here, if Mr. MacGregor so states."

MacGregor replied, "And that includes the foreseeable future."

Wall stated, "I have every confidence in what Mr. MacGregor would say."

Shew then said, "Thank you, Mr. MacGregor and Mr. Wall. That's all I need from you. If Your Honor, please, that, of course, is one of the two ingredients that is necessary in connection with Agnes Thompsen, exception to the heresy rule. Either that or a situation such as this kind, or insanity and so forth. Obviously, she is unable to be here. If she made certain statements in connection with this matter, which are prejudicial to her, it is my feeling that those are admissible evidence. There are a number of exceptions."

The Judge said, "There is some Connecticut Law on this first point, I believe."

Shew answered, "Yes, Your Honor, there is quite a bit of law on it. One of the cases is States versus Mosca."

The Judge said, "I am familiar with the case. The point he was interested in, is the rather broad language that was used. The Supreme Court said that Counsel for the Defendant admits that the great weight of authority is against their claim. If a third person, other than the accused, has confessed to the commission of the crime, it is admissible in favor of the accused. This is unquestionably true, and then it cites a few cases. Now, that is pretty broad language."

Shew said, "As far as the weight of authority, if you will consider it in number, it might be possibly correct. I think, "Wigmore", indicates clearly, that the better rule is to admit it on the basis that there is no reason to keep it out. Because a person admitting they committed a murder, obviously could have no financial reward or benefit there from. That is conceivable for making such an admission. Now, I think "Wigmore" states, it is their opinion definitely, that such statements as we are talking about here, should be admitted in criminal cases. That's the better and more sensible law. I would quote from the Donelly case which is one of the leading cases—"

The Judge stated, "I would make no comments on that. I agree with you most heartily, that he was, and I will make no further comment."

They mentioned several other famous cases, and then Shew said, "There may be some circumstances where it goes to the weight. I appreciate that, here. Mr. Wall may say that Agnes Thompsen didn't know, or something like that, or that she didn't know what she was doing. That is his privilege and is a matter of weight rather than admissibility. It is certain that the leading writers on the matter consider that the better rule is, undoubtedly, to allow such statements. No one can be harmed by it. As a matter of fact, as far as this is concerned, it isn't going to hurt Agnes Thompsen. It's just seeking the truth, and it helps to do so because this never could be used at a future time, if she were ever placed on trial. I am not claiming that it's something entirely different. There is an entire difference between statements she may have made against herself, and this statement of that sort. That theory of self-incrimination shouldn't even come into the picture, because obviously, any statement that might be admitted here could never plague her in the hereafter, on account of that, because they would be not admissible as far as she was concerned. I don't think there is any connection with the thought of self-incrimination. It's just a question of whether she made such a statement or not, and, if she did, it was much against her interests. Then why should it be eliminated?"

Wall replied, "I say, Your Honor, that this is definitely hearsay, and the reason that there are ever exceptions to the hearsay rule, is, if there is a guarantee of trustworthiness. In this case, Your Honor, I say that we have listened so far to find out what has been said by the interrogator to this particular person, and he has lied to her four times. He said to her, Your Honor, "There is blood on the sandpaper." Can you imagine a poor woman sitting there in a mental institution, and lying to her and telling her there was blood on the sandpaper? How did it get there? "There is blood on the towel," which was a lie, "Blood on the staircase," which was a lie. I show you, Your Honor, that he knew it was a lie, the interrogator, because—"

Shew then said, "If your Honor, please, I don't think we need to get—this has nothing to do with the law or the matter at all."

The Judges interrupting said, "I hate to interrupt, but what we are passing on now is not the circumstances under which this statement was taken. If it should be ruled, that this statement, whether it can be characterized as an admission, or a confession, or whether it is to be admitted at all, I will rule that the statements made by Agnes Thompsen be inadmissible."

At 4:15 Mr. Shew asked for an adjournment until the following morning.

19

The following morning while trying to recover from the latest setback in the trial, Shew began reading the morning papers. Gerald Demeusy wrote in the Hartford Courant: *Golberg defense fails in evidence strategy. Judge rules report by police, hearsay. Counsel for accused slayer Harry Solberg failed Thursday in his long-awaited attempt to get before a Superior Court jury, statements about the murder of Mrs. Dorothy Thompsen allegedly made by her mother-in-law.*

Judge Herbert S. MacDonald ruled that to permit the introduction of such statements about the murder of Mrs. Dorothy Thompsen allegedly made by her mother-in-law, would violate Connecticut's long-established hearsay rule. The mother-in-law, Mrs. Agnes Thompsen, was questioned by State Police four times about the June 15, 1965 killing of her son's 30 year old wife in her Barkhamsted home.

Shew finished reading Demeusy's column, then he went into the Court room to face the three witnesses scheduled for the day. Mrs. Carole Stadler was the first witness.

Shew started with, "Just to refresh the recollection of everybody, Mrs. Stadler, you testified for the prosecution in this matter earlier, did you not?", and you are the girl who lives across the road from the Thompsen house, and you were the first person to call the police?" Mrs. Stadler answered, "Yes," then continued, "Dorothy told me that she thought her mother-in-law was getting bad again, or she had gotten worse. She said her mother-in-law came home and couldn't open the front door. She had to wait twenty minutes for Dorothy to get home and open the door. From that day on, her headaches had come back, and she blamed that on Dorothy, for not being home to let her in."

Shew then asked, "And during the two and one-half months that you lived across the road from her, did you notice anything unusual about Dorothy when you had a an opportunity to see her?

"Yes, I had always noticed that she had a black and blue mark on her, one place or another. She always seemed to be black and blue."

"And did you get any impression as to how they were caused?"

"Yes I did, she looked to me as though she had been beaten or—"

"Been beaten by somebody?"

"Yes."

"And was there any way you can explain to the jury how they appeared to you?"

"Well, not really except that I noticed one time she had a great big black and blue mark here (indicating her neck) and another time she had a big one on her arm and she had several on her legs."

Wall asked, "Now Mrs. Stadler, this was a new home into which the Thompsens had moved fairly recently, isn't that so?"

"I think they had been there about two years."

"And she did very heavy work out in the yard, man-sized work isn't that so?"

"Yes."

"And any of these bruises, that you may have seen, might very well have happened as a result of the hard work, or the knocking down of trees, or things of that sort?"

"Yes, they could have.

"Did it occur to you before Mr. Wall asked you, Mrs. Stadler, that she might have received these bruises working around the house or around the yard?"

"Well, I had thought they might have happened that way, but I also thought they might have happened from a beating."

The next witness was Stanley Martin Bugge. He said he has been the minister of the Bethany Lutheran Free Church of East Hartland, Connecticut for five years, and Harry Solberg has been a member since he was baptized as an infant."

Shew asked, "What, if any, investigation do you make before they are admitted to your Church, Pastor?"

"Well, there is a general surveillance of each of our potential members. In Harry's case, he has been a boy in our Church since his childhood, and in his character—"

"Wall interrupted, "Your Honor, I don't see the relevance of this. It isn't responsive and—"

The Judge responded, "I assume that this line of questioning is going to be reputation and character, is that the purpose?"

Shew answered, "That is correct, Your Honor."

The Judge added, "And if so, I suppose this is foundation for the expression of an opinion."

Wall replied, "Well, I don't object to the foundation, Your Honor, but he is already going into the answer to the final question. The foundation I think—"

Shew said, "If I am hurting your feelings in any way."

Wall answered," You are not hurting my feelings one bit."

The Judge interrupted the juvenile behavior of the opposing Attorneys. "Gentlemen, gentlemen."

Shew answered, "I would be glad to do it differently."

Pastor Bugge continued answering the questions about Harry's reputation. He said, "Harry has been with the Church nearly five years, and during that period of time, I have seen him in Church three or four times a week, plus midweek bible classes, and Junior league, for High School students. He always attended Sunday morning and evening services, plus choir practice. All of the 95 members knew him, and he had their respect and high esteem for this young man who has maintained a high moral integrity in the community."

Cross Examination by Wall

"Pastor, you then, are testifying concerning what you have heard about him in the community, is that correct?"

"That's what I have observed and what I know and what—"

"Yes, now, do you know of an incident in a group meeting in New York, involving a young lady in Brooklyn? Do you know of that incident involving the accused? Did you hear of that?"

"Yes, I heard of that."

"And was that favorable to his character?"

"Well, I can clarify it by answering it—"

"You may answer it, if it was or was not?"

"What I heard, yes, was something which wasn't pleasant, but the next day he did seek out this person and apologize for what he had done."

Redirect by Shew

"Give us the incident, Pastor?"

"Well, again, what I heard, Harry was responsible for transporting some of the young people both to and from our Church to the Church in Brooklyn. Some of the girls, I understand, came extremely late, and Harry had to wait overtime with his fiancée for them. I don't know what excuse or reason the girls gave, other than probably, I just can't say what type of excuse they used, I didn't hear that. Anyway, Harry was somewhat upset and showed this in some way, what way I'm not really sure, but it caused a little friction, and a little tension when they came home. He apologized to them the next day, or the day after, I am not sure, but a day or two. Again, this is hearsay, this is all I have heard."

"Well, Wall asked you something about hearsay, so now I'm going into it."

Wall responded with, "Character is hearsay."

"Isn't it a fact, to clarify this before the jury, Pastor, that Harry Solberg proceeded to the Church in New York, or in Brooklyn with the girl that is now his wife?"

"Ummm."

"And two other girls, isn't that correct?"

"I believe it was, yes."

"And that he was under instructions from his parents and the girl's parents to be home, at East Hartland at a certain time, I think, no later than midnight. Is that your understanding?"

"That, I don't know, but I would assume so."

"And that the other two girls, who he brought down, went off on a date and did not return on time. That's what prevented him and his present wife from getting home on time, isn't that correct?"

"I don't know why they didn't come back on time."

"And that he got mad at them because they did it. Isn't that what Wall is referring to?"

"Yes, I imagine so."

"Is there anything wrong in getting mad at two girls, that went over, and prevented you from getting home on time when you should have?"

The Judge stated, "I don't think the witness should be forced to answer that question."

Shew remarked, "I, well, let's get it straight."

Recross examination by Wall.

"Is it true Pastor, that you had heard, that in connection with this, he roughed up the girls and pushed one of them into the car, and in so doing, ripped her dress, is that what you heard?"

"Heard the dress was ripped as she went into the car."

The next witness Phillips Skaret, was sworn in. He testified that he has lived in East Hartland for twenty-seven years, and has been an Elder, and also Chairman for fifteen years. He has been acquainted with Harry Solberg, since he was a child. And as the Pastor has brought out, Harry had a good reputation, and attended church and Bible classes several times a week.

"Do you know about his reputation, so far as having a violent temper is concerned?"

Shew remarked, "I object to that, Your Honor There is no evidence for the Court to question Mr. Solberg having—I think that is highly improper, and I think Mr. Wall should be censured for it. There is not a bit of evidence. If Mr. Wall wants to bring out—"

Wall responded, "I have the right to bring it out."

To which Shew replied, "Your not going to do it that way."

The Judge again had to censure the two attorneys, "Just a moment gentlemen. I think that the question is improper in its form. I don't think it should—"

Before the Judge could finish his statement, Shew remarked, "Most."

The Judge commented, "I don't think it's bad enough to warrant the actions suggested by Mr. Shew, however, I think that the question should be simply as to whether the witness knows anything about his temper."

Mr. Skaret said, "In all my dealings with Harry, I would say that Harry was mild tempered."

20

There was an air of expectation as, Samuel Sanford Rome, the long-awaited witness, was now walking towards the stand to be sworn in. Then the direct examination by Shew began.

"Your occupation?"

"I'm a State Police Officer."

"How long have you been serving in that capacity?"

"Twenty-eight years, it will be twenty-nine next week."

"And have you—what is your title in the State Police?"

"Major."

"And can you give us the different ranks of the State Police? Who is at the head of the State Police?"

"Commissioner Leo Mulcahy."

"And who comes next in rank?"

"Major Leslie Williams."

"And how many majors are there in the State Police Force?"

"There are three majors, and one acting major."

"And I asked you a minute ago, who is under Commissioner Mulcahy and you answered, Major Leslie Williams, is that correct?"

"Major Leslie Williams would be the Executive Officer. He would be the first major, and Major Carroll Shaw—"

"What does Major Carroll Shaw do?"

"He's the Fire Marshal, and then we come to myself, who is the major of the Detective Division, for the State Police."

"And will you go into a little more detail, major, as to what your duties consist of, and how your department is set up?"

"The department is set up, divided into eleven barrack districts. There is a lieutenant. We try to have a lieutenant in charge of each barracks, plus two Field Captains, one in the Eastern Division, and one in the Western Division. These Field Captains report directly to the Commissioner. Then we have the Detective Division, at the State Police Headquarters in Hartford."

And are you a head of that?"

"I am the head of it, and have been for six years."

"And tell us, major, what the Detective Division does? I want you to explain to the Jury, just what your duties are?"

"It is our duty to investigate major crimes, and unusual crimes throughout the entire State of Connecticut, when assigned by the Commissioner."

"And that would all be handled by the department of which you are the head, is that correct?"

"That is correct sir." major

"And how long have you been head of that department,?"

"I believe it has been six years."

"And before that?"

"I worked in that division ever since it was the Detective Division, and before that when it was Special Services, for approximately twenty-five or twenty-six years."

"And is it a fact that since you have been head of that division major, all the so-called difficult murder cases have come under your supervision?, Is that correct?"

"Not all. They are, when assigned by the Commissioner. If we have a case that appears to be difficult, he will invariably assign me and the men under my command to assist the barracks in the investigation of that crime."

"You mean the murder cases or other important cases that are handled by local police from the various towns and so forth?"

"You are not called in unless your services are requested, is that a fair statement?"

"Yes that is correct sir, Yes, sir."

"And I ask you whether or not you were called in on the Solberg case?"

"Yes, sir, I was assigned to take charge of the Solberg case. I was on leave the week the crime happened. I came back the following Monday, after June 15, and Commissioner Mulcahy assigned this case to me. I conferred with Captain Thomas O'Brien and later with—"

"Commissioner Mulcahy specifically assigned the case to you at that time?"

"Yes."

"And had you been on vacation or what?"

"I was on leave. I believe it was on vacation, but I wasn't on duty. I had the previous week off. I wasn't on duty at the time of the crime."

"And now major, when was the first time that I ever spoke to you about this case?

Will you describe the circumstances under which I first spoke to you about that case?"

"I could do that better—"

Wall spoke out, "I object to it as irrelevant, Your Honor."

Shew responded, "Well, it might be, Mr. Wall, except for certain—if you don't want me to go into it, I won't, but I think it may be proper."

Wall answered, "I feel the time should be saved for important matters."

The Judge stated, "I think the time element would be important and perhaps under the circumstances, brief."

The major testified that he received a telephone call from Shew who said he was the defense lawyer for Harry Solberg. Mr. Shew indicated he would like to meet with me to talk. The major explained it would have to go through channels, which means he would have to get the Commissioner's permission. The major didn't remember the timing when this took place.

"Now after you were assigned to this case by Commissioner Mulcahy, major, what did you first do?"

"I had a long talk with Captain O'Brien, Lieutenant Fuessenich, and the men from my office who assisted in the investigation. I went to the scene of the crime and met some of the Canaan men who had participated in this investigation and was briefed by—I think,—each person who had anything to do with the case, or anything important to do with it. I spent considerable time going through the house, studying the pictures and the grounds, and making every effort to get all the facts that were available at that time. And in furtherance of this task, I assigned various men to various jobs and we stayed on the premises well into the night. In furthering my understanding, and what the facts would lead me to, I went to the Connecticut Valley Hospital in Middletown and had a talk with Agnes Thompsen."

"How many times, major, did you—why did you go to the—why did you talk with Agnes Thompsen?"

"Because the facts that I had learned from reports, investigations, what I saw, aand what I had heard, convinced me, that I should investigate this individual."

"And do you recall when you first saw her?"

"I do not."

"Incidentally major, there was testimony here of an interview, and I believe it was Sergeant Ragazzi who testified as to that, and I am not sure whether you were in the courtroom or not. Were you in the courtroom yesterday when Sergeant Ragazzi testified?"

"Not the full time."

"Well, Sergeant Ragazzi testified that there was an interview, at which I believe you were present, and I think that Lieutenant Fuessenich was present, and maybe somebody else at the Connecticut Valley Hospital. My impression was that this is the first interview at this hospital that you had with Agnes Thompsen. Do you recall such an interview?"

"I recall an interview with her. I had talked to Agnes Thompsen maybe four or five times.

"Yes, but I want the first one."

"But this one—I'm trying to separate them Mr. Shew, but I do recall one occasion when Lieutenant Fuessenich was with us."

"And I believe the record will show, and I don't mean to lead Major Rome, Mr. Wall, but I am just trying to establish at what time, shortly after Agnes Thompsen was confined to the hospital, and among other things, was questioned concerning a substance that was taken from her fingernails, to which Dr. Stolman testified yesterday."

"Yes, sir."

"Do you remember such an interview with Agnes Thompsen?"

"Yes, sir."

Wall remarked, "Your Honor, I object to that as leading and I ask that the answer go out. If there is a first interview or a particular date of an interview, I have no objection to that."

Shew answered, "I was trying to save time, I realize it was a little leading, however, I thought it was harmless."

The Judge ruled, "Mr. Shew did give warning and did give you an opportunity to object for that reason. He was trying to place the date. If you object to that way of establishing the time, I will ask him to establish the time in another way. There was testimony that there was an interview which concerned this particular matter. If you'd like to have me check the transcript, and see if this was it—"

Shew replied, "If Mr. Wall wants to save time, Your Honor, and I do too, however, if we can't agree, we will go into a lot of things."

Wall said, "I am not asking for a lot of things Your Honor."

The Judge asked, "Do you object to the leading on this particular phase?"

Wall responded with, "Yes Your Honor, I object to it, but I have no objection to his referring to a particular date, June 21st., which was in evidence yesterday. If that establishes the time."

The Judge replied, "According to my notes which certainly are not infallible, the first interview was June 21st, at which Major Rome, Lieutenant Fuessenich, and Agnes Thompsen were present."

Wall said, "I don't object to the major having notes if he requires them Your Honor, to refresh his recollection."

Shew asked, "And do you remember, major, questioning Agnes Thompsen? There was some statement that she had cut her hand, or did it with a knitting needle or crocheting needle. I'm not sure whether it was a knitting needle or crocheting needle, but do you remember such a statement?"

"And what did you do to determine whether or not she was telling the truth at that time, if anything?"

"Well, we checked the admittance report It had been checked by someone, and we knew that this wasn't so, but I checked her hands myself."

Wall said, "I move that go out."

The judge responded with, "The portion about the examination of the report may go out. If the witness wishes to testify what he checked, himself, of course, that may go in. But the jury will be cautioned to disregard anything about the report unless the report, itself, is placed in evidence. He can testify to anything that he, himself, observed."

Shew inquired, "Did you check her hands, major? Did you see any marks or—?"

Wall came back with, "I object to that, Your Honor, this is long after the time that anything like that would have had any relevance, at all. This is the 21st. of June, and if it had any relevance, it would have been the 16th."

Shew remarked, "Mr. Wall, a big mark such as she is supposed to have had, certainly would have lasted that long."

Wall commented, "A trace of blood under her nails?"

The judge once again made a ruling. "It's a matter of weight to be given by the Jury, taking into consideration the length of time, and the type of injury that she claimed. Having been brought out what the time lapse is, and which would be brought out during cross examination anyhow, I will allow the major to testify as to what he observed on the 21st. of June."

Wall withdrew his objection.

The major continued, "She had no cuts, no cuts healing, no breaking of the skin of any kind on either hand. I had three, or four interviews with her during a period of a couple of months."

"Major Rome, I have in my hand State Exhibit "K" which on one side is a printed letter, and on the other side, an envelope with an address on it. Have you ever seen that?"

"Yes, I believe that this is the letter that was brought to my attention to my office from the Canaan Barracks. It is a letter that was mailed to Arnfin Thompsen and turned over to the State Police at Canaan and brought to my attention at Headquarters."

"Do you know when it was brought to your attention, major? Not exactly the date, but in point of time?"

"Not exactly, sometime early in the investigation."

"And whether or not you have had opportunity to study it and look at it?"

Wall said, "I object, your Honor."

The judge said, "Sustain the objection. This is not responsive."

To which Shew said, "That's right, I was going to correct that myself."

Wall remarked, "He's helping me."

Shew asked, "Did you, at that time major, I don't mean now, I mean at the time it came to your attention? And did you take any action in connection with that letter?"

"No. Later on I turned it back to the Canaan Barracks in hopes that attempts be made to trace the writer because I—and arrest, if they could find the writer—arrest the owner of being a crank or feeble-minded or something because I had no—."

Wall interjected, "I object to anything further. The question has been answered."

The judge sustained the objection.

Wall said, "I move that part go out."

The judge ruled, "The last part, the reasons may go out. Because—reference to the type of person."

Shew questioned the judge, "And why—can you tell us, from any statements made in that letter, why you gave that instruction?"

"Rather than censuring Shew for challenging his ruling, the judge said, "Yes, sir the person who wrote this letter did not have the facts in the case."

Shew again question the judge, "And why—can your point out any reason in that letter, or will you point out to us why you make that statement?"

Wall remarked, "Well, Your Honor, I object to that, Your Honor."

Shew replied, "I got it right from the Exhibit, Your Honor, that he said it, and I will find out why."

The judge remarked, "If this is a question of Major Rome to point out any differences in the letter from the facts, as he then found them to be, I suppose that he is entitled to do that."

Wall objecting again said, "Your Honor, I object because, any facts, so-called facts would be completely hearsay."

The judge, once again, attempted to give a ruling, "No, don't misunderstand me. What I mean to limit it to, Mr. Wall, is that a comparison—if Major Rome is giving his reasons for giving the instructions that he did, and he wishes to point out differences between the statements made in the letter, in fact, which he himself observed of his own knowledge, not through hearsay, or discrepancies, but of actual fact as he observed it to be having to do with the place, time, exhibits, matters which are—which were known to be fact at that time as distinguished from hearsay, he can do that."

Once again Wall responded with, "May I object further, Your Honor?"

The judge answered, "Certainly."

Wall said, "On the grounds that this witness has laid no foundation, whatsoever, as knowing any fact about this situation, except what he heard from reports or hearsay. He did not come on the scene until almost a week afterwards, that has laid no foundation of having any personal knowledge about the case, whatsoever, and also on the further grounds, Your Honor, I object to it on the ground that it is immaterial, what he believes to be discrepancies, if there are discrepancies, as there definitely are, Your Honor, there are discrepancies—it's up to the jury to decide what those are from the facts as they hear them here, not just such facts as this witness makes out of his head as being considered to be fact, Your Honor."

The judge, finally getting tired of these constant objections, decided to take the reins of his judicial authority said, "I am limiting it, and will limit it carefully, to matters within his own personal knowledge, based on his own personal investigation, and not the wide scope which would include his talking to other people to find out the facts. Mr. Shew probably won't like that limitation, but nevertheless, that's the limitation.". Wall objected again. This time he said, "My objection is further, there is no foundation. He should lay a foundation that this witness actually knows, of his own knowledge." The judge answered with, "I think that we can take care of that."

Shew said, "Mr. Wall, I know I could get a lot of lessons from you, for trying this case."

The judge, in his usual long winded convoluted statements said, "Gentlemen, let's skip that, even for the record, and I think objections can be made if the witness starts to make a comparison with something in the letter that he didn't know, of his own knowledge to be otherwise, and I will sustain the objection. If it has to do with something that he observed in the course of his own personal investigation, I will allow it. But I will have to take—I will have to make that ruling, Mr. Shew, because, otherwise, we could be—"

Shew replied, "Oh, I agree with you, Your Honor."

The judge said, "All right. Let's proceed."

The major then, was finally back on the stand, at which time he started to read the letter. "I killed your wife. She worked with me at the bank." I don't know of my own knowledge—I knew that when the individual who wrote the letter was found, that this was untrue. I couldn't have her—"

Wall interrupted, "I object to that, Your Honor. "This was untrue, this is his own knowledge."

The judge stated, "I think Major Rome can answer the question, whether he knew that of his own knowledge—"

Major Rome confessed, "I have to admit that was hearsay."

Shew said, "All right, major, will you pick out such statements in there, if you find any, that you know of your own knowledge—without basing it on hearsay or anything else, that in your opinion are incorrect, and tell us why they are incorrect, if there are such statements in there, and if you can base the incorrectness on facts that you know."

Wall said, "I object to the question, Your Honor, until there has been laid a foundation of what this witness knows of his own knowledge. Was he there and did he see something happen or did he see some physical evidence?"

The judge replied, "Mr. Wall, I think, maybe we would save time if we would work this way, not meaning to dictate procedure. If Mr. Shew asks the witness to do, what he has done, and he points out a certain statement and considers that incorrect, then, at that point, Mr. Shew will ask him the basis, upon which he knows it to be otherwise, and if that is based on hearsay, or something other than his own personal investigation, it can go out."

Wall said, "I think I'd like to make an argument in Connection with that Your Honor, and it's important enough. Maybe it should be in the absence of the jury."

The judge agreeing said, "All right. I will give the jury their morning exercise. The jury may be excused, and Major Rome may also be excused."

The judge stated, "Now of course, we all know, Major Rome knows, Mr. Shew knows, you know, and I know, that we are going to be careful about any comparison based on opinion. Opinion will not be admissible. I will say that right now. I would rule that Major Rome, as an investigating officer could point out discrepancies between facts, stated to be such in the letter, and facts which he of his own personal knowledge, based on his investigation, not on hearsay, but on his own personal observations were incompatible and were discrepancies. Now, if what you want, is to have Major Rome describe what he did, what he saw, other than what he heard, if you think that would shorten it, all right."

Shew remarked, "If I understand you correctly, that would be what Mr. Wall wants. I think what he is saying, and I think he should go over everything, and point out particular things he has seen, such as some of the evidence here, and then testify what constitutes a discrepancy, which will take us another two or three weeks maybe, or something like that. I don't think it's necessary, and I will try and get him to do that as he goes along."

The judge said, "Well, that was what I had in mind."

Wall said, "Your Honor, what I feel would shorten this matter is to exclude the testimony entirely because I don't see any right of the defense to put anyone on just to make comments about a particular exhibit, what he thinks of it, or what he believes, or anything of that sort This is an exhibit in this case, and it's a question for the jury to decide, whether or not there are discrepancies on what this witness says."

The argument was dragged out for approximately forty-five minutes, after which the judge said, "Well, you see Mr. Wall, what you are saying is substantially what I have said, although you may not recognize it because of my way of expressing it. My intention was to simply allow Major Rome to point out the reasons why he took the action that he did, with respect to this letter, and then referring the matters, which are in evidence before this jury, and the letter."

Wall responded with, "But, I object to any matter of discrepancy or difference that he himself might express."

The judge then replied, "Well, this is exactly what I have said. In other words he may point out discrepancies between statements in the letter, and facts, which are either already known here in evidence, physical evidence, exhibits, and so forth, or matters which he himself observed during his own personal investigation. Let's see just exactly what Major Rome intended or what Mr. Shew intended him to point out."

It was now mid-afternoon, and the two attorneys had been feuding the entire day. For every question Shew asked, Wall had an objection. The judge's patience was diminished by the minute. He said, "There will be no expression of opinion. It will be for the Jury to decide whether the items pointed out, are in conformity with the evidence. I don't want a mistrial in this case, and nobody else does!"

On the last statement that he made pertaining to this letter, his answer was, "'I turned it back to one of the men in the Canaan barracks, with the suggestion that he should have the writer of this letter arrested—for being a crank or feebleminded or something." The witness was the one in charge of the examination, and he gave the order with respect to this letter."

As usual Wall said, "Well, I object to it strenuously, Your Honor."

The bickering, and objections continued, until Shew finally seized an opportunity to question the major, at which time he asked, "Now major, will you try and give us the time that this order was made to the best of your ability?"

The major replied, "It would be difficult, but I believe it was after the first Coroner's Inquest."

Wall as usual, said, "I object, Your Honor."

To which Shew responded, "If Your Honor, please, may I have Your Honor suggest to Mr. Wall, that he allow me to try the case in the way I see fit."

The judge responded with, "Go ahead, Mr. Shew. So far, the answer is inadmissible."

Wall then asked, "May it go out, Your Honor?"

After a constant barrage of objections, the major finally got to answer a question. It was about a word used in the letter. He said,

"That is not a spike, that is a "nailset" and in the letter, the one who wrote it, used the word spike."

Shew asked, "Are there any other statements in the letter?"

The major said, "Yes. In fact, after studying the photographs."

And then Wall said, "I object to that your Honor."

Shew said, "If Your Honor, please, I don't, but apparently a "Donnybrook" is wanted around here."

The judge said, "A "Donnybrook" is the last thing that any of us wishes, Mr. Shew, and I am trying to prevent it. But, here again, we are getting information from a study. Now, if that isn't a matter of opinion, it's something for a jury to decide."

Shew said, "I understood the major to say, 'is a fact'." He started to say something about a fact, a fact which I don't know."

The judge then said, "Well, let him state a fact which he knows of his own personal knowledge, and not just simply from a study of the work of other investigators. That's what I am trying to get at."

Shew asked, "Can you tell me any other discrepancies, based on facts, which you have, of your own knowledge major?"

Wall once again interrupted with, "I object Your Honor. Discrepancies are entirely a matter for the jury."

Shew snapped back with, "Again Mr. Wall, whether you think it helps a jury is not any of your business. It's mine."

Wall then said, "It's up to the Court, Your Honor, whether or not it helps the jury."

The judge made a quick decision. He said he would substitute the word "statement" for "discrepancy." Then Shew asked the major to answer the question.

Wall remarked, "The answer shall be yes, or no, Your Honor."

Major Rome started to answer, but all he had an opportunity to utter was. "The letter", at which time Wall stated, "I object to any further statement at this time."

Shew now infuriated, shouted, "Mr. Wall, will you give the witness a chance!?"

Ordered to proceed, Rome said, "It's a fact, when you look at the photographs taken of the—"

Wall, in his usual manner said, "I object to that, Your Honor."

This prompted the judge to say, "major, I am sorry, but this is getting into a, an opinion based on examination of evidence, and not something what you yourself saw. Something physical, like a board, which is brought in here with a spike or a "nailset" in it, something that can be seen as tangible, is acceptable. Examination of either statements, or photographs taken at different times, statements taken from different people, etc., gets into a matter of opinion. This is a hairline distinction, that an awful lot of people, including the Court, are going to have a hard time distinguishing between. We, nevertheless will have to try, and draw the line the best we can."

Shew showed his disappointment, but not to be thwarted, picked up the white dress and passed it to the major, and said, "Now I show you an article, Major Rome, and will you inspect it please? Look it over carefully. I ask you, whether or not, you have ever seen this article before?"

"No sir," he answered. "Not outside of the courtroom. It was never called to my attention. I never saw it outside this room."

Shew realizing this was going nowhere, said, "If your Honor pleases, at this time I would like to withdraw Major Rome and call Lieutenant Fuessenich, but I know what the time situation is, and I would just as soon continue on next Tuesday."

Court was, therefore, adjourned until Tuesday morning.

21

The following morning, all the newspapers ran headlines about the trial, and reporters made sure the public was aware of the animosity between Major Rome and Wall. The Hartford Courant story was headed; *Sleuth Claims Letter Written by "Crank"*. It ran lengthy articles detailing the bickering between Wall and the witness: *Wall objected to almost every answer given by the major. When Wall leaped to his feet and exclaimed "I object to anything further," the jury was excused for the second time Attorney Shew didn't make much progress with his main witness either. It was a bad morning all around.*

The next witness sworn in was, Charles Von Salzen, a specialist in psychiatry, from Hartford, Connecticut. No sooner did Shew begin his examination of the doctor, when Wall interrupted, and said, "I might say, Your Honor, that I am acquainted with the qualifications of Dr. Von Salzen, and I consider him to have the highest standing in his profession, and I do not require any qualification although Counsel may wish to do so."

Shew responded with, "Thank you, Mr. Wall, I would like to have him qualify just the same, but I do appreciated your endorsement."

The judge said, "I understand."

The doctor testified that he graduated from Columbia Medical School thirty years ago, and in 1936 Trained in Psychiatry at the New York State Hospital for four years. He entered the Army in 1941, serving as a psychiatrist, for four and a half years. Following his tour of duty in the Army, he started work for the Veterans Administration in New York. His next assignment was as Branch Medical Director for twelve hospitals in New York and Puerto Rico. He relocated to Hartford nineteen years ago, to take the position of Executive Officer at the

Institute of Living, a private Hartford medical facility, for treatment of patients suffering from mental disorders.

Shew asked, "And have you, Doctor, had any connection with the Connecticut State Prison Service?"

"Yes, I have been consulted in various matters. For a period of about two years, I think, probably seven or eight or nine years ago, I was a consultant at the Connecticut State Prison in Wethersfield."

"Doctor, at the request of Mr. Wall and at the request of myself, did you examine Harry Solberg?"

"Yes, I saw him on a Saturday morning. He was brought to my office at 9:00 a.m. by two members of the State Police, at which time I examined him for nearly two and a half hours."

"Who was present at the time when you examined him?"

"No one."

"Did you talk with any of the State Police Officers, in connection with it, at that particular time?

"Yes, I talked with the lieutenant who had escorted the defendant, and I also discussed some of the aspects of the case with Lieutenant Fuessenich."

"And now, can you tell us Doctor what, if anything, in your own words you found out about Harry Solberg?

"Well, I discussed with him his early life history, the details of where he was born, family background, siblings, past history, and education. He told me he required six years to complete the four-year high school course. I then asked him in what year he graduated from high school, and he wasn't sure at first, if it was 1964 or 1965. He finally decided it was 1965. We then discussed his subsequent marriage. I believe that he lived a restricted narrow life. He seemed to have no interest in sports, dances or parties, and he didn't attend movies, or drink. He attended church from two to three times a week, and my general impression was that he was a rigidly inhibited and repressed youth."

"And when you say rigidly and repressed youth Doctor, could you in a layman's point of view, express that a little differently?"

"Well, he spent quite a lot of time reading the bible, and I questioned him about the contents of the bible. I am not a student of it, but I know something about it. He wasn't able to discuss the contents of what he had read clearly, with me. I also discussed any interest in girls. He told me that he had never fantasized, or thought about girls. I think at the age of nineteen, I would consider this unusual. He also seemed to have rigid feelings in the entire area of sex, and the normal male/female relationship."

"Did he make you aware of the fact that he kept company with one particular girl?"

"He told me he had married on January 15, 1966, that he had been very much in love with his fiancée, and that he had gone steady with her for sometime. Nothing abnormal about that."

Shew then asked the Doctor to explain to the jury what he meant by, "Repression". The doctor replied, "Well, I'll try. I think one has to understand, first, that in psychiatry, we are interested in behavior and the motivation of behavior. If that behavior is sick behavior, we try to modify it so that it is no longer sick. We believe that the behavior is motivated, not only by our conscious mind, but also by a large part of the mind which we designate as the unconscious mind. I will have to state here that no one has ever discovered the unconscious mind anatomically, so far as its existence in the brain is concerned. It has not been shown to exist anatomically. In large part, the content of the unconscious mind is harmless, innocuous stimuli which have come into our minds over the years of our living. Everything which has come into our mind through our senses or through our thinking has made an imprint upon our minds somewhere, and this is never abolished except in organic brain damage." The doctor continued about repressions, inhibitions, superego, until he was interrupted by Shew.

"Now, further, you questioned Harry Solberg about various aspects of his life up until that time, doctor? And did you question him about what, if anything, he knew about June 15, 1965, did you not?"

"Yes, I questioned him in detail about what his reactions were of June 15, 1965. He stated that on June 15, 1965, he left school on the school bus and arrived home about 12:30 or 12:45. He thinks he must have changed his clothes to working clothes, and that he had something to eat. He then said he helped unload a supply truck which was bringing plumbing supplies to his father. He then went to Simsbury to get a lawn mower repaired, or to see somebody about having it repaired. Then he said that he had been having trouble with an economic report for High School, and Mr. Thompsen had agreed to help him. So he apparently had planned to stop at the Thompsen home to get this report. He then said he walked up to the front door which was partially open, that he called out and knocked, received no answer, so he walked into the house and called out again. He heard the baby crying, and he walked into the hallway, then into the kitchen, and saw blood on the floor. He followed this blood into the living room. He told me he remembered nothing, until he saw himself climbing up a ladder outside the house, to the rear porch. I then asked him whether he had seen the body. He replied, 'I can't remember seeing her.' He doesn't recall leaving, but he does remember that he was going to stop at the home of a State Police Officer, who lives nearby. He didn't do this. Instead he went directly to his home and asked his mother where his father was working. He wanted to tell his father he was going to work with him, however, he decided not to. That is what he told me, initially in my interview, as to what transpired on June 15."

"That's what he told you initially. Did you question him further?"

"Yes. At the end of the examination, I went over the whole thing in detail, and questioned him again to see if any other memory could be brought to his mind, and there were no other memories—or no greater recollection of what he had seen."

"Did he give you a different explanation at a later date?"

"Yes, he did, Mr. Shew."

"And in a layman's explanation, can you tell me why he doesn't know?"

"Well, possibly yes, possibly no. I will try, and I would like to preface that by being somewhat subjective and in speaking of my own reaction."

Wall objected, "I believe that there has been no foundation laid for any facts upon which the Doctor could base this opinion. I believe it is obvious that certain facts have been left out concerning the Doctor's findings. I think—"

Shew commented, "If Mr. Wall is worried about that, I have no objection. Is that what you want Mr. Wall?"

Wall replied, "I don't want anything except the facts—all the facts."

The judge said, "It seems to me that the Doctor's testimony thus far has been, I think, illuminating. I think, however, that before he can explain why the different statements were made, if in fact they were made, and I gather that he says there were contradictory statements made, I think the only way the jury can get the full significance of it, would be to know what the conflict or differences were. If the Doctor can explain them on that basis, he certainly is entitled to."

The next statement from Shew was, "And I show you State's Exhibit "K", which is a letter claimed by the State to have been written by Harry Solberg. Have you seen this before, Doctor?"

"Yes, I have seen this before Mr. Shew."

"All right, confine yourself to the actual examination Doctor, of Harry Solberg, on the 25th, of September, and be a little more explicit as to what the discrepancies were that you observed in his statement, and then tell us why in your opinion, they were made?"

Wall requested, "May we have the first question read, Your Honor?"

Shew remarked, "I would prefer it the way I asked it. If you want help from Mr. Wall—"

Wall interrupted, "I object to it as being triple headed."

The Doctor said, "I don't know about the word discrepancy. It seems to me that from the story the defendant told me after walking into this home, and after seeing this blood, he then did not remember anything more after that, or his memory for it was spotty and very fragmentary. Is that what you were referring to?"

"Yes, And can you tell us in your opinion, why his memory was that way?"

"The Doctor's answer was, "I think so sir. I asked myself what would be the reaction of a human being walking in on a situation, such as this which is photographed in exhibit "V". Although I have been a Doctor for thirty years, and I have seen hundreds of corpse, when I saw this photograph I had a feeling of revulsion. I think that perhaps this would be the normal reaction. I believe that a person such as the defendant, walking in on a rural scene, on a June day, expecting to get a report on economics, and encountering a scene of blood, violence, and murder, and for all anyone knew at that moment, rape, would get the same feeling. I think this would be an enormous shock to the nervous system, and I think the mind could easily reject what the senses perceived."

Shew asked, "And what would be the effect of rejecting what it saw, the mind."

"The effect would be similar to what one sees in combat in war time. In traumatic neuroses when something happens, a man's buddy is blown up in front of his eyes, it's so repulsive, or so appalling that he cannot take it in, cannot accept it. In other words, it does not gain access to the conscious mind. This was rather common in war time."

Shew then asked, "Is it a fair statement, Doctor, that in your opinion, it is impossible for Harry Solberg to give a statement as to what took place June 15th, because he, himself, does not know at this time?"

Wall started to say, "Your Honor," but was cut of by Shew saying, "Claim it."

The judge, entered into another long-winded ruling, "He has just asked a question which, it seems to me, is based upon the overall picture, and the doctor has thus far testified as to only the first part of the interview. Now it seems to me, if he is going to express an opinion, as to whether or not, this accused could not remember what took place, that he has got to explain the entire basis."

Wall, answered, "That's my objection, Your Honor."

Shew countered with, "If your Honor, please, I object to Mr. Wall's whole attitude on this thing, and explaining to the jury."

When the bickering was over, the judge allowed the question. The doctor answered, "Well, that question is difficult to answer, Mr. Shew, there may be a great many people who have had temporary lapses of memory and gone through the remainder of their lives without any problem. Cases such as this, just as in traumatic neurosis from combat, every effort should be made to relive and recapture the lost memory. This is psychiatric treatment."

Shew then said, "Doctor, it has been testified here that Harry Solberg was apprehended by Detective Rebilliard on a Sunday morning at 9:30."

Shew then read through the testimony from the time Harry was apprehended until he was taken to jail. The doctor was then asked," Would you have any opinion as to his ability to make a correct statement?"

Wall objected to it.

Shew then said, "I claim it, Your Honor. Misrepresents the situation completely. Doesn't include facts?"

The judge commented, "I think the jury realizes this from having heard the evidence itself."

Cross Examination of Dr. Von Salzen, by Wall.

"I believe, Doctor, that you related quite fully what Solberg said to you relating to his memories of the circumstances of June 15, 1965, is that correct?"

"Yes, sir."

"And did you, in coming to your opinion, have regard to what he said later, in reaching conclusions relating to him?

"I have both the report, and my recollection. At the conclusion of my examination, I went over again, with the defendant the details of his entering the Thompsen house on June 15th, and then he told me the second story. He gave me a rather long, involved statement to the effect that it might be hard to convince the jury of the truth of his first story and, if the jury didn't believe him, he could spend twenty years in prison, whereas, he said, that he might get only six years if he told the second story. The second story was that—"

Wall interrupted with,"Wait a minute—Just hold it.—That's all—Continue."

"The Doctor continued, "He said when he entered the Thompsen house, Mrs. Dorothy Thompson greeted him, and offered him something to drink, such as orange juice or coke. He then stated that he sat with her in the living room, at which time Mrs. Thompsen made amorous advances to him. He kissed her and then when he wanted to retreat, she slapped him, and said something to the effect that no one could go half way with her. He said that at this point, he remembered nothing further." My report states, When questioned closely about these two stories, he said the first story was true, but that he might say the second story was true.

"Now, Doctor, did you deviate some from your report?"

"I don't see any deviation, Mr. Wall."

"Now, Doctor, are there any other observations that you made in your examination of this accused, in addition to these factors that you and I have just discussed?"

"Well, I didn't make myself as clear as I wanted to. We all operate under repressions. Repressions are important to our personality functioning. My report was that he was too rigidly repressed."

"Is that the principle finding that you related, upon which you have based some of the opinions expressed here?"

No, I think, sir, the major point was the walking in upon this scene and seeing the body. This must have had a tremendous emotional and shocking impact upon him, especially being an overly repressed individual."

"Were there any other observations that you made in your examination of this accused, which are in addition to the factors you and I discussed?"

The Doctor replied with, "I don't think that I am at all clear as to the question, Mr. Wall. For over two and a half hours, I observed many things, and I considered many things important, and I have not in my testimony condensed everything that took place during that two and a half hours."

"And whether you considered this young man to be an overly repressed individual, depended primarily upon what he told you in that two and a half hours, did it not?"

"Not entirely, no. There are other techniques. If you were worked up completely, medically and psychiatrically, other techniques would be utilized to give a clearer picture of the personality makeup. For instance, psychiatric tests such as the Rorschach Test and other tests of personality."

"But, you placed the principal reliance in your findings of an overly repressed individual, upon his answers to your questions, isn't that so?"

"No, in my report to you, I discussed showing him some drawings. This is one of our psychological tests. These tests consist of having the individual look at drawings or pictures of various kinds, and then have him make up stories about the pictures. The pictures have no titles, and there is nothing to indicate what it means. In making up a story, his own thinking is projected into the story, I administered a number of these pictures to him. I brought two of them along with me because they seem to indicate his marked repression of feeling, that I spoke of, and wrote to you about. I concluded from my knowledge of teenagers and from my examination, from this brief test that I gave him, and from my experience, that he is a rigidly repressed individual."

"Well, I think that covers a lot of territory, Mr. Wall. In my letter to you, I said he has repressed an awareness of these normal urges, and he has maintained repression, and then I described that an individual such as this, when confronted with a scene of violence, would react strongly. Do you want me to go on with the report that I wrote to you?"

"If it answers the questions?"

"I believe at that time, behavior, governed by rational thinking, would be suspended. Rational thinking itself would be impossible as a result of the panic. To go into that more deeply, and I'd be happy to, would require more discussion of psychiatric theory. In other words, it is not just viewing a scene, but it is what that scene does to a particular individual."

"I ask you Doctor whether a person like this, who commits a horrible crime, would have the same reaction, as that when he viewed the result of a horrible crime. Wouldn't it even be more probable, that having committed the crime—a repressed individual would then have memory gaps?"

"I think that is true, and I believe that this is pretty well known. That we do read about when someone commits a crime which is alien to his ego, entirely alien to his teachings, that he could well develop an amnesia for that?"

"In other words this amnesia is consistent with his having committed the crime, as well as just having viewed the corpse in its horrible state?"

"Yes, in my letter to you, I said since amnesia plays such a prominent part in each story, I would have no way of ascertaining the truth, except possibly by the use of drugs. I think it is a pretty accurate statement that amnesia was present in both stories.

"And in this particular examination of this accused, Doctor, did you have any personal history, other than what you have stated here in Court?

"No, only what he told me. I have some information about his High School record and intelligence tests, however, I have had no interview with his parents or teachers or minister, as to his historical background, which I obtained it from the defendant. I have already testified that a more detailed investigation would be in order."

"Now Doctor, were you able from the different stories he told you, to determine whether his lack of memory, or his claimed lack of memory, was untruthful or whether it was a defense mechanism?"

"You mean the ego protective defense mechanism against something shocking? I have no way of determining the truth or untruth of what Mr. Solberg told me. I did suggest the use of certain drugs, such as Pentothal, which is helpful. In my letter I stated that I would have no way of ascertaining the truth, except possibly by the use of drugs."

"Now, when he said to you that he had to submit a report at school, and Mr. Thompsen had agreed to help him, did you accept that at face value?

"I didn't question it. He said Mr. Thompsen was a bookkeeper and he was going to help him with the report That was why he went to the Thompsen house. To get the report. I think I certainly would want to know why he went to the Thompsen house, and when he told me he went there for the report, I assumed this was the reason he went to the house."

"Now, in his first story to you, he did not say anything whatsoever, about having any contact, or talk with the deceased, did he?"

"Well, in the first story, he stated he saw the blood, and he thinks he must have seen the body also. He didn't have any conversation with the deceased, that's true."

"Now, when you say a memory gap, can you, in point of time and circumstances, state where the memory gap began, and where the memory gap no longer applied?

"No, I really could not do that, Mr. Wall. I don't know the exact moment it began. I believe that seeing the body could be a sufficient trigger to blot out the recognition of what he had seen. I think that when there is a gradual return to what we call identity, or knowing who one is, and putting one's self in a proper place again, as it gradually returns. I think, at this time, it's not complete. It did, however, certainly begin to return when he found himself at home, asking his mother where his father was working. It is not a matter of memory rushing back in, and one moment it's gone, and the next moment it's all there. It is definitely a piecemeal type of thing. These memory gaps can be filled in various ways. For example, by things that he has read or heard. One might use this type of thing to try to fill in the memory gap. I might be able to explain this better if I take a clinical example, if you like, a different type of case."

"Wall replied, "If it would help, I am sure His Honor and the jury would—"

The Doctor continued, "There is an entity in psychiatry known as Korsakov's syndrome, which is an organic illness, there are profound memory gaps. The individual does not know where he was last night or any other time. If, in talking to him, one can put an idea into his head, and say, "Did you have a good time last night in Washington, D.C.," he will then pick up on this to span the memory gap. In other words, one is putting ideas into his mind. He may have been in the State Hospital two years, but this is what I mean by filling in the memory gaps. It isn't just the return of one's own memory because the gaps can be filled in by other stimuli."

"Doctor, in your examination of this young man, I believe that there were two occasions when he told you that he had no further memory, whatsoever, is that correct?"

The first occasion was at the time he said that he had viewed the dead body, and the second occasion was after the deceased had slapped his face? Is that correct?"

"Yes, sir."

"And could that memory gap have come as a result of either of those events?"

"Well, that's a question I have asked myself, Mr. Wall. I think for a state of complete blocking out of the personality, there has to be a sufficient stimulus. It doesn't happen from something minor, and the stimulus here was seeing the body. I just can't believe that a stimulus of a kiss is enough to cause a great change in one's personality."

"Or a slap in the face?"

"I don't believe so, no."

"Although he did state that his memory gap started with that slap in the face, did he not?"

"When he wanted to retreat, she slapped him and said something to the effect that no one could go half way with her. He said at that point, he remembers nothing further."

"And you believed him on both occasions, didn't you Doctor?"

"No. I didn't, I believed the first story. As I testified, a few minutes ago, I don't believe a kiss or a slap, is sufficient-stimulus to produce a profound change in the personality, in which a diffused state, such as these situations constitute."

"Then, he was lying to you when he told you that he had no further memory after she slapped him in the face, and made the statement that no one was going to go halfway with her, is that correct?"

"I don't believe I testified to that."

Shew interrupted, "I tried to let him have free rein, but I think the Doctor testified that the whole statement was a lie as far as the second statement was concerned, and he considered it so."

"The judge stated, "I don't believe he has gone quite that far, have you, Doctor?"

The Doctor replied, "I thought I had, Your Honor. I don't believe that two and a half hour examination is adequate to make a diagnosis and reach conclusions."

Wall then said, "That's all."

Shew asked, "Doctor, can you tell us the difference between the word diagnosis and opinion?"

Wall then asked, "When he first started to cross examine you, he asked whether you were able to make a diagnosis, isn't that correct, Doctor?"

"That is true. I have made no diagnosis."

"But, you had given your opinion on certain matters, Doctor."

"Yes, diagnosis in medicine is easy sometimes. If one is diagnosing a broken leg, and one sees that the bones are out of place, the diagnosis may be made by simple inspection. At times, a diagnosis is not so obvious and requires radiological examination to establish the diagnosis. In psychiatry, the same thing holds true. There are some conditions, or some types of mental illness which are so far advanced that the diagnosis, to a trained psychiatrist, is a matter of a few minutes observations or discussion. But there are many other things which are so complex that a much more detailed investigation is required. I don't believe my examination was detailed enough to establish a diagnosis. It has only established my clinical impression."

Doctor Von Salzen was then passed a paper, State's Exhibit "MM" Interrogation of Harry Solberg. The doctor read it and made a few notes. It was curious, that on page one, when the defendant was told about his constitutional rights, he disregarded those and went ahead with the interrogation. On page two he is describing how he went to the Thompsen house and he said, "So I went down College Highway and took another road home. I don't know what the number of that road is or anything, I know, but I can't think." Well, this to me was of some importance, that he knew the road, but he couldn't think. That was March 15th, At 12:13 a.m., and I thought that was rather important. He was asked a question as to how the deceased was dressed, and he didn't know how she was dressed. The Doctor was then asked to explain the so called "projective tests". He said, "The purpose is to have the individual who is under examination, make up a story about what he sees on a drawing or picture. Since there is no title, and the pictures are made somewhat vague, the story which someone makes up, will project his own thinking, and emotional response. Most people make up a story including some love or tenderness or affection and embrace between two people, this is the typical response. When I asked the defendant to make up a story about this—"

At this point Shew interrupted, with a suggestion that the jury be allowed to look at the pictures. This suggestion was acceptable. Then the Doctor continued, "The defendants interpretation, was something to the effect that, it reminded him of a birthday party for his seventy-five-year-old grandfather. This may be an acceptable interpretation, but which to me represents a suppression or repression of what I consider normal feelings of love. The interpretation of the second picture, was to the effect that, this was a boy who had been playing with a toy, became tired, and laid down to take a nap. This to me indicates again repression and suppression of feeling. There is an object in the picture which is shown in a vague manner, however, I believe most people would look upon it as a gun. He interpreted it as a toy, again not wanting to recognize."

It was obvious by looking around the courtroom that everyone, including Shew was bored to death. He interrupted the Doctor's explanation with, "I have no further questions, Doctor."

Re-cross examination of Dr. Von Salzen, by Wall.

Wall referred to the interrogation of Harry said, "He knocked on the door and Mrs. Thompsen answered, and he didn't remember much after that, except climbing up a ladder and running out. Doesn't that constitute a third story, when he said he stopped remembering?"

The Doctor, showing his irritation replied, "I think that I have already testified that there is a lapse of memory for a certain period of time, on the afternoon of June 15th, and I don't believe I can answer your question any more comprehensively than that, and I have testified to that fact."

Wall, not ready to give in, tried again." Well, your examination corroborated one of his stories to the effect that he saw a body, and that he then had a lapse of memory. That was your principal testimony, was it Doctor?"

"Well, he told me he doesn't remember seeing the body, but then I reported that he said. "I must have, but I don't recall it."

"Then he told you that he had a lapse of memory, and didn't remember any more after the slap in the face, and the statement that she wouldn't tolerate any halfway business."

"That's true."

And now this constitutes a third time when he said, "I don't remember too much after that. I knocked on the door and Mrs. Thompsen came to answer the door, and I don't remember too much after that, except that I went in, and I can remember climbing up the ladder on the back porch and running out. That's all I can remember."
"Now, that constitutes a third statement of his relating to his lack of memory, isn't that so?"
"Well, I have testified, Mr. Wall, that I believe that day he doesn't remember what happened, during that afternoon, and the trigger that started this lapse of memory obviously was seeing the body."
"Now, would you please answer the last question?" The Court reporter read back the last question, to which the Doctor replied, "It is certainly a third statement relating to lack of memory."
"And having made three different statements on the same subject Doctor, there is a pretty good chance too, that he lied on each of the three occasions, isn't that so?
Well, as a Doctor I have to say that we don't consider that amnesiacs are lying, we consider they have a loss of memory. They may make up things to fill the gaps."
"And these three statements are completely inconsistent, are they not?"
"They certainly are contradictory."
Further redirect examination of Dr. Von Salzen by, Shew.
"Now Doctor, the very fact that these statements are contradictory, which they obviously are, right?
"Yes, sir."
"And isn't that in itself caused by the fact that the accused can't actually remember?"
"In my opinion, yes."
"Thank you, Doctor, that's all."

22

Another week of court session was finally over. On this lovely Sunday morning, parishioners walking or driving to church talked about the trial. It was the topic of conversation, as a matter of fact, that's all they ever talked about. After the service, people formed into small gatherings and debated their opinions. The grounds of this handsome white clapboard church, with its spire reaching to the clear blue sky, just didn't seem the place to be discussing a brutal murder, but people being people, do what they do. The one point they did agree on was, that they all hoped the right person would be caught soon, and prosecuted.

Some country residents raise sheep, or other animals for a hobby and/or to get lower taxes, and a reduced rate on the electricity. One woman said, she has geese as watchdogs, but regardless, she is still afraid. She hoped the situation would clear up before the lambing season. Ewes, unlike other animals, require help when giving birth. She talked about the nights she spent in the barn alone, with the children alone in the house, a frightening situation during those frequent occasions when her husband was out of town overnight. Another woman said, that she hasn't been out of the house at night since Dottie was murdered, nor would she open the doors after dark. No one would go out, not even to the church suppers. When the discussions about their apprehensions and frustrations were over, they went home for the usual hearty Sunday dinner, always at one o'clock.

The next morning's headlines in the Hartford papers read. *Psychiatrist Sees Solberg as Repressed and Withdrawn. Accused slayer, Harry Solberg has been pictured to a Superior Court Jury here as a youth of few interests who has lived a restricted narrow life.*

The court opened with Doctor Robert B. Miller on the stand. He testified that he is Chief of Professional Services at the Connecticut Hospital, in Middletown, and had brought with him, the requested records pertaining to Agnes Thompsen. He told Shew that the records were confidential, however, he would provide them if he was instructed to do so by the Court. The judge so gave the order.

"Just let me examine them please, Doctor," Requested Shew.

"They represent the accumulation of information obtained by doctors, psychologists, nurses, and in fact, everyone responsible for patient care. In addition to this, they contain specific personal data, and this would include among other things, for instance, records of probating and such," said the Doctor.

"And you have such a record on Agnes Thompsen, have you. And whether or not you have anything in those files pertaining to an examination of Agnes Thompsen shortly after her admittance, either June 15, or June 16, 1965?"

"Yes," Was his reply.

"And can I look at that one, please?"

"Yes."

While observing the documents the doctor had carried with him, he asked, "For the purpose of the record, what do you call that book?"

"This is the hospital chart of the complete hospital record. It contains a record of the physical examination performed on Agnes Thompsen, on June 16, 1965."

Shew asked it that particular page could be detached, and the answer was, "Yes." Wall said, "I have no objection to this, Your Honor. Perhaps so as to not have the record mutilated, I would be willing to consent to a photostat being made of it and introduced if that is."

Before he could finish his statement, the judge interrupted, "I suppose the page would have to be removed."

When the question of copying the page was resolved, Shew asked the doctor, "Is it your practice at the Valley Hospital, to examine the patients carefully and could you explain how you have gone about it?"

"On admission to the hospital, the patient is first given a psychiatric admission examination by the admitting resident, then within twenty-four hours, a physical examination is given."

"Doctor, has your institution had an inquiry from the State Police, or County Detectives concerning this document?"

"Yes, if I recall correctly, it was Detective Holden. He has the same information. The diagnosis is appended to her chart, 'Schizophrenic reaction, paranoid type'."

"May we have the time of this diagnosis, Doctor?"

"Well, I am not too sure. I can give you a brief answer on that, because, in the general procedure of working up a patient, the first procedure, is to make a tentative diagnosis."

"Doctor, does that record you have there, include admissions made only from June 15, or 16, 1965, or does it refer to previous confinements of Agnes Thompsen at your hospital?"

"To previous admissions, as well."

Doctor Miller read from his papers, On December 22, 1964 there is a note indicating that the patient was sent out on an extended visit, which means that there were some attempts to find out if she would adapt to her home environment, instead of having to remain in the hospital. At that time there was a notation that on admission she had hallucinations and delusions, mainly of a religious nature. She was totally lacking in insight, and she felt there was nothing wrong with her, and she wanted to go home. In addition to auditory hallucinations, she had tactile experiences of spirits touching her fingers, and God touching her spine and head. Subsequently she showed signs of symptomatic improvement and was permitted to leave on home visits. She gradually improved and her visits were increasingly satisfactory. There was evidence that she was no longer experiencing her delusions or hallucinations and was able to do various forms of work at home, and to socialize to a moderate extent. Her son claimed that she was greatly improved, and in December expressed a desire for her to return home feeling that she was capable of making a satisfactory adjustment.

She was seen again on December 22. She was over-excite and over-talkative, fairly oriented, and showing no further evidence of hallucinations or delusions, she was permitted to try an extended visit home. Now, on June 16—

Shew interrupted, "Hold the June 16, for a moment,. You stated her son expressed a desire to have her home in December of 1964, is that correct?"

"Yes, that is correct."

Doctor Miller read the report of the resident in training, who admitted her on June 16, 1965, She was brought from her home by a policewoman and two State Police Troopers. She had an emergency certificate signed by her local doctors which read, history of present illness, acute agitation over violent death of daughter-in-law and pressure on head. Physical findings, none. Mental condition, acute agitation, violent and suicidal. The woman is seen to be spry and chipper, elderly, white, and appears to be somewhat agitated. She is neatly and appropriately dressed, with well-groomed hair.

She stated that she returned to the hospital because her family physician Doctor Cannon said she should come back because, "My younger Son's wife died." She said, "She was killed. I heard two hard bangs, and I saw a man lower something from the porch to the ground. it was dark. I saw a man in the back and I thought it was her brother. I was upstairs and I didn't know anything bad had happened. I can't believe it's true. I was the only one home, and I had to tell what I saw, to the detectives. I couldn't love anyone more if she were my real daughter. She was very nice and we never had any arguments. I never bothered them, They have their ways and I have mine." She also said, "The baby was left alone all afternoon, and I didn't hear any crying." She said that her daughter-in-law died between 11:15 and 2:30 and that her daughter-in-law was not found until her husband arrived home at about 6:15. She then said about the baby, "She will never remember her mother." She denies having any nervous trouble, however, complains of pressure in her head plus some stomach trouble. Patient was oriented as to time, place and person. She was coherent and relevant. It was not possible to detect any discrepancies in her story. There was no delusional material elicited. Patient frequently remarked about how happy she was at being at home and how well she got along with her son and his wife. She spoke about how she kept herself busy taking care of a garden and her African violets. She showed evidence of being somewhat agitated, and she was noticed to be frequently hyperventilating. Patient stated her fingerprints were taken here at Connecticut Valley Hospital after she was returned. Asked if she did not think this was strange, she said, yes, she wondered about it but didn't ask. According to the verbal information received from the Battell Hall Supervisor, and the State Troopers who accompanied the patient to the Hospital, she stated that she herself, had murdered her daughter-in-law.

Doctor Miller continued reading. On June 16 this patient who had been admitted by the resident in training, whose note I have read, was also seen by the Senior Psychiatrist in charge of the building to which she was admitted. The only outward signs of agitation during the conversation were a series of hyperventilation, when discussing yesterday's happenings at her home. No significant depression, no ideas of reference or persecution or grandiosity. She vehemently denied having anything to do with the death of her daughter-in-law and consistently held to her statement about a man in a dark green car being present in her daughter-in-law's apartment yesterday afternoon. She stated that she did not see his face but saw him throw some large bundle from the porch outside the porch outside her apartment to the ground below. She said she heard two tremendous bumps about 2:00 p.m. yesterday but didn't go downstairs to investigate. She said she spent the day in her room crocheting, reading and doing house work. She denied any interpersonal difficulties with her daughter-in-law, or her son, but said that by mutual consent, she and the younger couple lived rather independent lives. She had been working two or three days a week in the area as a domestic, earning twelve dollars a day.

Patient's sensorium is essentially intact. Memory, both recent and remote, shows significant impairment. General fund of information appears in keeping with her intelligent level, dull, normal range. Judgment is impaired. And here the diagnosis was schizophrenic reaction, chronic undifferentiated type. There is a note dated August 2. Patient appeared more agitated and volatile the on ward today. She had been interviewed at length by police officials two days ago, and in her comment on the interview she said, "They couldn't break me down because I'm "un-guilty"." They'll never get me to break down. They have lied so much. I'm at peace with the Lord. They blackened me down so terrible." She denied any pressure in her head. Then on August 23, it was indicated, patient shows more and more preoccupation with her Bible reading and she shows hyperventilation and athetoid-type twitching when attention is directed at her, even with conversation on neutral topics. She denies hallucinations, but her preoccupation, distractibility, and frequent listening attitude suggest otherwise. She has shown no aggressive or paranoid behavior during her interaction on ward 22 which is a closed ward, where she has been since admission. She still assists nursing personnel in feeding bed patients. But, in recent weeks she does things in a mechanical, robot-like fashion with little conversation and a glassy, faraway look in her eyes."

"What does that mean Doctor?"

"That means she was getting worse. She was becoming more preoccupied and withdrawn, and acting in a much more robot-like fashion. Now, on October 4, I examined her and my note simply states: On this date I examined Mrs. Thompsen and found her to be tense, anxious, manneristic, and with an extremely inappropriate effect. When discussing the possible Court appearance today with her, it became apparent that her reality testing was extremely poor and that she would not be capable of advising counsel. In addition, in reviewing the situation with her, it became apparent that she did not know right from wrong or the nature of her acts. In view of her current status, she is not capable of appearing for trial. Subjecting her to the confusing pressure of Court, might presumably exacerbate her illness.

Shew asked, "And what subsequent notes have you, Doctor? I would like to have the whole report, on the record, if it is possible."

Doctor Miller responded with, "Your Honor, the hospital has no objection to the entire chart remaining for whatever the usual duration, providing it is ultimately returned."

Shew said, "Well, I have none, offhand, and I would take a chance and admit it now.

Your Honor. I have not had an opportunity of going through it, but I don't know whether Mr. Wall has, or not."

Wall answered, "No, I have never seen it or heard of these things before, your Honor, and I would like, before it goes into evidence, to have an opportunity to look at it."

The judge said, "I would suggest that we continue along the line I suggested, page by page, until there is an objection, and then perhaps over the next recess, counsel can both have an opportunity to look at it."

Doctor Miller continued, "On March 1, 1966, there is entered an annual note." This patient is fairly good most of the time, but can become upset and agitated. Hallucinates at night and states that she is talking to a little dog. Can become assaultive to other patients. Helps with some work on wards, but does not attend any activities. Fully ambulant, neat, active, assists nurses on wards spontaneously. Affect is blunted. At times, appears preoccupied. She admits to occasional auditory hallucinations, but not in the past month. She denies depression, reads her Norwegian Bible for hours each day. Some improvement in the last six months.

"What else do you have in that book, Doctor, besides the admissions and progress reports?"

"Well, there is a report which I made to the office of the Commission of Mental Health, sometime in March, related to what had gone on with the case. There is a substantial amount of correspondence including a letter which I wrote to Mr. Wall, and there are various nurse's notes, forms which record electrocardiograms and other aspects of physical examinations, There is chart in the file, as well as the coroner's report and findings."

"Doctor Miller, did you say there is a copy of a letter which you, personally, wrote to Attorney Wall?"

"Yes."

"May I see that letter?"

"Yes, you may have to wait until I locate it, however."

"And the date on that letter is when, Doctor?"

"The date of that letter is September 3, 1965."

Wall asked, "With your Honor's permission, could I look at it?"

The judge responded, "Certainly."

Shew asked the Doctor, "You used the phrase Schizophrenic, paranoid type, correct?"

"Correct."

"What does it mean in reference to this case?"

"This patient had both hallucinations and delusions, which referred to concepts of persecution and bizarre phenomena. Now for the purpose of definition, a hallucination is a false perception. A delusion is a false belief. In other words if someone believes he is hearing voices, this would be considered an auditory hallucination. If he harbors some concept such as being persecuted by some unknown imaginary person, this would be considered a delusion."

"And Agnes Thompsen was such a type?"

"She was."

"And when a person such as Agnes Thompsen has delusions of persecution, are they dangerous, or are they apt to be dangerous?"

"Not necessarily, but possibly."

"Doctor, is there anything in the report concerning any communication that Agnes Thompsen thought she had, with the Devil?"

The Doctor turned to March 5, 1964. Review Staff Conference notes,' She responds to hallucinatory experiences. She stated that the

Devil had gotten into her spine and head. She stated that the devil had been walking around in her head, then touching her body. She tended to be paranoid, suspicious and expressed a lot of autistic thinking. No memory losses.'

"Are there any other references to the Devil, or to any other people that were bothering Agnes?"

"There was another evaluation on June 12." It states, 'She feels that God has influenced her to heal her spine and head. She talks about the Devil drawn to the leg, but then revelation in kingdom come and many religious places She has the idea that there is a spirit that touches her fingers, and that these spirits move around in her head. "I walk on my head." 'She feels that she is not ill, and she wants to go home. She said the doctor was mad at her, and he sent her there for no reason at all.'

"Is it a fact, Doctor, that from this time on June 12, 1964, that Agnes Thompsen might have so called remissions?"

"Yes."

"And what are remissions?"

"Remissions are periods of time during which the pathological symptoms diminish or disappear and the patient apparently improves, or gets better. However, the term remission is usually used, to indicate a period of time in the course of an illness during which there has been improvement, but following which time the illness continues with all the symptoms as before."

"I noted you used the word, apparent improvement. Doctor. Would a patient of this type, or take this particular patient, in your opinion is there a possibility of recovery?"

"I believe that there would never be a time when she would be considered completely normal. There might be periods of time during which she had sufficient improvement to effect some sort of marginal adaptation to the world around her. She would be considered as schizophrenia in remission. However, any additional stress beyond that, which her low level of tolerance might handle, would in all likelihood, push her right back into her symptomatic phase of her illness, once again."

"Have other discourses in which she might have in reference to the Devil?"

"There is no specific reference to the Devil."

"Doctor, were you present on any occasion when this woman was interviewed by the State Police?"

The Doctor replied, "On several occasions. I remember that a substantial number of police were on the premises at the time. I remember several of them, however, I don't remember them all."

"And during these interviews, can you describe the manner in which she was interviewed by the State Police. I mean, as far as consideration for her was concerned?

Wall objected at this point, "Your Honor, I object. There is no specific time no specific occasion—no specific person."

The judge stated, "I think if the Doctor indicates the times when he himself was present, and can observe them, and the dates, I think that is what Mr. Shew is getting at probably."

Shew asked to see the chart, however, Wall objected." I don't consider it part of the hospital records. It is interdepartmental mail and includes a great many conclusions that do not appear to be relevant here." Shew argued that the chart was part of the hospital records. Wall being true to form, objected.

Shew said, "I feel it's very important Your Honor, but I suppose you've got to identify the letter, in order to get it on record as the basis of an exception. There are statements in there which are already in evidence. It's the records of the Middletown Valley Hospital." He then asked the Doctor, "Is there anything in this chart indicating that you yourself had any interviews with Agnes Thompsen?"

"Yes there are. There is a note of mine indicating this."

"And when was that?"

"Well, there was an extremely brief interview at the time that the warrant was lifted, or whatever the appropriate term is, at which time

Lieutenant Fuessenich wanted to speak with Mrs. Thompsen, and he spoke with her, while I was present."

"And was there more conversation between Lieutenant Fuessenich and Mrs. Thompsen at that time?"

"Well, the lieutenant attempted to explain to Mrs. Thompsen what had gone on. The fact that the warrant was no longer in operation, and she was no longer under suspicion, however, he had some difficulty conveying this to her. Ultimately, while waiting for a response, he asked her whether she was in fact, pleased by this. She made no spontaneous indication of this at all. That was the day he came to remove the warrant."

Shew stated, "I think I am almost through with the Doctor, but I may or may not be, depending on the recess."

During the recess, pages of the Connecticut Valley Hospital record of Agnes Thompsen were marked as Full Defendant's Exhibit, and received in evidence.

At that time Shew asked, "Just one or two more questions Doctor. Do your records show whether or not Agnes Thompsen, at the time of June 15, 1965, was discharged from your hospital, or on an extended leave?"

"The records show she was on extended visit. And she was directed to make visits to the Outpatient Clinic in Hartford, run by the Norwich State Hospital."

"And do you have anything in your records to show whether there was anything in Agnes Thompsen's behavior previous to her coming back, to indicate that she should have come back to the hospital?"

"There is some tangential reference to this fact—" To which Wall objected.

Shew then stated, "It's on identification, Your Honor."

The judge then said, "Well, then, it is not before the Jury, of course, if it is only for identification. Now, if you wish him to refresh his recollection, are you objecting to having it read, Mr. Wall?"

Wall answered in the affirmative.

The judge then said, "Maybe he won't."

Shew then said, "He doesn't know what I want, yet."

The Doctor was permitted to tell roughly about the condition of Agnes, ten days prior to her having been readmitted to the hospital, "She appeared to be acting in a bizarre fashion and seemed to be hallucinating. The people for whom she worked felt somewhat uneasy, and discharged her. She had been told by the outpatient department to return to the hospital because her case had worsened."

Shew thanked the doctor, and said, "That's all."

Cross examination by Wall

"Doctor, when a person is admitted to the State Hospital, is there not usually a commitment?"

"Yes."

"Well, perhaps I could ask, what was the situation, in this case, and what kind of adjudication was had?"

The Doctor repeated the now familiar testimony. "On February 25, 1964 Agnes Thompsen was admitted to the Hospital on an emergency commitment, which empowers the Hospital to hold an individual for thirty days. This is not through the court, but by any licensed physician Upon re-admission, Mrs. Thompsen was examined by Dr. Louise Rucker, who was assigned to the patient. There were no cuts, bruises or mutilations on the patient, however, she had fingerprint ink on her fingers."

Trooper Allan Yuknat was the next witness for the defense. Before the testimony started, Wall asked, "Your Honor, there was a witness on the stand last time, and he was taken off. I was wondering whether the request was made to put this witness on "out of order", as preliminary. Otherwise, I think the witness, who was on the stand, should be recalled to the stand."

Shew replied, "If Mr. Wall objects to the State Trooper, and I don't want to keep him around here, therefore, if Wall wishes the other witness to go on, I will be happy to go on with him."

The judge responded with, "There is no objection. Proceed."

Trooper Yuknat testified that he is assigned to the Connecticut State Bureau of Identification, and took part in the Thompsen investigation. He said, "He arrived at the house about 8:30 on the evening of June 15, 1965. He further stated that they had a pair of black shoes belonging to a male. He didn't take the photographs of the items in evidence, but Sergeant Chapman did. He stated that said he looked for identifying characteristics within the imprint left on the floor, which would correspond to a similar characteristic on the shoe itself, and if such a characteristic had been found they would have gone further.

"And can you tell us whether the imprint on the floor in the exhibits just referred to, were similar in size and shape to those of Arnfin Thompsen?"

"They were similar in size and shape."

At that point Shew said," That's all."

Lieutenant Cleveland Fuessenich was recalled to the stand for continued direct examination by Shew. He was asked, and answered the previously asked questions, about the white dress and the hairs. And he stated that other toxicologists besides Dr. Stolman examined the exhibits. And that the Alcohol and Tax Division in Washington, D.C., also did some analysis on the hairs. More questions followed about the dress, and a towel that was in the dryer. He stated that, "Two pieces were cut out of the dress and sent away to be examined."

Shew then asked, "How did the detectives get a sample of Harry's hair?"

The lieutenant replied, "He gave it to us at the Hartford Barracks."

"Did he know you had taken it?"

"Yes, sir, he gave it to us."

23

Major Rome was recalled to the stand, with continued direct examination by Attorney Shew.

"Now major, do you remember how many times you interviewed Agnes Thompsen at the Connecticut Valley Hospital?"

"As I testified last time, I believe it was around four times."

And now, on August 5, did you interview Agnes Thompsen?"

"I believe it was August 5."

"Who, if anyone, was present besides yourself?"

"Sergeant Ragazzi, myself, Valerie Hageman, and Detective Lester Redican. There was always some member of the hospital in attendance, such as the nurse, Miss Butterworth, Dr. Miller, or some other members of the staff."

"And how long did this interview with Agnes Thompsen take?"

"Two, to two and a half hours."

"Do you remember whether or not Dr. Miller was present at the interview, or in the adjoining room?"

"He was there. We had a microphone in the room where we were talking, and we had a speaker in the other room, where the Doctors, or other troopers could listen."

"And at that time, can you describe her condition, as she appeared to you. Just her appearance?"

"I thought she was nervous. She is a very excitable woman, although she appeared to be strong and in good health physically."

"And whether or not, on this interview, or any other interview you had with her, you ascertained, whether or not the authorities in the hospital felt that it would not do her any physical harm?"

Wall objected to the question.

Shew then asked, "Now, what's your objection, Mr. Wall."

He answered, "The phrasing is too indefinite. The who, somebody, whether he got some information, etc., is vague and too indefinite, that's why I object."

The judge then replied, "Be more specific Mr. Shew."

Shew continued the questioning. "And at any time did you interview Agnes Thompsen without the approval of somebody on the staff. And whose approval did you have on August 5, if you remember?"

"Permission would be sought through Dr. Miller to Dr. Lowney, who was the Superintendent."

"And who was, Miss or Mrs. Hageman?"

"She is a member of the State Police force."

"And she was present at this interview? Did you ask certain questions of Agnes Thompsen at this interview, major?"

"I asked many questions."

"And during this interview, did you have Valerie Hageman do anything or take any action?"

"Yes, I asked her to lie down on the floor."

"And what was your purpose in asking her to lie down on the floor?"

Wall said, "I object to the purpose, Your Honor."

To which Shew said, "I claim it, Your Honor."

Wall replied with," What's in this witness's mind?"

Shew came back with, "I'm not asking what's in his mind. I'm asking what was actually done."

The judge sided with Shew by stating, "No, I think it requires an explanation, and if he states what his purpose was in setting up the scene of this interview in a certain way, I think the jury should know what it is."

Wall started to say, "Your Honor—", at which point the judge interrupted him.

"There are some limitations to this, I realize, as to what was in his mind, but where a certain setting is provided for the interview with this person, I think the reason is probably important to understand the circumstances, the settings and the validity of the interview, therefore, I will allow it."

Shew stated, "I feel very strongly that the jury should have it."

The judge once again had to ask of Wall, "If you have some additional reason that this is prejudice."

Wall replied, "There are, Your Honor, and I wish to develop those by cross examination of this witness relating to the circumstances that existed at this time, so that Your Honor can then determine what those circumstances were, and whether or not this is admissible, and with Your Honor's permission, May I inquire of the witness, relating to these circumstances?"

The judge then asked, "Is this going to develop into something that should be in the absence of the jury?"

Both attorneys agreed on having the jury hear the testimony.

Wall resumed his questioning." Major Rome, I believe you have testified that you are, or were, at that time, a third or forth in command in the State Police Department in the State of Connecticut? Which was it, third or forth?"

"Fourth."

"And in accordance with that, major, did you call upon the services of various people, who were not directly in your detective command, in connection with this work which you were doing on the fifth of August, 1965? And you requested the services of policewoman Valerie Hageman to assist you in this investigation, on that day?

"Yes, I did. Well, I actually asked her to assist. I believe it was on that morning."

"And had you interviewed Agnes Thompsen that morning before you called Miss Hageman to come to the Connecticut Valley Hospital to assist you?"

"If I was at the hospital, I was there to interview Agnes Thompsen."

"And had you then questioned her for some time that morning?"

"I don't know what you mean by some time."

"Did you question her all that morning?"

"I don't know."

When you had occasion to see Miss Valerie Hageman on that day, did you issue instructions to her, relating to what her what she was expected to do on your behalf in connection with this investigation, and would you tell us what that was?"

"I will be glad to."

"Well, I will be very happy to have you."

Major Rome answered in his usual sarcastic manner, "Very good. Make us both happy."

"Your Honor, and ladies and gentlemen, I had talked to Agnes Thompsen on at least three previous occasions."

At this point Wall interrupted the major with, "May I ask, Your Honor—", To which the major screamed out loud, "Will you let me finish!?"

With that there was a gasp from the visitors gallery. For a moment it appeared that the judge was going to sensor the major for his rude behavior.

The judge was now really getting annoyed with this blatant disrespect for the Court and replied, in an outraged tone, "Just a minute!"

Wall said, "I object to this answer as not responsive. May the question be read Your Honor?"

The judge answered with, "Read the question. I want to hear what the question is, Mr. Shew, before I can rule on whichever you gentlemen wish it to be ruled on."

Wall asked, "What those instructions were?"

The judge responded with, "I might say I know what Mr. Wall was objecting to in the beginning of the answer, and that is, background as to what the instructions were. That can be brought out if the counsel feels that one thing leads to another, but at the present time, the question is, just what the instructions were. Does that answer your question?"

Major Rome answered the next question with, "Miss Hagemen was to pose as Arnfin Thompsen's girl friend."

"And will you relate in your own words, what instructions you gave, and amplify the statement that you made, that Miss Hageman was to pose as Arnfin Thompsen's girl friend?"

In his typical cocky manner, the major replied with, "Amplification I will be glad to give you Mr. Wall."

"Just amplify what your instructions were," said the judge."

I explained to—now, this is all from memory, I have no notes on this. I explained to Miss Hageman, that I was of a firm opinion."

At this point the judge was getting more impatient with the major, "Now, this is not responsive major. Just answer as to the instructions."

"I am sorry. It is all part of the instructions."

Wall interrupted again with, "May I move it go out Your Honor—I have a firm opinion?"

The judge, really getting enraged, once again had to instruct the major to, "Just answer in regard to the instructions."

Major Rome continued with, "I instructed Miss Hageman to pose as Arnfin Thompsen's girl friend, in order to get, not a confession, but some information from Agnes Thompsen, from which we could later determine whether she was guilty, or innocent."

"Now, and is that all you recall of importance in the way of instructions which you gave to Miss Hageman?"

"Well, if you refresh my memory, I'll go on, but this is all I can recall right now. See, I made no notes myself."

"You have been in this courtroom for about ten full days, haven't you?"

In a rather stern voice, Rome shouted, "No, I haven't!"

"Shew remarked, "Objection, Your Honor, just hold it right there. Mr. Wall asked Major Rome to even stay out of the courthouse. Let's get this straight."

Wall answered with, "I never said any such thing."

The judge then said, "Gentlemen. This is one of those things that I am not going to get into, in front of the jury. If the purpose of the question is to ask whether Major Rome heard certain testimony here, that's one thing, but not simply to the blanket question as to how much time he has been present in the courthouse."

Wall said, "I withdraw the question."

"Major, what other instructions did you give to Valerie Hageman when she arrived at the Connecticut Valley Hospital, other than the instructions which you have mentioned already here in testimony today?

"I have to repeat, Mr. Wall, that's the only thing that comes to my memory. I will be glad to go on, but I am hiding absolutely nothing."

Wall asked, "May that remark, "I am hiding absolutely nothing," go out, Your Honor? Me thinks he protesteth too much."

Shew then replied, "I can make just as many wise cracks as he can, Your Honor. If we're going to have that, and I don't think they are very good."

Judge MacDonald immediately excused the jury. He said, "I realize the hard feelings between the attorneys in this case, however, I'm not going to allow them to disrupt the trial or to erupt into anything that could cause a mistrial. I think that answer of Major Rome was unnecessary, in which he said he had nothing to hide. I also think the observation of the State's Attorney is even more unnecessary. Now, so far I don't exactly see what the purpose of this part of the interrogation of Major Rome, has to do with the merits of the case, because so far I have barred from evidence over Mr. Shew's objections, and with his exceptions, certain statements that were made by Agnes Thompsen. One of my purposes in doing so under the ruling of our Supreme Court, which I quoted at that time, was to avoid confusing the jury with certain collateral issues that had nothing to do with the trial of this particular accused. I think that possibly the circumstances have caused Major Rome to be overanxious to explain that he has no axe to grind, and I think that some of these statements, then understandably provoked the State's Attorney into adding comments that are uncalled for. So let's just call a halt on all of it, and proceed as though you two have never had words before, or even seen each other.

"The jury was called back, and the cross examination of Major Rome continued.

Wall asked, "Now major, you requested Valerie Hageman to pose as the girl friend of Arnfin Thompsen?, and to pose as a prospective daughter-in-law, correct?"

"That is correct sir."

"And did you give any further instructions as to the strategy to be used, if any, by Hageman in connection with her contact or conversation with Agnes Thompsen?"

"I'm sure I may have, Mr. Wall, but I don't recall. We talked and I explained the reason for bringing her up there. I also explained the type of person we had to deal with, and I asked her if she could go along with a certain strategy, to open the mind of an insane person."

"And now, you had with you, another man who was on your staff, whom you had to pose before Agnes Thompsen, in another capacity, did you?"

"Yes, I did."

"And is it so, that at your direction he went in, to Agnes Thompsen, and told her that he was a lawyer? That he had been hired by the girl friend, and to see that he would protect her interest in this matter, is that so?"

"Well, exactly what he said, I have no recollection right now, but I was dealing again, with a woman who had been committed, an insane woman, and I had to resort to subterfuge to find the truth, and find the facts in this case, and I did."

"And that subterfuge—involved your denial of that woman of counsel, isn't that so? That poor woman."

"That was discussed with Superintendent Lowney of the hospital. Either Arnfin, her son, or Theodore, another son, or the hospital, who was her guardian at the time, was present. The members of the hospital were present."

"And then at your direction, this member of the State Police department deceived that poor woman into thinking that he was her lawyer, to protect her rights."

"That is not correct. She didn't fall for it at all, she was too smart."

"That wasn't your fault was it major?"

"I tried."

Wall said, "I move that the latter go out, especially the last statement."

The judge then directed that the statement go out.

Wall then asked, "Did you offer to get Agnes Thoinpsen out of the institution that day, if she would answer your questions the way you wanted her to?"

"No sir, it is only part true what you are reading. I told her to open her mind, because I felt the woman had the secret to this case, in her mind."

Wall asked, "May that go out Your Honor?, that portion that is not responsive"

The judge agreed, "That last portion, about the last twelve words, may go out."

Wall continued the questioning, "Did you promise her that you would get her out of the institution that very night?"

"Yes if she was telling the truth. I was dealing with an insane woman, and I had to resort to deception, I will admit to that, Your Honor."

"And you told her she would be in the best position to get out, go free, and go home, and forget about it, didn't you? You knew that she had never been before any judge, did you not?"

"I was dealing with an insane woman, Mr. Wall."

"And did you say, "You tell me where the piggy bank is, and you and Jean can go right home. I'll bring up the papers." Is that correct?"

"I would say that is a correct statement, yes."

"And did you say to her, "You going to continue to lie to me, huh? Then you have to stay here for the rest of your life. Did you say that to Agnes Thompsen?"

"I used every kind of deception to get the truth of this case. This wasn't a confession against Mrs. Thompsen. I wanted the truth of this case. I'll go along with that."

Wall once again asked, "May that latter remark go out, Your Honor, that part is not responsive, that last sentence."

Shew said, "It might as well stay in, because I'm going to bring it in anyway."

The judge said, "Well, I think it came out, and I'll allow it to stand."

"Did you say to Mrs. Thompsen, I am going to stop the marriage between Arnfin and Jean?, or did you say that to Miss Hageman? Did you say that to her?

"I don't remember everything I said to her that day."

"Well, did you say to Agnes Thompsen that, if she said she did it, then Jean—so called Jean, could marry Arnfin?"

"I'll go along with that. I used everything in my bag of tricks to get the truth from this insane person. Opened the bag wide."

"Did you say, "Agnes, I will bring Arnfin here tonight? You tell me where the bank is, and I'll get a minister here to marry them. As a matter of fact, I'm a State Policeman major, I can marry them"

"Yes, I think I did, yes."

"Did you say, anybody that doesn't remember has to stay in the hospital?"

"Yes, I was trying to get what she did, out of her."

"Did you say, remember this, Agnes, and get it straight, if you can't remember anything, they are going to keep you here. This is a hospital for people who can't think, who can't remember. You know that don't you? If you can't remember, stay in the hospital, goodbye. I'm not able to help you."

"I would go along with that one hundred per cent. I did everything possible in the legal manner to try to extract the truth from this lady. I could have said that too."

"But you don't recall whether you did or did not?"

"I resorted to every kind of subterfuge that I knew, to try to get at the truth. Because, in previous statements, she had stated to me, she knew I was there to try to get at the truth, and I eventually did."

You said, "Jean is entitled to know. She is going to be your daughter-in-law, maybe tonight. Did you say that?"

"I think I did. But the—I—I—I cannot picture—I don't remember—really saying that to her, but I am sure that I did. I feel sure, that is—this is—let me finish."

"Wall said, "I'm sorry."

The major continued, "This is in line with everything I was trying to do to extract the truth—not a confession, nothing illegal, but to extract the truth. Yes I would go along with that."

Did you say, "I don't want to tell the doctors you can't remember? They are going to keep you here, and these nurses are worse than the doctors? Did you say that?" At this point the judge interrupted the questioning with, "Perhaps—perhaps—that particular answer should not be put into the records, because it might be the basis for some action against the major, or by the nurses."

"I'll take the chance, "said the major, "Your Honor. I remember saying that. That means—may I explain that?

The nurse was present and I was just—it was just a pun to the nurse at the time. Miss Butterworth was present, and I did that more to break the monotony for this poor girl that was sitting through all this."

Wall then asked, "Was this an occasion of levity to you, major."

"At that instant, that moment, Yes, sir."

"Did you say, "Agnes, we're telling the truth now, your memory has got to be good or you stay here, "did you say that to her?"

"Yes, I go along with that one hundred per cent. I was trying to extract the truth, not a confession, but the true instances, true statements that could be verified or corroborated, Yes, sir, that would be in line with what I was trying to do. I'm sorry I had to use this kind of subterfuge."

Wall then asked, "You are devoted to the truth?"

"I am sir," Was the major's answer.

"Did you say, "I don't want to have to tell the doctor you can't remember because all I have to do is tell him you can't remember and you are going to stay."

"Yes, sir, because I didn't want to make up anything. I wanted the truth."

"Now, you may wish to answer that question, major, if you are devoted to the truth. Are you, and would you like to answer that question?"

"If I didn't, I wouldn't be here," was his sarcastic answer.

"I see. You mean, on the witness stand?"

"That's correct."

"Aren't you under subpoena here, today?"

"Because I want to get the truth out."

"Aren't you under subpoena today?"

Using a sarcastic tone once again he answered, "I said I am!"

"Then you would have to be here whether you wanted to be or not, would you not?"

"Mr. Shew knows—"

"Wait a minute. Answer my question, please."

"No."

"In other words, you could defy the law and defy a subpoena?"

"No. But if I told Mr. Shew some other facts or something else, he wouldn't have me here today."

"Did you say, "I don't want to tell the doctor that you can't remember. Look what you are doing to me, Did you say that?"

"That doesn't make sense. I don't understand that question."

"All right. Did you say, Jean, she can remember, and I am going to make a note to the doctor?, Now stop and think. I don't want to have to tell the doctor you are not thinking clearly. Did you say that to her?"

"I could have. I feel reasonably sure I did."

Did you say, "I just want to know where the bank is, and we'll get your clothes?"

"I may have said that."

"And did you say, "We got your footprints and fingerprints right here," "And you pointed to the bay window. Did you say that to her?"

"That, I don't recall, but if someone with a better memory than mine says I did, then I did. I was talking to an insane person, seeking the truth, put me down as, yes"

Did you say, "Don't let the doctor know that I am talking to you, and if you say you don't know? I'm a dead duck."

"That I don't recall, but if someone else does, I will go along with it."

"You started the interrogation of Mrs. Agnes Thompsen in the morning, on the morning of August 5, did you not?"

"I testified before, I don't know the exact time."

"And you know that it was late at night before you completed your interrogation of Agnes Thompsen that particular day, isn't it so?"

His sneering answer was, "If you explain to me what hour, late at night means."

"And was it not—had there not been darkness come upon you at the time you just completed it?"

"No, I don't believe so, anyway, this was under the control of the Superintendent of the Connecticut Valley Hospital, the hours I talked to her, when she was fed, and the time taken out, and et cetera. This is all under their control, and it was all strictly legitimate."

"Now, this question that was asked of you, as to whether or not Miss Hageman lay on the floor, on one occasion?"

"Yes."

"This was this a question which was asked, after you made all of these statements to Mrs. Thompsen, isn't that so?"

"I would again say yes. Yes."

Wall said, "I object to the question, Your Honor in view of the circumstances, on the additional ground, that only is it hearsay, but anything which might have been said under these circumstances, would have no trustworthiness whatsoever. On these grounds I move that it—"

The judge, totally confused at this point, cut him off with, "Well, it has been so long ago that we had the question, that I'd like to know from you, what that question was to which the objection was made, that called for the last half hour of interrogation. Just what was it?"

Shew interjected, "May I make a suggestion Your Honor. Mr. Wall has taken Major Rome over as a witness, and I propose to Cross examine Major Rome on his statements now."

Wall agreed, "I'm perfectly willing—Perfectly all right."

The judge said, at this point, "I might make this observation before I take a recess and I am going to, shortly. I think I am going to reverse a former ruling that I made concerning the admissibility of statements."

Shew said, "I'm certainly going to ask you to, Your Honor"

"After recess, the judge said, "I'll give both counsel an opportunity to think about the reasons for it. Keeping out certain statements made by Agnes Thompsen were based on our Supreme Court decisions that in my opinion, stated one of the reasons for keeping such statements out, were that they would only confuse the issues before the jury and bring in collateral matters and make it look as though somebody, other than the accused, was on trial. I feel that since the opportunity arose and questions were asked, concerning the circumstances surrounding the interrogation, that the jury, in my opinion of the moment is entitled to know what the statements were that were objected to, so that they can decide for themselves what weight should be given to the statements, whether they were made voluntarily, or whether they were made under compulsion. My inclination is to allow the results of that interrogation to come in, although that reverses a prior ruling that I made, and if Mr. Shew was going to ask that."

Shew confirmed, "I was going to ask that Your Honor, and I feel I'm entitled to it."

Wall said, "Your Honor has indicated an intention to take certain action in connection with this matter. I'm not at all sure just what it is, although I believe that it might be that Your Honor wishes to reverse the ruling relating to hearsay that was previously made."

The judge, responded with, "I indicated that I was going to think it over and decide just how far I should go. I haven't made up my mind as to just how far I should go, and I assumed I would hear from counsel on that subject."

Wall started to say, "Now—.", and the judge cut him off before he could finish his sentence, with "Now, through certain circumstances that arose, much of that has come out and I don't know how much of it will be left after this further questioning on it, but at any rate, a picture has been presented to the jury of the circumstances under which Agnes Thompsen was questioned. I'm beginning to wonder whether the fairest way to present it to them, would be to have them know what exactly this woman said under the circumstances that have already been partially described to them, under the mental condition that they know of from the Testimony of the witness here, and to evaluate those statements, and decide what weight to give to them. That's my present line of thinking, Mr. Wall. I will be glad to hear arguments from you and Mr. Shew on that subject. I believe you had started, and I interrupted you, so continue."

Wall continued with, "I'm sure, that if Your Honor allows such testimony to come in, it will bring up not only some of this, which is only a preview of what might happen. The counsel for the defendant had claimed he was going to appeal on this ground. He said that he felt that the Supreme Court would have to decide—"

Shew said, "Let's stop right there Your Honor. That is incorrect."

The judge expressed an opinion that they were getting into unrelated matters.

Shew said, "I made no such statement and I don't expect to appeal. Let's put that on the record. I never made such a ridiculous statement Your Honor."

The judge responded with, "Let me make this statement clear for the benefit of both counsel, that if I had not had the decisions of the Connecticut Supreme Court. This is not—nobody else is on trial here. We are not trying State Police Officers, we're not trying Mrs. Agnes Thompsen, we're trying Harry Solberg. The jury knows now from the remarks made by other witnesses, from all the implications that have arisen from the controversy over the circumstances. The only question was as to whether or not this evidence was admissible. Now the next thing to do is to allow Mr. Shew to question Major Rome on the circumstances that have been brought out. I am making no change in my ruling at this time."

Shew stated, "In the first place your Honor, regardless of what your own observations are, obviously Mr. Wall has opened the door. I'm going to insist in every way, shape and form, to bring out the whole business now."

The judge replied with. "Excuse me for interrupting you, but if I don't, I'll forget these things. How about the fact that we would be hearing statements of an important nature made by a person who is not in the presence of the jury, no opportunity for cross examination, and we are hearing only the statements that she made in answer to questions asked under what, apparently are, rather high pressure circumstances."

Shew remarked, "Your Honor, she's not on trial. There is no self-incrimination."

The judge said, "That's what I keep reminding everybody."

Shew said, "It' merely a matter of weight. Now, it has been clearly brought out by Mr. Wall, that the door was opened to the rest of it Your Honor, and the jury is entitled to know it, and I certainly, under all circumstances, feel that it must. We are trying to get the truth of this. Why is it an insult to the jury, when Mr. Wall says they would be confused by this?"

The judge once again tried to explain his position, "I think I have said it too, because I think we are getting dangerously close to trying Mrs. Thompsen, instead of Harry Solberg."

Finally the next witness, Philip Salafia, was sworn in. Unlike Major Rome, he answered all questions briskly and without hesitation. He stated that he has been a Connecticut State Policeman for four years, and had worked on the Thompsen case. He arrived at the Thompsen house at approximately 8:00 p.m. on June 15, 1965. It was early the next morning when he left the homicide scene, and two other officers were with him, Detective James Jacobs and Policewoman Butler. They took Agnes Thompsen to the Connecticut Valley Hospital in Middletown, which was about an hours drive. They didn't waste any time and drove straight to the hospital. While there he obtained some dried substance from the cuticles and from underneath the fingernails of Agnes Thompsen, while Policewoman Butler and Detective Jacobs were present. He sealed the scrapings in a white paper bag, and put his identification and date on it. He further stated that there were no cuts, or bruises. Her hands were clean.

Cross examination by Wall.

"Was the substance which you took with you from the a substance from the cuticle of the right middle finger?"

"Yes, sir."

"Did you observe something particularly relating to the cuticle of the right middle finger, as distinguished from the other fingers?"

"No, sir. It was a "gloppy" substance, clearly visible."

"Yes, and you saw something that was clearly visible on the right middle finger. Is that correct? The cuticle of the right middle finger?"

"Not as much, sir."

"And did you make any observations of any specific examination to determine whether there were any pinpricks or any types of small wounds that might possibly have caused this?"

"No, sir. The scraping, itself, was a delicate procedure, business. I didn't notice anything."

"Well, Officer, if you had seen some other source that might contribute or make blood on Mrs. Thompsen's fingers, you would have so noted in your report, wouldn't you?"

"Yes, sir, I would."

James M. Jacob was the next witness for the Defense. He gave the same testimony as Officer Salafia. He witnessed Officer Salafia scrape all ten fingers of Mrs. Thompsen's hands. He stated that he didn't see any cuts or bruises on her hands, and it would have been in his report if he had.

Policewoman Virginia Butler, of the Connecticut State Police, was the next witness to be sworn in. She stated that she arrived at the Thompsen house about a quarter after nine, June 15, 1965, and was upstairs with Agnes Thompsen most of the time, until they took her to the hospital, in Middletown.

Shew asked. "And was anybody else there, Mrs. Butler, besides you and Mrs. Thompsen?"

"Yes, The Captain and the lieutenant, however, they were walking in, and out."

"And did you have any conversation with her?"

"Not pertaining to what happened in the house. She talked about her religion, her crocheting, her friends. She was aware of what had taken place."

"And whether or not she had viewed the deceased?"

"No, sir. I kept her upstairs."

"But the statements she made were concerning things other than that."

"She asked me if it could have been the Boston Strangler, and said it was too bad it had happened. And, she would get a little excited, so I'd get her off the subject and she would calm down again. She also said, there was a green car parked in front of the house that day."

"Do you remember, Mrs. Butler, if it is possible to see out front from her apartment?"

"No, I know there wasn't a good view."

"And did you see her use her hands for anything during that entire evening?"

"No, outside of reading her bible and looking at some old photographs of the family taken in Norway."

"She didn't do anything that would get dirt or any foreign substance on her hands, other than dust?"

"She did pick up. When somebody would bring in dirt on their shoes, she would pick it up."

"And tell us what happened after she was checked in at the hospital?"

"Scrapings were taken from underneath all her fingernails. There were no bruises, or marks on her hands."

Shew asked, "Would you give me a moment Your Honor?"

The judge replied, "Surely."

Shew then read through some parts of Mrs. Butler's report, after which he asked," There were other statements made that night, weren't there, Mrs. Butler?"

"Well, let's see. She talked about her crocheting, and about her daughter-in-law. She said that it was too bad it happened."

And she was perfectly well aware of the fact that her daughter-in-law was dead, at that time?"

"Yes she was, however, she didn't show any remorse, and she wasn't crying."

"Will you refer to your report, Mrs. Butler?"

"She did make the remark that she would stay there and take care of Christa."

"Now, did you make a remark, that she took exception to, while you were with her?"

"I don't recall just what the remark was. It had something to do—"

At this point Wall asked her for the second time, to refer to her report.

"I am not asking what the remark was," he said, "I'm asking whether she took exception to one of your remarks."

"Yes she did. She jumped up and glared at me. I then changed the subject and she calmed down."

"Now, the last sentence in this report, Mrs. Butler, will you read it out loud please?"

"Well, that particular evening, I felt that this woman would be—"

"Now, Mrs. Butler. Please. I asked you if you would just read that statement in your report."

"It would appear that this woman could be capable of going from various moods, up to one of violence. As stated she showed no grief, sorrow or any emotion of any kind over the death."

Cross examination of Police Woman Butler, by Wall.

"Now, Mrs. Butler, will you describe the apartment?

"It was immaculate. Absolutely immaculate, except for the dirt brought in by people going in and out."

"And when you say dirt brought in by people going in and out, you mean the investigating officers. And what happened as this dirt was deposited on the floor?"

"She picked it up with her fingers."

"And now what can you say concerning her personal appearance on that night? Was she disheveled or well groomed?"

"Well groomed. She had a home permanent that day, and her hair was up in pin curls."

"And did they appear to be disturbed in any way?"

"No sir."

"Was there any indication of anything that could have happened to her hair, from the condition that night?"

"No sir, in fact as I said, she had gotten this home permanent, and I believe it was either her daughter or daughter-in-law that had given it to her. It looked like the same person who had given her the permanent, had also done up her hair in pin curlers that looked like they had just been left there."

Shew said, "I object. I don't object to anything except—"

The judge ruled, "Excepting that part after, they looked like, may be stricken."

Shew remarked, "I don't know if Mrs. Butler has testified here saying it looked like her daughter-in-law had given it to her."

Wall responded with. "We expect to have evidence that will clear that up Mr. Shew."

Redirect examination of Police Woman Butler by, Shew

"When did the question of the hair and curlers first come up Mrs. Butler?, When did you discuss that,? this morning?"

"Someone asked me about it. I think it was Trooper Pennington who asked me about it."

"Mrs. Butler, did you discuss the time, when that might have been done, and with whom did you discuss it? Was it Trooper Pennington?"

"Yes, something was mentioned about that, that she did have a home permanent and her hair was up in pin curls."

"And you hadn't called it to anyone's attention until this morning, until trooper Pennington called it to your attention, right?"

"Yes, I hadn't thought of it anymore." At that point shew expressed his thanks.

After lunch, and before the jury was recalled, Judge MacDonald said, "Before we call in the jury, gentlemen, we shall settle this question, right here and now as to what's going to happen to the statements by Agnes Thompsen. I am ready to rule on that without any further arguments. The reason I asked the question in that way, is because there were certain things during Mr. Wall's questioning of the witness, that were stated in the jury's presence, which may call for an opportunity on the part of Mr. Shew to ask further questions in connection with the circumstances. I believe he indicated he didn't think it was necessary, however, I think that the issue better be settled right now, so that we don't call the jury in and have to send them out again. I am ready to make a ruling on that, if there is nothing else preliminary that counsel wishes to argue on that point."

Wall started to say, "Your Honor—" however, was interrupted by the judge who said, "I will state, that I am more firmly convinced, more that ever, that my prior ruling was the correct one, and that the statements are not admissible. I say this now, so that it will perhaps save some time in our argument, and I just as soon have it on the record why I feel that way. The main argument against the admissibility of the evidence, and the fear of perjured testimony, is minimized in this case. The witnesses are Connecticut State Policemen with no motive to falsify."

Shew indicated his disagreement with the judge in part, by saying, "Well, then Your Honor, I feel that the jury should be made aware of the fact that certain statements that Mrs. Thompsen made are being kept from them, and I think they are entitled to know. And why did Mr. Wall have that long dissertation with Major Rome. It took three quarters of an hour. Mr. Wall used Major Rome as his witness, absolutely and unequivocally. It was an unusual request which I conceded to him, after which he then proceeded to use Major Rome as his own witness, obviously with a slight subterfuge. He took this opportunity to get on the record that he might not have otherwise, and he used it as a subterfuge to ask Major Rome leading questions and everything else. This boy's life—"

The judge responded with, "It bothered me, Mr. Shew, and that is why I thought long and carefully before making my decision."

The judge then recalled the Jury and said, "Ladies and gentlemen of the jury, before we resume the testimony, I would like to explain something to you that I think you are entitled to know. This is a little out of order, because of the line of questioning, and the extreme care with which certain circumstances of the interrogation of Agnes Thompsen were gone into, and so you won't think that counsel are lying, or the State's Attorney is trying to conceal or withhold anything from you, which is pertinent to this case. You are all aware, I am certain, from the testimony that has been given, and from the remarks that have been made during the course of the testimony of the other witnesses, that an interrogation was made of Agnes Thompsen. In fact several interrogations made of Agnes Thompsen by the State Police, and that during the course of those interrogations she made certain statements. Certain statements, for which there has been an attempt to get into evidence. I have excluded them because, I feel bound by the rules of evidence as laid down by our Supreme Court, which clearly bind me to, in the observance of the law of the State, to refuse to admit those statements in evidence. The reasons for which, I won't go into here, but, for reasons which the Supreme Court goes into, which I think apply here. So, I am simply pointing out to you for your better understanding of what is going on, that certain statements made by Agnes Thompsen during the interrogation by the State Police have been excluded, and will not appear in evidence before you. I hope that clarifies it.

Shew stated, "Your Honor, may I add that I am the one that requested the statements."

The judge said, "That, I think was apparent Mr. Shew has been attempting on behalf of the defendant to get certain statements into evidence, and the Court has excluded them under the rules of evidence, does that clarify it?"

With that question settled, Mrs. Butler was recalled to the stand for re-cross examination by Wall. Major Rome was still standing in the back of the Courtroom looking frustrated, due to the constant repetition of the questions. Mrs. Butler again testified about Agnes Thompsen's hair, and the pin curls, and she read the report of the admitting doctor, which included the statement, her hair was in pin curls and perfectly groomed, we didn't touch it.

Redirect examination of Mrs. Butler by, Shew.

"Now Mrs. Butler, this morning I asked you whether there are any other things that you considered of importance in this statement of yours. Do you remember me asking you that?"

"Yes, sir."

"And up until that time, what had you told me?"

Wall objected, "I object to going over it again, Your Honor."

Shew explained, "I have a reason. This witness has definitely turned hostile your Honor, and I want to have the privilege of asking leading questions."

"And I asked you, what the conversation, if any, with Agnes Thompsen consisted of?"

Do you remember me asking you that?"

"Yes, sir."

Wall objected once again, "I object to that, Your Honor, It's repetitious. This is all in evidence and if there is any conclusion to be drawn, the jury has every fact necessary to draw that conclusion."

Shew, showing evidence of being "ticked off" said, "Again, I will ask Mr. Wall, to let me try my own case. If there is anyone around here that repeats, he does. I am entitled to this question and I am going to insist, unless your Honor prevents me from doing so."

The judge agreed, "Go ahead Mr. Shew."

Mrs. Butler answered the questions with the same answers. She was with Agnes Thompsen for a good four hours, they talked about everything. It was the only way she could keep her calmed down. They talked about the child, about her daughter-in-law, and about seeing a man out on the back porch. She showed no grief, sorrow or emotion over the death. She appeared capable of going to various moods, including one of violence. Shew thanked her and dismissed her.

At this point Wall commenced his cross examination of Major Rome.

"And now, major, I believe you made an observation to the effect that the piece of metal driven into the board was a "nailset" and that it was not a "spike". Did you make such an observation sir?"

"I believe I did."

"Well, is it not so that you were making an analysis of an error that was made in calling, what appeared to be a "nailset", as a "spike"?"

"I don't believe I understand your question, Mr. Wall."

"On direct examination by Mr. Shew, did he ask you to make some observation relating to the fact that the piece of metal driven into the wood, was a "nailset", and actually it was stated to be a "spike"."

"Yes, sir."

"And actually, though, wasn't the function of that "nailset", the same function you would expect from a "spike", since it was driven into the wood in the same manner as a "spike"?"

"No, I wouldn't say so. To me, a "spike" is a "spike". I know the difference. I know what a "nailset" is, and I felt that was a discrepancy. I still do."

"It didn't occur to you, did it, that a "nailset" used as a "spike" might be called a "spike" by somebody?

"It didn't say "spike" in there, did it sir?"

"It does not."

"You gave an order in connection with that State's Exhibit—you issued an order?"

"If I did, I don't remember it right now."

"And did you issue an order to trace the writer of this letter and arrest, if they could find the writer—arrest the owner for being a crank, or feeble minded?"

"Yes, I was talking about this letter being sent to the home of a man who just lost his wife, and that in my opinion, sending this kind of letter would be the work of a crank."

"Did you issue a press release at or about this time, that was widely published, relating to the fact that this was a work of a crank and that it had no connection with the case?"

"I don't print the newspaper. I don't know whether or not this is accurate or correct. I don't remember having given that statement. I do have a recollection of returning that letter. After examining it carefully, I realized that the individual who wrote it, did so without facts."

Wall asked, "Your Honor, may I ask that the witness,—what the witness has said go out?

The judge agreed, and dismissed the major.

The next witness sworn was twenty four year old Richard G. Gower. He said he has lived in East Hartland for sixteen years, and has worked at Hayes' Store for eight years. "Because Hayes' is the only store in town, you know almost everybody." He also said that he knew Harry Solberg. He used to ride on the same school bus with him, and he is a quiet person who is always around town. The only negative thing he had heard about Harry, was the incident in New York.

"In your capacity of working in this store, if there was anything happening around town, you probably would have heard of it?

"Well, we heard quite a bit of what went on."

Shew, Wall and the judge all agreed that the witness had given sufficient testimony, at that point.

Dr. Gertrude Lucille Rucker, resident in psychiatry at the Connecticut Valley Hospital, for two years and ten months, was the next witness to be sworn in. She read from her reports, and explained every detail of the examination she had given Agnes Thompsen, which according to the admission form, was at 3:10 a.m. on June 16, 1965. She said she examined Agnes Thompsen's head for abnormalities, also her skin and glands, her general body build, and her extremities. Then she asked, "Do you want me to read the whole report?"

Shew asked, "Would you say her—is it a fair statement to say that her physical condition was pretty good at that time?

"Yes."

"Now Doctor, I noticed that you mentioned something about her hands in that report."

"The stains on the palmer surface of fingers from the fingerprint ink."

"And whether or not you saw any cuts or things which could produce bleeding on her hands at that time, Doctor?"

She answered, "I found none."

Wall then started his cross examination of Dr. Rocker

"And a slight puncture wound caused by a knitting, or a crocheting needle, or something of that sort, might escape your attention?"

"I am not sure that I am familiar with the wound of a crochet needle."

"And you didn't find anything that would cause blood to accumulate on her fingernails, did you?"

"No, I did not."

The Doctor was then excused. After recess, Shew asked permission to recall Major Rome for one more question, assuming Wall expressed no objection.

The judge agreed, "All right, Mr. Shew, I believe you wanted to recall Major Rome."

Shew started his questioning with, "major, up until the start of this case, and I mean by that, the start of the impaneling of the jury, and so forth, had you ever talked with Mr. Wall about this case?"

"Maybe—at the start of the case just before they started impaneling the jury, I did."

"And just one other question major, what was the purpose you had in questioning Agnes Thompsen during the interview, that Wall questioned you so much about this morning? Why did you do it? What were you trying to find out? What were you doing it for?"

Wall said, "I object to it, your Honor. I see no relevancy as to why, or what mental processes this man went through."

"The judge replied, "I understand Mr. Shew's question to be, what was the reason for the interrogation."

Shew added, "Why did you interrogate Agnes Thompsen, major?"

"To extract, if I may use the word, information from this individual which could be verified and corroborated, and to determine whether or not it was factual and truthful, and whether or not she did, or did not commit this crime."

Shew said, "That's all, major."

Wall began his cross the examination of Major Rome.

"Wall, addressing the major said, "I am not unknown to you, am I major? And you know sir, that I have been the State's Attorney in Litchfield County since 1953. And that I have, before that, been Public Defender in this County for a number of years, and defended a large number of criminals in this County—you knew that?

"I did, yes, sir."

"And you felt you had information, did you, that was relevant to this case, is that so, is that what you want this jury to understand?"

In a very caustic tone of voice he replied, "No, sir, I don't. I want this jury to understand that you had my reports in your possession, which were contrary to the reports you had gotten from others, and at no time was and at no time was I called to your office to see why I arrived at a different opinion."

"I see now, Mr. Rome."

"Is that a demotion?"

Wall looked about, puzzled. Shew explained, "You addressed him as mister. If you have been accustomed to using that title for all of your witnesses, I assume—"

Public Defender Wall then said, "Major Rome, you will have your title, sir."

"Now major, you saw then, no necessity not even propriety in getting in touch with me as State's Attorney in this county, knowing that I was proceeding with a prosecution against Harry Solberg, is that correct?"

"Yes, sir, that's a true statement."

"And it is well known, major, that you believe, in working for the state, that you have the right to lie?"

The judge stated, "If there is objection to that, I will sustain it."

Shew, now getting hot under the collar, replied, "That's dirty politics, Your Honor! I think it's absolutely unfair of Mr. Wall."

Wall replied, "I can connect it up, Your Honor. May I show you what I have here?," as he passed the transcript to the judge.

"I see nothing in here to justify that question," answered the judge.

Shew said, "I certainly object to it, Your Honor, and I am willing to have everything before the jury, except that Major Rome is a liar. May I see that transcript?"

The judge replied, "I have already ruled that the question is not justified by the document, so that I don't think it has any further place in the—"

Shew interrupted the judge and said, "I think I would like to see Mr. Wall's source of information, here, Your Honor, for my own purposes now. Do I see it, Mr. Wall?"

Wall replied, "When I am finished with it, sir." He then mentioned another case in 1964, in Middletown, Conn. He asked the major if he had been examined by Attorney Jacobs. Shew pleaded, "If Your Honor pleases, I don't know what this could possibly have to do with it., if there is a personal—Wall is trying to carry on a vendetta with Major Rome."

Wall replied, "There is no vendetta."

The judge then said, "I don't consider that this is relevant. I think it could only lead to much trouble, and confusion, which would serve no purpose, other than to confuse the issues."

Wall explained, "Your Honor, that is not my purpose. My purpose is to answer the inquiry that has been made, and the reflection that has been made upon the State's Attorney's Office. The State's Attorney did not go to Major Rome himself to ask about this particular case, and I felt, Your Honor, that the reason for it, should be made apparent to the jury."

The judge getting agitated, said, "I will state right here and now, that I don't consider that any reflection has been cast upon the State's Attorney, or the State's Attorney's Office. There has been a great deal of argument, I won't use the word "vendetta". I think the curtain should be dropped, here and now, on this entire line of questioning."

Wall wouldn't drop it. He said, "I respect Your Honor's judgment, however, in this case, I feel that even though Your Honor has stated that there is no reflection upon the State's Attorney's Office, the only purpose of this testimony by this witness, was to reflect upon the State's Attorney's Office, in his neglect of duty, in not going to see the major about this case."

The judge really getting perturbed, said, "It could be argued, Mr. Wall, that the only purpose of your asking the major certain questions, were to reflect on him. So let's call a halt to it, here and now!"

Wall resumed his questioning, "Now major, you never had any reason to believe that I, as State's Attorney was not completely cooperative with you as a major of the State Police, in any of your official actions, is that not so?"

"That's correct."

Major Rome was excused. The next witness was Solveig Solberg. Mr. Shew asked comparable questions, and her answers likewise parallel. The addressed the subject of family and children, and the fact that Harry was the oldest. Then Shew asked, "And now Mrs. Solberg, do you remember July 15, 1965?"

"Yes, I do," She answered.

"And, will you, in your own words tell the jury just what your recollection was."

"He came home from school about one o'clock, and had a frozen "TV" dinner. He then went upstairs and changed into his work clothes. A few minutes later he went to the shop for the lawn mower, after which he helped his father load the truck." Mrs. Solberg also said. "I didn't notice anything unusual about Harry's appearance when he came home from the lawn mower shop, nor anything unusual about his clothing when I did the laundry."

"Mrs. Solberg, do you remember the last time you saw Dorothy Thompsen?"

"Yes, I do. It was about two weeks before this happened. I was outside and Dorothy came by in the car. She had the baby with her, and groceries in the back seat. She said she could not come in, because she had to get the baby back home for her nap, then she started to cry. I asked her what the problem was. I said, "Dottie, don't you feel well?"

She said, Yes, I feel all right, but I don't look forward to going home. I asked, "What are you afraid of?" She said, Well, my mother-in-law acts so funny towards me, I'm just afraid she is going to do something. I have the baby there and if something happens, what will I do? "Every time I turn around, she just stares at me and doesn't say anything." I asked her why she doesn't discuss it with Arnfin? I said, "After all, his first responsibility is to you and the baby." She said, "We just can't seem to talk to each other anymore."

Shew asked, "Mrs. Solberg, do you know how well Mrs. Agnes Thompsen knew your son, Harry?"

"She knew Harry well because he used to cut her grass every week, and she always made him a big lunch."

Cross examination of Mrs. Solberg by, Wall.

Wall basically asked her the same questions, and Mrs. Solberg kept her composure as she repeated the answers. When Wall suggested that she told Trooper Pennington that Harry left the house at 1:20 or 1:30. She repeated her testimony about the "TV" dinner. That she put it in the oven at one o'clock, it took forty minutes to cook, then Harry sat down and ate his lunch. She did agree that Harry left the house in the black Ford, to take some soda to his father who was working in Granby.

Harry Johnson, Jr., a State Trooper with the department three years, was the next witness, however, he didn't have much to offer. He said he was sent to the Connecticut Valley Hospital to pick up a sample of blood, taken from Agnes Thompsen, and deliver it to State laboratory in Hartford, for Dr. Stolman. Trooper Johnson was then dismissed and the attorneys and the judge sat at a table huddled together, conversing about something pertaining to the case. Everyone in the court room waited eagerly for some indication that the trial was near an end, and ready for the Jury. Could this be it?

24

The trial continued to be the lead story in all the papers, with story leads such as; *Rome, Wall Pull, No Punches in Flareup at Solberg Trial.*

Gerald Demeusy, of the Hartford Courant wrote: *State Police Major Samuel Rome and State's attorney Thomas F. Wall broke into an angry argument at the first degree murder trial of Harry Solberg in Superior Court here Thursday.* All of the newspapers in the area carried details of the trial, and everyone, who couldn't attend the trial, was, therefore, able to read what transpired in the courtroom each day, especially the friction between, the major and Wall. *Rome clearly indicated he feels that Solberg is innocent,* was one line. Others included such tidbits as, *Attorney Wall went at Rome with a vengeance. And, Is it well known, major, that you believe, in working for the state, that you have the right to lie? Will you repeat that question? said Rome, leaning forward as though ready to leap from the witness stand. Attorney Shew objected, charging that Attorney Wall was trying to carry on a vendetta with Major Rome. The judge said, Let's put a halt to this, right here and now.*

The State's Attorney then asked Rome to tell about the role Miss Hageman played in the interview with Agnes Thompsen at the hospital. Rome said he instructed Miss Hageman to pose as Arnfin's Thompsen's girl friend. He wanted to get some information from Agnes Thompsen which he could verify and determine whether or not she was guilty or innocent. The papers used terms such as *Rome's Bag of Tricks. Wall said he still intended to object on the grounds that Mrs. Thompsen's statements, if given by some other person, would violate the hearsay rule. The animosity between Wall and the major, was revealed as never before.*

The local people, who couldn't attend the trial, had to rely on the newspaper for an account of the court proceedings, that were accurate in every detail, and was the next best thing to being there.

Everyone was ready for the morning proceedings. Jury and spectators were seated, and judge MacDonald stood talking to the attorneys. There was a feeling of anticipation as Arnfin was recalled to the stand.

Shew began the direct examination of Arnfin Thompson."Just a few questions," he said. "Mr. Thompsen, what was your mother's attitude when she found out that your wife was dead?"

"She Just had a glassy stare."

The next questions concerned Christa, whether her pants were wet, or dry, and about Arnfin, and his new wife. He said he discussed marriage with his present wife about three or four weeks after Dottie's death. There were more questions about Dorothy being afraid of her mother-in-law. Also, questions about Agnes losing three of her jobs. "Did she think she was going to stay home and take care of Christa?"

"Not that I know of."

Wall said he had no questions, but would like Arnfin to remain.

Dr. Stolman then resumed the stand. Shew had some questions about the hair found on the edge of the patio door, also about hair taken from the bottom brace of the baby's highchair."

And will you tell us about that hair?"

"The comparison test I conducted, indicated that the color characteristics were similar to the hair samples taken from Mrs. Agnes Thompsen at the State Hospital."

Cross examination by Wall

"Doctor, I believe you said that these hairs had the same color characteristics. Did you also compare them with the hairs of the victim?"

"Yes, sir. They were quite different. One was dark hair, similar to the victim's hair, and Mrs. Agnes Thompsen has light hair."

"And now, with two hairs of this type, can you draw any definite conclusion?"

"No, sir, it simply classifies. It has some value differentiating dark colored hairs from light colored hairs, or Negroid from Caucasian hairs, and so on. You can't pinpoint it like blood typing, you simply divide it into groups."

Wall then asked the doctor about blood types. The manner of identifying blood samples, and the function in identifying them.

"The doctor explained, "Mainly blood typing is one of exclusion. When we find a blood type "B", it means, any individual of the other types like "A", or "0", have to be excluded as the source of this type "B" blood. That's the primary purpose of blood typing."

"On any samples of blood, that were submitted to you in any of these Exhibits, was there ever any blood found of the type group "A, RH" positive?"

"No, I only found two types of blood. There was one exception to type "O" which I found on all items. The blood on the shoelace, that was found in the driveway, was type "B"."

Neither Wall, nor Shew had any further questions.

Direct examination by Shew.

His first witness was Karen Thompsen, Ted Thompsen's wife. She answered the same questions, Yes, she was a hairdresser, since 1958, and yes, she gave Agnes the permanent. In answer to their relationship, Karen said, "My mother-in-law used to take care of my daughter every Wednesday. Her daughter, Sonya, was two years older than Christa, and the children played well together."

"When you cut her hair, what happened to the cuttings?"

"Well, I just threw them on the floor, and swept them up later."

Do you recall what your daughter and Christa were doing?"

"Well, they were running back and forth between rooms. Especially my daughter, who kept running up and down the stairs."

"And when you completed the permanent, will you describe the appearance of your mother-in-law's hair?"

"I put her hair up in pin curls, and I put two bobby pins in each curl. I put a hairnet on her, and she put a scarf on over that."

Wall then asked several questions about the relationship between Dorothy and her mother-in-law.

Karen said, "We were talking about it, because her condition was worsening We were discussing the possibility of bringing her to the doctor, to see what could be done for her."

"Did Dorothy ever express to you any fear of her mother-in-law?"

"No, sir."

"Do you remember an incident from having some soup your mother-in-law gave you?"

"I wasn't scared of that. My mother-in-law was a good cook, and it was unusual that she served anything reheated."

"And did you remark to anyone in town that you were afraid to eat the soup because you were afraid something was in it?

"No sir. Not that anything was in it, but reheated pea soup, can be hard on ones stomach."

"Did you ever use a poison in connection with that soup?"

"No, sir."

"Mrs. Thompsen, do you realize that you are under oath?"

"Yes, sir."

"Did you talk this over with your husband?"

"Yes, I believe I did."

"Didn't he go to Wall, to give him this same information?"

"I don't know anything about that."

"And you want this jury and the court to understand that you and Dottie, have never mentioned the fact, that you were afraid of your mother-in-law?"

"I wasn't afraid of her, no."

"Did you ever hear Dottie say she was afraid of her?"

"No sir."

"Well you were discussing taking Mrs. Thompsen to the doctor, isn't that right? And didn't Dottie tell you, she was afraid of her at that time?"

"She said she made her nervous. She didn't say she was afraid of her."

"She did? And what is your definition of nervousness? What do you mean when you say nervous?"

"Well, I got nervous looking at her, because she was so nervous."

"As a matter of fact, you were both frightened to death of her, were you not?"

"No, sir."

Shew asked again what she meant when she said it made her nervous to be with Agnes.

Karen replied. "Well, it made me upset to look at her, to see to see how sick she was."

"Why did it make you upset to look at her?"

"She was close family, I mean, after all she was my step-daughter's grandmother. I felt sorry for her. She was mentally disturbed, and I was afraid she might hurt herself, or do something to herself."

"And were you afraid she might hurt somebody else?"

"I never was, sir."

"You did make a remark about the soup she gave you?"

"Yes. That was after."

"So, you just happened to remark that it was re-heated soup."

"Yes."

At that point Shew said, "That's all."

Redirect examination by Wall

"Mrs. Thompsen, have you ever met me before today?"

"No sir."

"And when was the first time you and I had ever spoken to each other?"

"In the Courtroom this morning, sir."

The questioning continued about the meeting with Attorney Wall, with repetition of the questions about the condition of Agnes Thompsen.

The next person called to the stand was Raymond J. Fitzpatrick. A part-time employee with Hartford Plumbing Supply Company. He was under direct Examination by Wall. He described, briefly, his duties, such as making deliveries, working in the warehouse, and the showroom.

"And on June 15, 1965, did you have occasion to go to the home of the Solbergs' in East Hartland?"

"Yes, sir, Toby's house."

"You are referring to the father of Harry Solberg?"

"Yes, sir."

"Before and after June 15, on these occasions when you made deliveries to Toby Solberg, did you bring along any assistants, or did you come in a truck by yourself?"

"I come by myself"

"And on any occasion when you went to the Solberg residence did you ever have any assistance from anyone other than Toby Solberg?"

"He's the only one that ever helped me unload at the house."

"Do you know Harry Solberg?"

"I have met him, yes, sir."

"Did he ever assist, at anytime that you were there, in removing any of the articles that you were delivering?"

"No, sir."

Cross examination by Shew.

"Mr. Fitzpatrick, do you remember talking with me over the phone?"

"Yes, sir. I told you that I made deliveries to the house, and that the only one that ever helped me unload there, was Toby."

"You weren't sure that you even delivered that day, were you?"

"No, sir, I said that when Trooper Pennington came over to the house I checked the invoice and I come to the conclusion that I made the delivery."

"Now what refreshed your recollection?"

"On the day that I made the delivery, when I got the invoice, there was three bathtubs to be exchanged. I had to drop three off, and pick three up. I only talked to Trooper Pennington one time before today."

On redirect examination Wall asked Mr. Fitzpatrick, "Is this an invoice?"

"Yes, sir, these items that are crossed off here were exchanged."

Shew said, "I object to it Your Honor. I object as not being proper evidence. Your Honor, I don't know whose handwriting this is, I don't know what this is, or where he got it. I am not a bookkeeper. I have established the fact that this man himself, didn't know."

Wall resumed his questioning, "Does this paper, which I show you, actually refresh your recollection as to what you delivered, and what you did on June 15, 1965?"

Shew spoke out, "I object to any refreshing from that Your Honor, it is not in his own handwriting. I don't know where it came from—and it is—"

"Wall then asked, "And does it refresh your recollection as to what actually occurred on that day between you and Toby Solberg?"

"Well, I don't think I seen Toby that day."

Re-cross examination by Shew.

"Now Mr. Fitzpatrick, you say you are not sure whether you saw Toby that day, and why are you so sure you didn't see his son?"

"Because Toby is the only one that ever helped me unload."

"And you are not sure whether he was there that day or not?"

"No sir."

William Howard Zimmer was the next witness. He testified that he lived in North Granby, and has been in the building business seventeen years. He further testified that he was building a one family house, on his own land for speculation.

"On June 15, 1965 was Mr. Solberg senior, working on that job?"

"He was."

"Now Mr. Zimmer, do you keep a diary?"

"Yes, sir I do. I keep track of the weather, temperature, where I work, how many hours I work. I also keep track of cash expenses, especially when I don't have cash receipts."

"And does your diary also record, whether other people work with you, or whether other people are working with you in connection with your work?"

"It does, but not in all instances."

"And now having regard to the date of June 15, 1965, do you recall what day of the week that was?"

"I wouldn't just by your asking, but I checked my diary, it was a Tuesday."

"Now, on that day was Mr. Solberg, Sr. working on that job with you?"

"Yes, he was."

"And what was he doing in connection with his work there?"

"Well, I have been trying and trying, and I cannot recall what he was working on. It could have been finish plumbing or it could have been finish heating. I've been trying to figure out what I was doing myself, and I can't remember. That would be a big help, I know."

"And on that day did he have anyone helping him at all?"

"I'm not certain. I checked last night through the first few months of the year and I discovered, that quite a few names of people who had worked there, were not in the book."

"Was his son, Harry Solberg working there on that day—June 15, 1965?"

"As far as I know he wasn't. He wasn't there all day, nor was I."

"And what part of the day were you present Mr. Zimmer?"

"After I received the subpoena, and going through my diary, trying to refresh my memory, as I said, I keep track of cash expenses, of course that includes my traveling time. I have no idea how long I was there. I just don't remember. I do have a notation that I made a purchase at Beeman Hardware, in Granby center that day, and I don't remember how long I was there either. I didn't put it down, because it was a small purchase of thirty-one cents. The store is only about four miles from the job."

"And did Mr. Solberg have helpers on other occasions Mr. Zimmer?"

"Yes."

"And on June 15, did he have any helpers at all?"

"I don't know whether he did it himself or had help. It was a difficult job to do alone.

"Did you know who the other helpers were that did come at various times to help Mr. Solberg?"

"Yes, one was Harry Solberg and the other, I don't know."

Wall asked, "Is there anything in the diary relating to him.?"

Mr. Zimmer replied, "Solberg all day. That's all it says."

25

During the lunch break, several small groups of spectators strolled around the village. One of the most interesting places, was the Tapping Reeve Law School. A little Cape Cod house, next to the Noyes Memorial library. The Tapping Reeve Law School was the first in America. It was founded in 1784 by Tapping Reeve, who married Sally Burr, a sister of Aaron Burr, and granddaughter of Jonathan Edwards. Being appointed to the Superior Court bench in l798. judge Reeve associated judge James Gould with him. The school continued about fifty years and more than one thousand lawyers were educated there, including one vice-president of the United States, two judges of the United States Supreme Court six Congressmen, Cabinet Officers, Ambassadors, etc.

An interesting place to visit, especially for those attending a murder trial, and listening every day to testimony being given, and to lawyers squabbling with one another.

Some of the reporters and visitors ate lunch at The Phelps Tavern, the oldest hotel in continuous service in the country. The tavern was popular for the famous ballroom where brilliant social functions were held, especially the ball given in honor of General LaFayette in 1824. So many interesting places to see and lots to talk about; however, it was time to return to the courthouse.

Doctor Von Salzen was recalled to the stand, and asked to read from his psychiatric report on Harry Solberg, which was prepared at his office on September 24, 1966. It was a repeat of the evidence given when the doctor testified previously. After the intravenous administration of Sodium Pentothal, his examination was complete enough to conclude that Solberg was not psychotic. Solberg said, on June 15, 1965 he left the school on the bus at 11:30, and a arrived home at

12:30. He changed his clothes, had lunch, and helped unload a truck. He then went to Simsbury to see about a lawnmower, and on his way home he stopped at the Thompsen's house, because Mr. Thompsen had agreed to help him with economics report. He knocked, and upon receiving no answer, walked in through the partially open door. He heard a baby crying, while he walked through the hallway and into the kitchen. He then told the story about the blood on the floor. He remembered nothing else until he found himself climbing up a ladder to the rear porch. He then went home and asked where his father was working. He wanted to tell his father about this, however, he didn't, and he didn't remember if he had gone to school the following day. He did remember, however, writing the letter. He said, he visited his girl friend, now his wife, at about 3:30 that afternoon. The doctor continued, the psychological interpretation of Solberg's behavior at the time of the murder must be based upon theortical considerations since the workings of the human mind are based largely upon theory. Solberg reflected an unusual amount of repression, hostile urges, and normal sexual urges. When confronted with a scene of such violence as this murder, the average person would react strongly with revulsion. Rational thinking would temporarily be suspended. At the time he saw the body, he was incapable of thinking or acting rationally. He was a victim of panic, of irrational guilt.

The next witness was Mr. Hamilton Pitt, who cited his address, and other pertinent information. He had been a teacher for thirty-one years, and this past year he has been working as a Real Estate Broker.

Direct examination by Wall.

"And during the year of 1964 and 1965 where were you teaching?"

"Gilbert High School, in Winsted."

"And on June 15, 1965, did Solberg have any assignment to submit a report in the economics course?"

"No."

"Well, did he ever submit, prior to June 15, 1965, any report to you in an economics course? And was there any assignment due, or expected from him on June 15, or thereafter?"

"No"

"As of June 15, Mr. Pitt, had Solberg completed the course?"

"Well, the examination was on the 15th, yes."

"And was there anything else expected in connection with this course from Solberg?"

"No."

Cross examination by Shew "Now Mr. Pitt, do you remember a discussion with Harry either that day, the 15th or maybe the day before?"

"About what?"

"Would you remember any discussion that you had with all your pupils at that particular time?

"There would be no discussion on the 15th, I merely passed out the exams, and he completed the exam, and left the room."

"And there could be a discussion, that you do not now remember, isn't that correct?"

"Well, he had done pretty well in mid years, and had fallen off a bit in the second half. To pick up some marks, he had to write a theme, or something like that. Book reports, library work, reference papers, or a talk on a certain topic. Those papers were due on the eleventh. His written work was done by Friday, the eleventh or it wouldn't have been accepted. All my classes knew that."

"Do you remember whether or not you talked with Harry Solberg on the 14th, or a day or two before?"

"No, I don't."

In redirect, Wall asked the same questions about Harry's examinations. The dates on which papers were due, and about Harry's assignments.

Then Wall asked, "And is it possible that he understood that he could write another theme, isn't it?"

Mr. Pitt was really getting hot under the collar, and showing his agitation, he snapped back, "No! His written work had to be in by the eleventh, or it wouldn't have been be accepted."

"And he wouldn't necessarily know that would he?"

"He had been with me two years, he should have."

"Do you act that way in class?"

Mr. Pitt was now really getting fed up with the verbal harassment from Wall and answered. "Yes, if I have to repeat something three times to an intelligent person."

"And who do you have reference to?"

The judge said, "I don't think we need to pursue that further."

Wall then asked, "Why did you stop teaching, Mr. Pitt?"

"Personal reasons."

Wall recalled Arnfin Thompsen for rebuttal.

"Mr. Thompsen, in June 1965, or at anytime within a few weeks prior to June 15, 1965, did you have any conversation with Harry Solberg, relating to any assistance you might have given to him in an economics course?"

"No."

"Is there any reason that you would know of for Harry to come to your home on June 15, 1965?"

"No."

Cross examination by Shew.

"Arnfin, at various times, had you helped Harry with his schoolwork?"

"Yes, I had."

"And whenever he needed help, he couldn't get it from his parents, could he?, You are aware of that fact?"

"No, I didn't know. I imagine they helped him some."

"Well, anyway, you had been in the habit of helping him on his various problems in school over the past four or five years, isn't that correct."

"Possibly about three or four times during that course."

"And you wouldn't know whether or not he asked your deceased wife, at anytime, to intercede in his behalf, to get some help from you, would you? Is it possible he may have asked her, and you wouldn't know?"

"Not unless she told me."

"That's right, but she might not tell you. You didn't speak much to her just before June 15, did you?

"Sure I did."

"Well, you were only home a couple of nights a week."

"I was home weekends."

Wall then called Asa Burdick, Dorothy's father to the stand for a few final questions.

"At anytime when you talked with your daughter, prior to her death, did she ever say anything to you, about any fear of her mother-in-law, Agnes Thompsen?"

"She did not."

Then Shew asked, "Do you recall you and your wife talking with Major Rome, in connection with this? And do you know whether she was getting along with Arnfin?"

"They were getting along."

"And she was happy in the house she was in.?"

"That's right."

At this time the State finally rested their case. Wall began his presentation to the jury. He instructed them regarding their duty to decide whether the defendant was guilty, and the degree of guilt, of murder in the first degree, murder in the second degree, or manslaughter. He then read the anonymous letter, mailed two days after the crime.

I killed your wife. I *stabed* her with a meat fork. I stomped on her face. I *draged* her with an electric cord. She fell to the ground. I bashed her head in several times with a large rock. I used a *nabors* car, a 58 Ford. I'll kill the baby too, and my wife.

Handwriting experts established the fact that Solberg had written the letter in which he confessed to the killing.

Next, Wall talked about Agnes Thompsen. He acknowledged the fact that she was an early suspect. The piggy bank was found a few miles away, and she didn't drive, but she couldn't possibly have walked walk that far with the bank.

Then he talked about an interview between the accused and Lieutenant Fuessenich, commander of the Canaan Barracks. In it, Solberg again admitted the crime but said he could not remember how he did it. In one statement he said, "She was "too full of fight." You know, and I know, that there was never any question that the victim was dead by the time she landed on the ground.

There was complete silence as Wall continued. He lied to Doctor Von Salzen regarding the economics papers, which were due in one of his classes. The doctor said Solberg told him he came upon the murder scene when no one answered his knocks on the front door. The sight so shocked him, the doctor said, he suffered a loss of memory similar to that experienced by soldiers in battle. Solberg also told the psychiatrist another version of the story.that he had gone to the home for the same reason, but was greeted by Dorothy. He said she made amorous advances to him, and slapped him when he repulsed her. Here again,he said his memory went blank. There was one pertinent observation by Doctor Von Salzen, I think, that impressed all of you as it did me, that memory gaps could be caused just as easily if he had actually committed the crime. At this point, Wall yielded to Shew.

Shew started with, The defense attempted to show that Agnes Thompsen was the murderer. Shew maintained Solberg was suffering from a lapse of memory and could not tell the police how the crime was committed because he didn't know. The doctor said Solberg told him he came upon the murder scene when no one answered his knocks on the front door. The sight so shocked him, he suffered a loss of memory similar to that experienced by soldiers in battle. Solberg also told the psychiatrist another version of the story, that he had gone to the house for the same reason but was greeted by Dorothy. He said she made amorous advances to him and slapped him when he repulsed her.

Here again, he said his memory went blank. The Doctor said he believed the first story.

Then Shew mentioned a yellow cloth with blood stains, that was found in Agnes Thompsen's apartment. Her hair found on the sliding door, and a bloodstained dress was found in the clothes dryer. Would Harry put a dress in the dryer? Shew described the killing as the work of a woman. The fact that kitchen forks were used to stab the victim, and her body was dragged across the floor to a porch and hanged over the side with an electrical cord from the electric toaster, indicated the crime was not the doing of a strong man, like the accused. Another thing, Dottie told Carole Stadler that she was deathly afraid of her mother-in-law. And Karen Thompsen said, "We decided to take her to the doctor." And Bob Stadler heard the mother-in-law say, "Is she dead yet?" Yes, the mother-in-law said. "Is she dead yet?" Doctor Opper said the killing took about ten minutes. Would this boy hang around all that time, when he knew Agnes was upstairs? Would he use a fork? Would he drag a body? He was strong enough to carry the body.

What motive would Harry have for murdering Dorothy Thompsen? Agnes, however, had a motive. There were hard feelings about the baby, and she wanted to have Christa with her more often. Dorothy didn't like that. The fact that Christa was dry, indicates that someone had changed her during the afternoon. Christa wasn't hungry, someone obviously fed her, and only Agnes could have done that. Shew pleaded for an acquittal. "You can't give back this boy's lost freedom. Let him go back to his wife and baby."

26

Charge to the Jury.

"Ladies and gentlemen of the jury, you have listened patiently and carefully to the evidence in this case during these last weeks, and you have listened attentively to the arguments of counsel; and it is now your duty to give your attention, carefully, to the instructions of the Court, on the law involved in this case. A charge but, if you will follow it, step by step, I hope that things will be made clear to you, that this is a first degree murder case. It is somewhat involved, and unfortunately longer than the ordinary charge. There are a few general rules which apply in all criminal cases, and I will start with those.

In the performance of our duties here, you, as the jury, and I, as the Court, have entirely separate functions. It is my duty to state the rules of law involved in the decision of this case, and it is yours to find the facts. Insofar as I do state the law to you, what I say is binding upon you and should be carefully followed by you in accordance with the oath you took. You are to understand that if I should, in stating the law, differ in any respect from the claims that may have been made by counsel in argument, you will dismiss from your minds what they have said to the extend of any such inconsistency. I might add that you need not worry about any mistake of mine causing an injustice. If I state the law incorrectly to you in any respect, you can be certain that one of these gentlemen will see that the Supreme Court takes care of that error. I have already said that it is the duty of the Court to state the law in pursuance to which the guilt or innocence of the accused may be determined by you, and it is the exclusive province of the jury to deal with the evidence and determine the facts and reach the final conclusion upon them as to the guilt or innocence of this accused. The law presumes an accused person innocent, unless and until his guilt is established by the evidence. In a criminal case, guilt may not be established, and the jury is not warranted in finding it established, until proof of it, on all of the evidence removes all reasonable doubt of its existence. Now, the term "reasonable doubt" is one which can hardly be improved upon by any further explanation. Any person qualified by natural attainment for a juror's service must know what is meant by an honest doubt and must know what is meant by the qualification, reasonable doubt. The State, of course, is not required to prove the guilt of an accused person beyond any doubt or beyond all doubt. Proof beyond a reasonable doubt does not require proof beyond a possible doubt. In weighing the testimony of a witness, you should consider his or her appearance on the stand, and you should try to size him up.

You will recall that upon a number of occasions certain evidence was offered, and perhaps you could really see the nature of it, but when it was offered it was stricken out. For example, you will recall that the State offered in evidence as to certain statements made out of Court during interrogation by this accused Solberg, which it claimed were in the nature of a confession or admissions by him tending to show his guilt of the crime charged. You will also recall that you were excused while I considered the question of their admissibility, and that I did eventually hold that testimony to be admissible.

The confessions and statements of the accused which have been admitted as evidence are to be considered by you in connection with all the other evidence in this case. Made, as they were out of Court, they are not like the sworn testimony offered to you. They are to be considered by you as declarations inconsistent with the accused plea of not guilty. It is, therefore, for you to determine what weight you will give to these statements under which each was given, and, of course, also considering them in the light of all the other evidence in the case, and the testimony of all the witnesses.

Now a few words about what you all know as circumstantial evidence. What a man's purpose or intent or motive is, or has been, or was, is necessarily largely a matter of inference. A man may take the stand and testify directly as to what his own purpose or intention was. By that, I mean any witness can testify as to his own intention or knowledge, but no witness can be expected to come into Court and testify that he looked into another man's mind and saw therein a certain purpose or intention or motive.

Now, I think, ladies and gentlemen, that this rounds out my full measure of duty to you."

This concluded his charge to the jury, after which the Jury was escorted into the Jury Room to deliberate.

At nine o'clock that night, the judge called for the return of the jury. He said to them, "It has been a long day, and I know I promised not to keep you after nine o'clock. Do you think you can reach a verdict within half an hour, or would you prefer to come back in the morning? "The foreman of the jury, Mr. Ronald E. Glander replied, "I think we would rather return in the morning, Your Honor."

The judge agreed, "Then we will adjourn until ten o'clock in the morning." At that point all the newscasters and reporters rushed back to their respective offices.

Headlines the following next morning read, *Solberg Jury disagrees, Will Try Again Today Panel studies unique case.* One newspaper carried the following story: *Litchfield—The jury in the first degree murder trial of Harry A. Solberg resumed deliberations in Litchfield Superior Court today in an effort to reach a verdict in the case, before the court is forced to recess until Wednesday. Normally the case would be continued until Tuesday, but Judge MacDonald expressed concern about the delay since court officials will be attending the State Bar Association meeting that day. He said he did not want the jury out for four days after the evidence was completed.*

From the beginning, the case was one of the most unusual in Connecticut Courtroom history. Never before in this state have two persons been accused of the same crime at different times.

There was also a rift in the thinking and attitude of State police Major Samuel S. Rome, who headed the first probe of the murder of Dorothy

Thompsen. He never felt Solberg was the killer. His colleagues at the Canaan Barracks differed and arrested the 20-year-old East Hartland man seven months after Rome had secured a warrant for the arrest of the victim's mother-in-law, Agnes Thompsen. Rome never wavered from his original conclusion and was called as a defense witness.

Rome's appearance in the small, second-floor courtroom prompted several heated exchanges between himself and Attorney Wall. Both on the stand, and off. It began when Rome alleged Wall had ordered him not to consult with the defense, even though he was there under a subpoena issued by Shew.

The major sought a ruling from Judge MacDonald at which time Wall charged Rome's contention was a lie The judge ruled the major could consult with Shew but, nevertheless, the hard feelings were evident. During cross examination the two clashed again and at one point Judge MacDonald ordered the jury out of the room so he could calm the situation. When Rome was called by the defense later that day, and stated under examination that Attorney Wall had never conferred with him about the case, Wall lashed out at him again, contending the major had once made the statement that he had the right to lie because he worked for the state. The judge ruled him completely out of order, and the question was stricken from the record.

The Newspaper columns contained most of the court transcript.

Today, the reporters and spectators are patiently waiting for the next episode in this tragedy. The big question on everyone's mind is, will the jurors reach a verdict this time?

After lunch, the jurors had a question. It was necessary for them to return to the jury box to hear the answer. The question was, would it be possible from the window of Agnes Thompsen's apartment, to see a person at the edge of the porch lowering some object? The judge replied, "Such a statement by Mrs. Thompsen was in the record," The judge read it again; "She was killed. I heard two hard bangs, and I saw a man lower something down from the porch to the ground. It was dark, but I saw a man in the back and I thought it was her brother. I was upstairs and I didn't know anything bad had happened."

The judge said, "This is the only testimony on the question. You will have to decide for yourselves whether Agnes Thompsen could have seen this."

In response to the question, "Were they at an impasse?" Mr. Glander replied, "I think we can reach a verdict in about a half hour." They then filed back to the jury room.

Later that afternoon, another call from the jury. The judge came in from chambers, and the attorneys walked to their tables. The jury filed in, and Harry's mother, father and wife were seated. Judge MacDonald read the note handed to him by Mr. Glander. "We regret to inform you that we cannot reach a verdict and we feel that more time will not help us."

The judge said, "Do you feel there is hopeless disagreement?"

Mr. Glander answered, "Yes, Your Honor, I'm afraid so."

The judge said, "I am unhappy and unsatisfied. It doesn't help the accused, and it doesn't help the state. The accused will have to stand trial again."

Harry's mother, who had controlled herself all during the trial, sobbed on her husband's shoulder. Harry showed no emotion as he looked across the room at his wife. The dismissed jury went out slowly, the judge rose, and the sheriff escorted Harry out by the arm. Because Harry's wife, Sharon, was screaming so much and obviously in a state of shock, the clerk escorted the Solberg family out through a side door to an office, where a doctor administered a sedative.

The people moved away slowly, as though they were stunned. They couldn't believe the outcome. The judge, attorneys, reporters, spectators, police officers, and the twenty eight witnesses were now gone, and Harry was back in the jail near the courthouse.

27

The animosity between Attorney Wall and Major Rome was one topic of conversation from Litchfield to Hartford. The other was concern and disappointment over the trial. Almost everyone believed that Harry was guilty. Now they would experience the tension and uncertainty of another trial.

The women talked about little Christa. How lonely she must be without her mother. How her life had changed, now that her father had remarried, and she was living with relatives.

Another thing bothering the women was fear. They naturally were anxious for the case to be settled so they could feel safe again. They wanted to return to a normal life, to be able to go home after dark, and not be afraid to get out of the car, or to go into the dark house alone. One local housewife said, "We know that Harry is in jail, and that it must have been a man who committed the murder, but suppose, just suppose, he's not the murderer. If that's the case, then there is a murderer on the loose, somewhere, out there in the countryside."

Another of the locals said, "I could never believe that Agnes did it. Whenever we went into Hartford for a social event, Agnes always took care of the children. She was wonderful with them." And, so it went, in houses, stores and town meetings, just one topic, the trial. In the Litchfield Courthouse, the attorneys and judge were making preparations for the retrial, and a change of venue.

The next morning, the headlines read: *Solberg Trial Re-opens January 10th, In Bridgeport*. One reporter wrote; *Retrial of the bizarre Harry A. Solberg murder case will be held January 10th in Bridgeport. The scene of the trial will be the Federal Courthouse where a courtroom has been made available. Superior Court Judge Douglass B. Wright will preside at the trial, with Thomas F. Wall, Esq., representing the State, and William D. Shew, Esq., Attorney for the defendant with John McKeon assisting.*

Along with the familiar figures, Mr. Wall, Mr. Shew, representatives of the media, the Canaan police, and the Solberg family, everyone was experiencing a state of nervous anticipation.

In contrast to Litchfield, Bridgeport is a dismal dreary setting. Once a booming industrial city, now it is a depressed factory town. It was, in fact, the chief industrial city in the New England area, sixty miles northeast of New York City, where industrial plants once manufactured sewing machines, helicopters, phonograph records, hardware, brass goods, plastic items, household appliances, typewriters, etc. The once proud industrial plants of well-known household items have now, for the most part, become either abandoned or multi-tenanted. The new trial will be held in the former old Underwood manufacturing building, that has been converted into a court building, surrounded by dilapidated factories.

The other side of the city boasts Seaside Park with a sea wall, two family houses, a boulevard and playgrounds along two miles of the shoreline. There is also the University of Bridgeport, the Junior College of Connecticut, and trade and business schools. From this diverse environment, the new jury will be picked, and on this dismal January day, the time-consuming task will begin.

On the fifth floor, near the courtrooms, Shew was looking for a room that he and Mr. McKeon could use. There was an office for the State's Attorney, but none for the Defense.

Wall requested a meeting. He said, "Mr. McKeon was not here to represent Solberg, he was here at the request of Major Rome and Demeusy, columnist for the Hartford Courant." Wall then read an article from the Hartford Courant, *"Defenders confident of Solberg acquittal. New evidence has been brought forward that fully supports Solberg's claim that he is innocent, and will help them to identify the real killer."* Shew denied that he, or Mr. McKeon had made those statements. A rather heated argument ensued. Wall's expression showed his anger as he walked out of the room, with Shew, and McKeon following behind. So before the second trial even began, the two lawyers were at each others throats once again.

At lunch, Wall picked up a copy of the Bridgeport Post. The lead story was the Solberg case. The similarity to the Hartford Courant copy and this story angered Wall. He requested another conference. He made notes about the arguments with Shew. He wrote, "Mr. Shew stated I was out of the jurisdiction of the Litchfield Court, and I could no longer be a little Hitler, as I was in my own bailiwick. If anything like this were resorted to, he would have me cited for calling one of the witnesses a liar."

In chambers, Wall again referred to the story being planted by the Hartford Courant. He wanted to put Gerald Demeusy on the stand. Judge Wright said, This is the trial of Harry Solberg. The media is not on trial. So far, only three jurors had been selected, out of twenty-three examined.

Lieutenant Fuessenich was instructed to appear in court the next day with the tapes. Mr. McKeon said, "I want to be sure the tapes remain in the custody of the court."

Wall said, "The defense will have them at the proper time."

The judge asked, "Are you claiming the tapes might be altered? Do you oppose the defense seeing and listening to these tapes now?"

Wall answered, "I do, Your Honor. They're not entitled to them."

The Hartford Courant headlines the following morning read, *"Solberg Defense Wins Point. Police Must Surrender Tapes.*

Mr. Demeursy's article in the paper was as follows: *Bridgeport (Special) Over the protest of State's Attorney, Thomas F. Wall, Judge Douglass B. Wright ordered the production in Superior Court today of tape recordings made of accused slayer Solberg, by police last spring when he was being questioned about the mutilation slaying of Mrs. Dorothy Thompsen of Barkhamsted. These tapes must be brought to the courthouse by Lieutenant Fuessenich, commander of the Canaan Barracks. A demand that the tapes of Solberg be produced in court was made by Defense Counsel John*

McKeon who complained that Lieutenant Fuessenich apparently disregarded a subpoena. McKeon countered that the tapes are vital to the defense. Judge Wright asked Wall if he had any objection to the defense listening to the tapes. Wall said, he did not object.

The judge ended the conversation about the tapes by ordering trooper Gerald Pennington to bring the tapes to the courthouse today. McKeon did not elaborate on what he expects to learn from the tapes made of Solberg while he was being interrogated about Mrs. Thompsen's death.

Earlier in the day, the state's attorney charged an attempt was being made to prejudice the jurors against the state in Fairfield County. He said a page one story which appeared in the Bridgeport Post was highly inflammatory. He charged that the Hartford Courant "planted" the story in a deliberate attempt to create the same prejudicial atmosphere that existed in Litchfield during Solberg's original trial which ended in a hung jury.

Mr. Demeusy's column ended with, Rome Expected. It is expected that Major Rome, who testified for Solberg at the first trial, will be subpoenaed to the stand, by the defense at the retrial."

That afternoon the trial began, as Clerk of the Court, Mr. Ralph Scofield, read the indictment. Lieutenant Fuessenich was the first witness. Through Mr. Wall's questioning, the lieutenant gave all the horrifying details, and was shown a picture of the mutilated body. The jurors showed surprise and revulsion as they viewed the picture and passed it along. Not many ordinary, everyday people, are exposed to anything so graphic.

It is expected that the defense counsel will press for playing the interrogation tapes in open court to set a foundation for the claim that Solberg's confession was improperly obtained.

The defense, once again will revolve on a contention that Mrs. Thompsen was slain, not by Solberg, but by her mother-in-law, Mrs. Agnes Thompsen, who occupied an apartment upstairs in the Thompsen home.

That night, at the Howard Johnson Motor Lodge in Stratford, Connecticut, the attorneys and judge met to play the tapes. It began with

Officer Rebilliard reading Harry his rights. This was at the Canaan Barracks. Then Lieutenant Fuessenich took over the questioning.

Mr. McKeon said, "Conversation on the tapes will prompt the defense to claim that Solberg's constitutional rights were violated after he was picked up, and there appears to be a good chance the tapes will be stolen by interests adverse to the defense." He also said that he learned that someone had tampered with the lock on the door to the room. This drew objection from Wall who said the tape playing session was unpleasant due to the rude remarks by defense counsel, and Fuessenich should be permitted to retain control of the tapes.

Judge Wright countered, "The tapes will be in proper custody. If the clerk has them, that's his responsibility."

Wall protested, "There is misconception about the lock being tampered with."

It is expected that defense counsel will press for playing of the interrogation tapes in open court to set a foundation for the claim, that Solberg's alleged confession was improperly obtained. Earlier Friday, it became obvious that the defense once again will revolve on a contention that Mrs. Thompsen was slain, not by Harry Solberg, but by her mother-in-law.

Through Lieutenant Fuessenich, Wall put into evidence more than twenty-six exhibits, ranging from the murder weapons to the body photos, and first floor plans of the house.

"How about plans of the second floor?," asked Shew, as he as he rose to cross examine.

"We felt it wasn't necessary," replied Fuessenich.

"Did you know who lived there?"

"Yes, Agnes Thompsen."

Then Shew asked, "What had you determined about Agnes Thompsen?"

"I knew she was Arnfin Thompsen's mother, that she lived upstairs, and at one time had been a patient in the Connecticut Valley Hospital."

"Did you learn when she had been discharged from that hospital?"
"Yes, roughly six months before."
"Who was the last person to see Dorothy Thompsen alive?"
"We felt it was the victim's two year old daughter, Christa."
Shew continued along this point.

The lieutenant said, "It might have been a little child who was visiting the Thompsen's home, Randy Stadler, who lived across the road."

When Shew asked what Randy had told the police, Wall objected on the grounds such testimony is hearsay. This led to another bitter clash between Shew and the State's attorney. Judge Wright had to intervene. He asked Lieutenant Fuessenich to tell what his records showed concerning who had questioned Randy Stadler. The lieutenant answered, "Capt. Thomas O'Brien, Detective John Buonomo and Detective Lester Redican."

With the agreement of Wall, the official state police record concerning this interview was turned over to Shew to study over the weekend.

When Shew began to question the lieutenant concerning the articles found in Agnes Thompsen's apartment, Wall objected on the basis that this was outside the scope of the direct examination.

Judge Wright ruled that it was proper cross-examination because Lieutenant Fuessenich had testified he was in charge of the investigation from June 15, until June 21, when State Police Major Rome took over, on orders of Commissioner Leo Mulcahy.

Major Rome, who issued a warrant for the arrest of Mrs. Agnes Thompsen and lodged it against her at the hospital, is under subpoena by the defense to testify at Solberg's retrial.

Lieutenant Fuessenich, who was on the stand all day, was grateful when Judge Wright said, "We will reconvene tomorrow at ten o'clock." The jury of six men and six women filed out slowly. They looked relieved that the day was over. Judge Wright and the lawyers retired to chambers, while reporters lingered to talk things over. This time, there was no rush to file their stories.

There was no crowd of spectators outside this former factory courtroom. The local people showed little interest in the case. Unlike Litchfield, Bridgeport has a diverse mixture of nationalities, many of whom are of low income, live in old three decker houses, and work in the factories. Many couldn't care less about who murdered some old "broad" in the country.

28

"I'm glad you could get up today," said Margaret, as she helped Kay lift her bags from the car. "There's so much to talk about. I can't wait to hear all about your wedding. After all these years, and then a quick trip to the Justice of Peace, no big ceremony. Where's Charlie today?"

Kay laughed, "He had to go to South Hampton on business this weekend. He suggested that we get together for some 'girl talk'. No, there was no big wedding. I said to him, "We didn't get married in front of the altar. We got married in front of the typewriter." They moved a small table to in front of the fireplace, and started to eat lunch. Kay looked around the room, "A country place has fireplaces everywhere, even in the kitchen. It's cozy on a cold January day, but, you can't have all the city excitement and country comfort too."

Margaret said, "Either one would be nice, with a man to share it. Come on, eat up, and tell me everything.

"I told you over the phone about Jim. He died from a sudden and unexpected heart attack. When everything was over, Charlie was like a lost person, with no one to take care of now. Then, one night he said, 'How would you like to go to the Marriage License Bureau tomorrow? I thought I was hearing things. I didn't answer, and he repeated the question. I said, yes, meet me at lunch hour. When the five-day waiting period was up, we went to the Justice. There is still a lot of planning, and deciding what we will keep, and what to give away. One thing I will keep, is my bedroom furniture. Either that, or buy a new set."

They ate, and talked. Then Margaret said, "The roads are all plowed, and dry, let's take a ride up around Winsted and the hills." As they drove along route 44 towards Winsted, the conversation turned from personal to the trial.

Kay said, "I drove through Bridgeport on the way up. I wanted to see where the courthouse was. From what I saw, I wouldn't want to live there.

"Margaret replied, "There are some nice sections of the city where the affluent live. Like every city, it has good and bad.

Did you go to the start of the new trial?", Kay asked.

"Yes, for two days. It's a long drive, especially in bad weather." I explained, "It looks as though it will be over in a couple of weeks. There's a new judge, and another attorney to assist Shew. Wall is still the state's attorney. There is so much repetition. Sam Rome is expected to take the stand next Tuesday, and I expect he and Wall will be at each others throats again."

The roads up in the hills were deserted, and the women stopped to admire a flock of sheep. Mr. Brown saw the two visitors, and he came over to the fence to talk to them. They introduced themselves, and he invited them into the barn to look around.

He said, "I was just getting the heat lamps ready, I expect to be up most of the night, it's lambing time. Next year I'll build myself a shepherds room in the barn." He smiled as he watched the expression on the faces of the women. He said, "It's a constant vigil, back and forth from the house to the barn. They're the nearest thing to humans. Someone has to stay with them during delivery, so I play midwife." The first room he showed them had sixty sheep in it. He pointed to the bins that lined the walls at one section of the barn and said, "This is the maternity ward. I do the doctoring, castrating and shearing. We average eighty lambs born here every year."

Margaret asked, "Isn't January a cold month for lambs to be born? We usually associate the gentle little fellows with spring."

"No," he said as he smiled, "If we keep the ewes warm, and get the lambs on the mother as soon as they are born, we keep the mortality rate down to about five per cent. Lambs born in January are the best doers."

"Are there different breeds of sheep, like dogs and other animals?", Kay asked.

"Yes, selecting and discarding, are most important. By selecting ewes that are twins or daughters of twins, the yield is 150 per cent." He said, "I imported Shropshire rams from England to start this project, because that particular breed is versatile. Shropshire yield both wool and meat. Pedigreed stock has to meet high standards, for seed purposes, and 4-H groups. The ones not meeting these requirements go to the butcher."

The next room Mr. Brown showed the women had two interesting looking enclosures, called Creeps. This allows the lambs to creep through and feed at their leisure. While the ewes are feeding from the trough, the lambs will sneak up and nurse from any mother near them. The nursing period is 120 days, and they are self weaning. They are grass eating animals. Once weaned, grass constitutes about 90% of their diet.

"Here I am talking your ears off about my sheep," He said, "I must be boring you girls to death. City folk are not usually interested in farm life."

"Oh, but we are, that's why we took a ride up here,." Kay said.

Margaret asked him about wool production.

He said, Each ewe gives about eight pounds a shearing, It takes about twelve pounds to make a blanket. Heredity is important in wool producing also."

They shook hands with Mr. Brown and thanked him for showing them around, and explaining all about sheep.

Then Margaret looked around and asked him, "If you are out in the barn all night, who is with your wife. Isn't she afraid to stay in the house alone now? If Harry isn't the murderer, there must be someone else out there."

He nodded his head, "He's the one. He's guilty. Everyone thinks so. My two sons are home at night. If they go out on a date, they're home about midnight. We have two dogs. Oh, you didn't see them. They don't bark much in the daytime, but at night they hear every sound. We all knew and loved Dottie, and feel sorry for her family, especially poor little Christa." He walked to the car, and again said, "Goodbye. It's been a pleasant afternoon."

All the way back to the house they talked about the farmers they had met when they were out driving around. "What an isolated life it must be, but they seem to like it better than working for someone else."

After dinner they watched television until ten o'clock. Then Kay said, "All day we talked about Charlie and me, and the trial, and all that time we spent at the sheep farm, and not one word about you. Here you are up here alone another winter. Have you made any decision?"

Margaret sighed, and walked to the fireplace to put up the screen for the night. Then she said, "I'm thinking about accepting his offer. Remember he wanted me to go to London and live in his flat on Nottingham Court Road, in the west end, not far from downtown. There doesn't seem to be much hope for anything else. I think he's become a family man."

29

The following day the papers were full of stories such as: *Judge to query Rome before he takes stand, and Prosecution seeks to block testimony.*

Although a long argument between the defense counsel and State's Attorney Thomas F. Wall ended in some confusion about what will happen next, it is likely that Major Rome will be in court today for questioning by the judge.

Wall, charging that Rome does not at this time represent the type of justice we want in this country, told Judge Wright he intends to remain mute and refrain from cross-examining Rome, no matter what he says.

Defense Counsel William Shew said, "If Rome doesn't appear, I will subpoena State Police Commissioner Leo J. Mulcahy, to find out why Rome has been instructed to keep away until he is summoned to testify.

A court order to compel the major's appearance in Bridgeport was requested by defense counsel. Judge Wright reserved decision until defense was able to produce proof that a subpoena had been served on Rome. This proof of service was shown the judge by defense counsel Mr. McKeon. He said, Rome's presence was vital to the defense, because the major can tell what records in Wall's files will be of help to Solberg.

Wall stated that he could see no reason for such exercise of judicial power to bring Rome to court. There was an abuse of the major's subpoena at the trial in Litchfield when this so-called witness was in attendance every day, even while the jury was being selected. The newspaper article described Rome's actual testimony in the first trial as: *Nil, infinitesimal and immaterial.* To order Major Rome in court here, it said, would only be to repeat the abuses at the last trial.

Shew accused the State's Attorney of making false statements to Judge Wright. "Wall is not qualified to state what's important for the defense. He's got all he can handle on his own end."

Judge Wright asked, "Mr. Shew, Do you want Rome to sit with the defense at the Solberg trial?"

Shew replied, "If Wall's fear about Rome being in court is, that this will leave the people of Connecticut unprotected, then there's some question about the safety of Canaan residents, because six, or seven of the officers have been here since the trial started."

Then both Shew and Mr. McKeon urged Judge Wright to issue an order for Rome's appearance, because they needed the records in Wall's files which Rome knew about. "A Man's life is at stake, your honor," said Shew.

Wall said, "There isn't a single written record in the files submitted by Rome." Earlier he had charged that the major had a personal stake in the outcome of the Solberg case.

McKeon told the judge that, "Solberg's constitutional rights are being threatened if he is deprived of the right to obtain witnesses in his favor."

To the surprise of everybody, Judge Wright called Lieutenant Fuessenich to the stand, and asked the lieutenant, "Does Major Rome, or any members of his division have a separate file of records on the murder investigation?"

"There is no separate file, but the file in court is the complete file of the case."

"Was there a private investigation, running contrary or opposite to your investigation conducted by other members of the State Police?"

"Not after December 31, 1965."

When questioned by Shew, the lieutenant said, "He was assigned to pursue further investigation into the Thompsen murder on December 30, 1965, when the missing piggy bank was found in a field about a mile from the Solberg home."

"Who gave you this assignment, lieutenant?"

"It was Captain Thomas O'Brien, a field officer. Although Rome outranks O'Brien, the captain was my immediate supervisor."

Judge Wright said, he intended to reserve decision on his power to compel Rome's attendance until today when he determines from Rome, in the absence of the jury, what help he can be to the defense.

Wall exclaimed, "I feel strongly about this. The trial might be prejudiced by Rome's appearance, because of his propensity for getting into the limelight."

McKeon said, "Rome's appearance in court today is even more necessary because of a reckless assertion by Mr. Wall, accusing me of being in a conspiracy with Major Rome. I will demonstrate this is untrue."

Judge Wright interrupted to state, "I have no intention of getting into extraneous matters, when questioning Rome today."

Wall, in the absence of the jury, predicted, "Your Honor will get into extraneous matters if he is here."

By late afternoon, Lieutenant Fuessenich was showing fatigue and impatience. He had been on the stand all day, answering the same questions over and over, and repeating the same answers. This afternoon the questioning was all about the footprints in the blood on the kitchen floor. With a photograph in hand, he pointed out the blood outlines on the edge of the shoe, and indicated several heel prints and a full print in the blood, drawing away from the toe.

Wall then asked, "By reason of your training and experience, lieutenant, are you particularly able to interpret photographs with relation to what they represent and what interpretation can be obtained from them?"

"I believe so, sir."

"Will you then describe what you observed in relation to the photograph?"

"Examination of the footprint showed that the blood, at the toe, had been drawn away from the print and it was thin and dried. The thicker blood forming the outline of the footprint had not dried as much as the thin portion."

"From your observation, do you have any ides as to when this footprint was made?"

This started another round of bickering and objections, as to whether or not, the Lieutenant was qualified to ascertain the hour the footprints were made.

The judge asked Shew if he wished to cross-examine, and Shew replied in the affirmative.

"Lieutenant, will you tell us, what qualifies you to estimate as to when the print was made?"

"My experience investigating crime, seeing blood, and knowing how long it takes to dry."

"Then you are not in any position to make an estimate, are you?"

The judge excused the Jury. He then asked the lieutenant, "Can you tell from your experience, lieutenant, how long it takes blood to dry?"

"No, sir, I can't say that it would take a certain time for blood to dry on any occasion. In my opinion, that print was made soon after the blood was placed on the floor. This print was made by blood adhering to the sole of a shoe. The blood around the outside is quite heavy. The blood on the toe, which had been dragged away, was thinned out and it dried faster than the blood around the outside."

Shew continued the questioning about the blood.

"Lieutenant, when was the first time you came up with this theory?"

"It was before the Coroner's Inquest, sir."

"Did you testify at the Coroner's Inquest?"

"No, sir, however, I did discuss it with the Coroner and Mr. Wall."

Shew then asked the lieutenant, "Did you give this testimony at the Litchfield trial, and wasn't it Trooper Yuknat who gave the testimony regarding Arnfin's shoes, size, shape, and nail holes?"

"Yukriat did not say the prints were made by Arnfin's shoes, only that they were similar."

Shew then said, "I feel, your Honor, that I've demonstrated he isn't qualified. He allowed a man under him, to testify at an official hearing. He hasn't had any other situation similar to this, and he hasn't testified to any matters like this before."

The judge replied, "Well, have you seen other footprints, or hand prints, that you can pinpoint as to time?"

"I have investigated breaking and entering where perpetrators cut themselves and left blood. I have investigated homicides where blood was left, and knowing the time this took place, and I've had experience seeing how that blood dried in a known period of time."

Judge Wright asked, "Are there any further questions?"

Shew said, "I'd Like to spend a lot of time with this man because I think it's absolutely outrageous that he should pose now, to have such qualifications."

Wall said, "Your Honor, I move that remark be stricken from the record. It's absolutely uncalled for."

Shew came back with, "What difference would an increase of temperature make in the coagulation of the blood, say an increase of 20%, and what was the humidity that day?"

"It was a warm June day."

Shew asked, "All you know about the footprints is that they were made between the time of the crime, and the time you got there?"

"Yes, sir."

"Have you ever posed as a blood expert before?"

"I'm not posing as an expert on blood, now sir."

Shew, turning to the judge said, "Your Honor, this man is not qualified to give an opinion. He has no qualifications as an expert on blood in his past experiences."

Wall interrupted, "Your Honor, there is no claim that this witness is an expert on blood. But, he is an expert, and trained observer when it comes to crime."

The jury returned for about half an hour. It was then five O'clock, and court session was concluded for the day.

The next morning, Wall requested that Lieutenant Fuessenich return to the stand, at which time the examination continued. The previously asked questions were repeated, and once again, resulting in the same answers; about the blood, shoes, footprints, blood at toe of footprint, smeared forward towards dining room, etc. The testimony about the body been dragged from the kitchen to the porch, head first, face down, feet last, was repeated.

Wall sighed, and said, "Thank you, I have no more questions."

Cross examination by Shew.

"Lieutenant, were there dishes in the kitchen sink?"

"Yes, sir. There were dishes in the sink."

"Were the dishes washed?"

"I don't know, sir."

"Wouldn't your training as a detective bring you to some conclusion concerning how many dishes were in the sink?"

"No, sir."

After a short recess, the questioning began about what time Agnes Thompsen had sanded the stairs. The lieutenant said he got his information from other officers, including Captain O'Brien. He believed it was between 1:15 and 2:00. Mr. Shew showed him the transcript of the first trial. The time there varied from 1:00 to 3:00

"Now, do you wish to change that?"

"Only to say it was early in the afternoon."

Wall began questioning the lieutenant again, about the blood and footprints, and received the same answers.

The squabbling between the attorneys continued all day and at five in the afternoon, the lieutenant was excused. Another day had passed without any new information materializing.

The following morning, Trooper Enrico Soliani took the stand. He was one of the Troopers who did not testify at the first trial. He told of arriving at the Thompsen house, seeing blood all over the kitchen, following the blood marks through the dining room, out to the porch and finding the body. He looked at the photographs, and said, "Yes, that's what it looked like." When asked, what the weather was like that day, he replied, "Warm and sunny."

Then Arnfin Thompsen was called to the stand. Wall began his examination slowly. "Tell us about the day of the murder, Arnfin."

"The usual, breakfast, then to work at Carpenter Brick company, and home at 6:15. No one was home so I ran to Bob Stadler's house, across the road. He came back with me, while his wife called the State Police. I found Dottie dead, in the yard, and Christa upstairs with my mother."

Wall asked, "You found your wife, dead, before you went over to Stadler's?"

"Yes, I followed the blood through the dining room to the back porch. Dottie was down there on the ground."

"Did you walk through the blood?"

"You had to walk through it, you couldn't get around it."

"Did Harry Solberg ever come to you asking for help with his studies?"

"Yes, it was in the winter of 1964 or 1965. He came four or five times."

"And about the time of June 15, did you have any contact with him regarding his economics papers?"

"No."

"Do you know of any reason why the Defendant might come to your house on June 15, 1965?"

"No, there was no reason for him to come to the house."

Shew began his examination after lunch. He asked Arnfin, "What can you tell me about the night of the murder?" He repeated everything that the lawyers and judge had previously heard.

"How many trips did you make across the kitchen floor that night before the police came?"

"Probably five, or six."

"And how many trips did you make from the kitchen to the dining room?"

"Just one"

Shew passed Arnfin the transcript of his testimony at the Inquest, and waited while he read a part of it. Then he asked, "Did you state at that time, well, I stepped into something here. I had to get a glass out of the cupboard'?"

"Yes."

Shew then read some of the transcript, and asked Arnfin, "At that time you stated you didn't notice whether you made them or not. I realize you were terribly upset, and at that time you were unable to tell us whether those were your marks, or whether they were there before you arrived home?"

"I couldn't tell, no."

Shew then asked about Arnfin's relationship with his present wife before Dorothy's death.

Wall said, "I object to the use of the word affair, Your Honor."

Shew remarked, "I don't insist on it. I will call it anything he wants. Have you a better name, Mr. Wall?"

Wall responded with, "If his Honor asks me any question, I will answer it."

"The judge asked, "What word would you like, Mr. Wall?"

Wall replied, "I wouldn't like to use any word, your Honor. I don't know what he's driving at, when he's talking about an affair."

The judge said, "Let's call it friendship."

Shew said, "Mr. Thompsen, you stated that you came home at 6:15."

"Yes, Dottie wanted me home at a quarter after six."

Shew then repeated the questions about; breakfast, Christa's lunch and afternoon nap, the daily routine, the soap operas, and the nature of Agnes Thompsen's illness."

"That afternoon McKeon asked about the restrictions on Major Rome by Commissioner Mulcahy. As he produced the major's subpoena, he said, "If an intermediary such as the Commissioner of the State Police thwarts our right, the Court is empowered to issue an order for his appearance."

The request was granted, and the major was ordered to be in Court every day for the remainder of the trial.

Wall protested, "Your Honor, there was a definite abuse of a subpoena in the last trial, in a claim that this so called witness, should be in court every day, at all times. If this happens, he will be photographed on a daily basis, and be displayed on the front page of all the local newspapers This request can only be an attempt to repeat the abuse that took place at the first trial."

Shew commented, "Your Honor, I wish to correct the false statements that Mr. Wall just made. Judge MacDonald had ruled that if Mr. Wall had the members of the Canaan Barracks in constant attendance, then Major Rome was entitled to be there also. Major Rome is the only person we have to help us get these police records."

Wall said, "I think there should be some evidence, Your Honor, that Major Rome knows something about this case. There isn't a report that I have seen submitted by Major Rome, in connection with this case."

Judge Macdonald agreeing said, "I will instruct him to be here tomorrow. If he does not come, I will subpoena Commissioner Mulcahy to find out why."

The three attorneys engaged in a argument, concerning a difference of opinion, which prompted the judge to interrupt them, and call the lieutenant back to the stand."

The judge asked him, "Did Major Rome have a separate file on this case?"

"No sir, this is the complete file."

"Was there a separate investigation?"

"Not after December 31, 1965, when the piggy bank was found, and Captain O'Brien instructed Lieutenant Fuessenich to pursue the case."

Wall then asked, "lieutenant, you are familiar with the State Police files in connection with the Dorothy Thompsen case? Is there a report anywhere that was made by Major Rome?"

"No, sir."

"Are there any records to prove that the major made any investigation on his own?"

"I haven't seen any."

At this point Wall started his redirect questioning of Arnfin Thompsen. He realized that Arnfin had been questioned for five hours by Detective Rebillard on the night that Dorothy was murdered, and the next day, by Rebillard and Fuessenich, and on the next Monday by another member of the State Police. "Who questioned you on Monday," He asked?

Arnfin answered, "I don't remember the name." Then he reconsidered, and said, "About five minutes with Major Rome."

Wall's next questions were about; the dishes in the sink, the lunch routine, the Soap Operas, Christa's lunch and nap, the housework while the baby slept, and now, to the partly ironed shirt on the ironing board. Arnfin said, "She usually started her ironing about 1:30." Harry was seen going into the house about 1:30.

Wall asked that the jury be dismissed while he made a statement. "Your Honor, I would like you to reconsider bringing Major Rome here tomorrow. I feel that it would be an unfortunate diversion of the trial, and a waste of time. I think that the man's propensity for the limelight is well known. He doesn't seem to represent the type of justice that we like to think we have in this country. My feeling about this Your Honor, are very strong. It could serve no purpose, and could possibly, do a great deal of harm."

McKeon said, "On the opening day of this trial, a reckless assertion was made in Chambers by Mr. Wall. He said I was in this case through a conspiracy with The Hartford Courant and Major Rome. I will demonstrate in Court tomorrow that I have never exchanged a greeting with Major Rome."

The judge interrupting said, "If Rome appears tomorrow, I will hear him for one purpose. To see whether, or not, he has access to certain records, that could help the defense. After that, I will tell him to remain, or to go."

Wall vowed not to say one word on the following day, while Rome is present. "I will make an argument afterwards. I hope your Honor will do what you can."

The judge replied, "The Court has certain powers which the Court will enforce. At that point, the judge adjourned until the following morning."

The next morning, Mr. Slattery from Pratt and Whitney Aircraft Corp., East Hartford, was on the stand to identify Harry's handwriting on his job application.

Shew asked for a short conference, during which he suggested, "We might be able to shorten the examination."

Judge Wright said, "I would welcome anything that would shorten the trial." At that point the Court was reconvened.

McKeon said, that he and Mr. Shew would make a judicial admission that the letter was written by Harry Solberg.

The judge said, "Thank you.", and ordered the jury returned.

Wall objected, and the Sheriff hesitated at the Jury room door. Wall continued. "The State is interested in justice, even though counsel are not concerned in doing justice for him."

McKeon, in a stern loud voice said, "That remark is out of order, Your Honor!"

Wall then stated, "Any judicial admission is absolutely out of order. Defense Counsel conceded that the letter was written by the defendant, who claims a loss of memory. We don't know if the loss of memory is a concern in this document. It would be negligent not to put it to proof."

Shew replied, "This concern of Mr. wall's for the defendant is touching. In the first trial, a claim in summation or argument was entered, that Harry did not write the letter."

The judge said, "I can't direct the State's Strategy. If Mr. Wall will not accept your concession, I have no power over that. I am mindful that Judge MacDonald wrote out suggestions which might shorten this trial to one week."

Wall said, "Not because of the State, Your Honor, I think that the motions have taken a great deal of time, and they are matters that have little reference to the trial."

Mr. MeKeon came back with, "I would like to submit authority on the nature of judicial admission. I notice Mr. Wall never cites authority for his propositions. I am prepared to offer legal theory behind a judicial admission."

The judge then said, "I can't tell Mr. Wall what to do. Do you still want the concession made in front of the jury?"

McKeon answered, "The reason for judicial admission was to dispose of the need for this expert, to shorten the trial, and to minimize the effect of witness Liberi."

Wall complained, "We had Liberi here for two days."

McKeon parried with, "What difference does that make?"

Shew said, "I told him he could go home when he first got here."

Wall, now really getting upset, yelled, "Why doesn't Counsel speak to Counsel instead of speaking through the witnesses. I think there is a duty on the part of the State in fairness to the defendant as a person, rather than to rely on what might prove to be a temporary admission."

The attorneys quarreled about, Rules of Law, Judicial Admission, and Harry's statement that he didn't write the letter.

Judge Wright consulted his papers. Shew and McKeon walked to their seats, while Wall remained standing. When the judge finished what he was reading, he said, "Perhaps Mr. Wall is correct. To be cautious, we should go on with the evidence."

McKeon said, "The judicial admission is withdrawn. I ask Your Honor, as it pertains to evidence, that it is not publicized."

The judge repeated his ruling, and the jury returned to the courtroom.

Wall then turned towards the judge and said, "Your Honor, Mr. Anthony Liberi."

The witness was sworn and answered the familiar questions about Harry's handwriting and the letter. He explained the similarity in the writing on the job application, and in the letter. In the rear of the courtroom sat, Holden, Rebillard and Fuessenich. The three officers listened attentively.

Suddenly, there was a rush of excitement, as someone exclaimed, "Rome's here."

With the jury out to lunch, Judge Wright asked to see Sam Rome. Wall then asked to make a statement, and also requested that the major leave the room before he spoke. Major Rome left the room, after which Wall stated, "I consider this to be a combined enemy force. Two Defense attorneys, Demeusy of the Hartford Courant, and now, Major Rome."

The Headlines read: *Wall Wants to Keep Rome From Testifying—Judge to Query Rome Before He Takes Stand—Prosecution Seeks to block Testimony.*

Wall looked straight at the judge and said, "I told your Honor that if Your Honor had Rome testify, I was going to stand mute. I shall say nothing if he is allowed to testify. Your Honor. Major Rome is here today because Counsel wanted him for something other than window dressing."

The judge turned to Wall and said, "He is here by order of Defense Counsel." With that, Wall returned to his seat.

Shew's annoyance was beginning to manifest as he said, "Your Honor, if Mr. Wall had come into Chambers when he was invited, he would realize that he's now talking through his hat, as usual. The Defense needs help in this case. Wall has Officer Pennington, and his own private detective, Samuel Holden. He has all the available resources at Canaan Barracks. Now I am willing to take an oath, Your Honor, that Major Rome knew nothing about this. If Mr. Wall wouldn't make these stupid statements, he wouldn't get himself boxed in as far as the press is concerned."

The judge announced, "Bring in Major Rome."

Judge Wright then asked, "Major Rome, what records or documents do you have under your control?"

"None."

"And where are the records as far as you know?"

"They are in the custody of the Canaan Barracks or the States Attorney's office."

"The Defense claims that your presence is vital to the Defense. In what way is your presence so important?"

"Your Honor, I was in charge of the investigation from a week after the crime was committed until December of 1965. Commissioner Mulcahy instructed me to appear here, only to testify."

The judge asked the attorneys, "Do you have any questions along these lines? I mean limited lines, if so you may ask them."

Shew answered, "We will stand on Major Rome's statement. Your Honor. It is the duty of the State to seek the truth, not necessarily get a conviction. For example, in the first trial Mr. Wall ended his case without introducing Dr. Stolman's report. Isn't that right Mr. Wall?"

Wall answered, "Yesterday I stated that I would stand mute if Your Honor had the major testify, therefore, in keeping with my promise, I will say nothing."

Shew said, "If a member of the State Police feels that a man on trial for his life is innocent, he should be available for the Defense. I think Mr. Wall has started these fights to keep the major out of the case, and he should be available to us. If the major is willing to be here, he should be available to us."

After lunch Mr. Liberi finished his testimony, answering questions pertaining to Harry's handwriting, after that he had nothing more to contribute.

The next witness was Mr. Richards, the jeweler. His testimony was the same as he gave during the first trial in Litchfield, about Harry making a $25.00 down payment on the rings. He produced the sales slip. Rings plus tax of $71.10. He said again, that Harry took the slip home for his parent's signature.

The last witness for the day was Mrs. Clark, whose grandchild found the piggy bank. She had nothing further to add to her previous testimony, and was, therefore, excused. This now being the end of the week, Court was recessed until Tuesday morning.

30

As Margaret put another log on the fire, she looked around the large comfortable kitchen. Yes, she told herself, she had made the right decision. This would be the last winter up here in the woods alone. always waiting for the phone calls, and the not too frequent visits. John's trips to New Hartford were growing less frequent. How she missed him, and how she loved him. She realized he had to be with the children, but, when the kids are out of college and married, if he ever does get the divorce, she and John will be middle-aged.

Yes, she had made the right decision. She would accept John's offer to use his flat in London for as long as she wished. She would make the move in the spring. It might be interesting to make a new start.

She wished Kay was here this morning, but she was glad that Kay was happy now with her Charlie. After breakfast Margaret decided to go to the city, look around the stores, and go to a movie. With all the roads plowed and sanded, and light traffic, the driving was pleasant for a change. She drove on Rte. 44, then down Asylum St., and then to the G. Fox Department Store parking lot.

The day in town wasn't a treat as she has expected. Being in town alone, wasn't the same as being with her friend. She noticed several changes and other things that didn't bother her before. The G. Fox Department Store had changed drastically, since the owner, Mrs. Auerbach, had died, and the business was sold to the May Company. The large lounge that used to be the meeting place in town for ladies to meet, wait for their friends, write letters, or read while waiting, was now another department. The spacious Ladies' Room was reduced to a lavatory. Across the street, the Wise-Smith Department Store was sold to a discount store company. As people said, that won't affect the city, the steady customers will still go to G. Fox. Yes, thought Margaret, everything is changing, even the movie was a disappointment.

She stopped at the Canton Center General Store on the way home to buy dog biscuits to put some out at night for the little creatures that came searching for food. While there, she couldn't help but overhear conversations about the trial. Everyone was of the same opinion, "He's guilty as hell."

The next morning the telephone rang. It was Charlie. In an excited voice he said, "This is Charlie. Sit down, I have something to tell you."

Now, Margaret was excited. She said, "Oh, Charlie, at last you won the Irish Sweepstake."

He started to sob. "It's Kay. She's dead, she's dead. I looked in on her this morning to tell her I was leaving for the office. When she didn't answer, I thought she was asleep. At ten o'clock the police called and asked me to come home. It seems that Kay was going to a card party and lunch with some people. When a woman came to pick her up, and no one answered the door, she called someone. I don't know everything yet. Someone got the door unlocked and they went in, and found Kay dead in bed." He sobbed again.

Margaret trying to recover from the shock, said, "How could this happen? She wasn't sick. We talked last night and she was fine. She told me she was going to bed early because there wasn't anything on TV worth watching. I can't believe it. I'll come down and be whatever help I can."

Charlie just said, "She's gone, she's gone, there'll be an autopsy, according to what the police said."

The following week Charlie called again and explained to Margaret, that the autopsy had shown that Kay suffered a massive coronary attack, and died in her sleep. At least there was some comfort in knowing that she had died painlessly.

31

Over the weekend, social groups, church groups, neighbors, everyone was waiting for the next session of court. The big question in everyone's mind was, will there be a decision this week?

Tuesday morning Shew requested a copy of the bind over files, and said, "I assume Mr. Wall has a copy, but there is another. Major Rome doesn't have a copy in his possession." Shew mentioned Detective Redican's report regarding the interview with little Randy Stadler.

Wall said, "Your Honor, I have only one copy of my bind over file."

Shew said, "May I have Lieutenant Fuessenich, or Mr. Pennington on the stand to find out?"

The judge then interrupted and said, "Our law is that his file is privileged. If he refuses, I will uphold him."

Shew remarked, "Mr. Wall said 'I'll produce anything they want', and now he has changed his mind."

The judge then reprimanded them both. He said, "Gentlemen, we shall keep personalities out of this, and get down to the law. The law states that the prosecutor's file is sacrosanct." Wall apparently looking for the last word said, "Your Honor, asking me for the whole file is ridiculous, therefore any such offer would be improper on my part."

Shew turned to the judge and said, "I don't know that it is ridiculous to try to save a man's life, Your Honor. These statements should be available. If it's the only way, we will subpoena every officer who investigated the case."

The judge responded with, "Motion denied."

McKeon spoke, "Your Honor, Major Rome, will have his ability to testify impaired, if he is not allowed to see the notes that he, himself, had prepared. There is evidence that Major Rome was never relieved of this case, it is, therefore, necessary that he have that file to prepare himself for being a witness."

Wall not willing to give in said, "Your Honor, no report has been made by Major Rome to the State's Attorney relating to this case. He's a red herring being dragged into court to help the defense. There is no report, and I can say it categorically, none has ever been made to the State's Attorney by Major Rome.

The judge addressed Shew, "Apparently the document you want is not in existence." The judge ended the discussion and ordered the sheriff to call in the jury. Mr. Flagg, the water district patrolman was the first witness of the day.

In the first trial, Mr. Flagg had been called by the State. He testified that he had seen a man get out of a black 1959 Ford two-door sedan. The time, he said was about 1:30 or 1:45 in the afternoon. Mr. Flagg said he was sure of the time because he left his father's house about twenty, or twenty five minutes after one, and it is only two, or three miles away.

Doctor Murphy was now on the stand, to repeat every detail of his testimony. Dorothy's parents, the Burdicks', left the courtroom, with Mrs. Burdick in tears, crying her heart out. She couldn't bear to listen again to the heart-breaking, brutal account of the autopsy. The Doctor didn't omit anything. When he finished reading his report, Mr. Shew asked, "Doctor is there anything in this report that would change your ideas as to what happened?"

Doctor Murphy answered, "No."

Shew re-read the important paragraph about the green vegetables. Then he asked the Doctor, "After ingestion, food is passed into the Duodenum, if lettuce, greens, and salads takes only minutes, what time elapsed between the time she ate, and the time she died?"

Wall said, "I object, Your Honor, this is no part of the Direct examination."

Shew insisted that time is most important to the defense.

Dorothy and the baby ate about ten minutes to twelve every day. Doctor Murphy said that the lettuce wasn't digested, therefore, Dorothy was murdered a few minutes after she ate. The Ford was seen at the house about 1:30 or 1:45. According to the doctor, Dorothy was dead then.

The judge asked, "How does this become important, Mr. Shew?"

Shew answered, "We expect to establish the time she had lunch, Your Honor."

The judge responded, "Mr. Wall said there is no other possible evidence on this score. There is no such evidence, so far at any rate."

Shew then said, "If Your Honor please, I spent a great deal of time with Arnfin Thompsen, establishing the fact that his wife had a schedule of eating lunch. He said she ate at a quarter to twelve, after which she watched TV programs, while ironing."

Wall stated, "The fact that there is evidence of a habit of eating lunch at a particular time, doesn't mean that she didn't eat just prior to her death. The evidence shows that she did eat just minutes before her death. I dislike having to call the Doctor down to Bridgeport again, however, I think that this is proper Cross Examination of him as a medical examiner. This is an important matter."

Wall said, "My objection is that it's certainly no part of the Direct."

Shew stated, "That's what we're talking about."

Judge Wright said, "I am satisfied that there is proper claim, by the Defense with relation to the lunch hour and how soon after that she died. The only question was whether it must wait for the case for the Defense. It was not part of direct examination. Is the pathologist who prepared t the autopsy, going to be present at this trial?"

Wall said that he hoped Doctor Opper would be here. He had made several phone calls and was informed, that the Doctor was having trouble getting away.

Shew said, he had called Doctor Opper, who informed him, that Detective Holden told him, he wouldn't be needed. "I told the Doctor, he would be needed." Shew was once again showing his impatience.

The judge declared, "I have ruled that this is a matter for the Defense. They may bring back Doctor Murphy later, to answer more questions about the green vegetables, and how long after eating lunch, she died."

Mr. Robert Stadler, Jr. was the next witness. He repeated almost verbatim, the testimony he had given in Litchfield. Arnfin running across the road to his house for help, going across with Arnfin, seeing and covering Dorothy's body on the ground behind the house, and Christa with Arnfin's mother.

Wall then asked, "Tell us what happened next."

Mr. Stadler thought for a minute, then he continued, "We went to the living room. Arnfin said he wanted a drink. I told him not to touch anything, or walk in the kitchen. He reached around and got the bottle and a drinking glass."

Wall then asked about the time he entered the house, and if Agnes Thompsen was at the top of the stairs?

Mr. Stadler answered, "Yes, and she asked if she was dead yet?"

Cross examination by Shew.

Shew asked Mr. Stadler, "Do you know what time Arnfin Thompsen came home that night? As far as you know, Christa could have been upstairs all the time?"

"I don't know what time Arnfin got home, and I don't know what time Christa went upstairs."

"About Agnes Thompsen, do you remember how her hair was done?"

"It wasn't done up. It was in curlers."

"You went into the house—into the living room. "Did you sit down?"

"That's when Arnfin said he wanted a drink."

"Was he within sight when he went to get a drink?"

"I went with him."

"How long after that, did Trooper Soliani come?"

"Ten, or fifteen minutes. Then Soliani ordered everyone out of the house, and he went upstairs for Agnes and Christa. Did Mrs. Thompsen make any remarks at this time?"

"When a State Policeman asked her if she had seen, or heard anything, she said she heard two loud thumps, and then she saw a green car in the driveway. She said she thought it might have been her boy friend. She didn't say Dorothy, she just said her boyfriend."

Shew now got to the Police interview with Randy. Mr. Stadler said, one officer was John Bonolo, but he didn't know the names of the other two. He admitted that he also asked Randy some questions. Like who was in the house. Randy said, "Christa, her mother and her grandmother." He didn't see a man, or anybody else around the place.

Wall shouted, "Objection, hearsay. There is no guarantee of trustworthiness in a child of tender years."

Shew said, "I think it's trustworthy. It was made in the presence of the State Police."

Then Shew asked that Mr. McKeon be allowed to present the argument for the defense.

Judge Wright said, "To do what? What are you talking about now? To talk about what Randy said? Or to have this argument of law? I will hear you."

Wall said, "I object Your Honor, to the questioning by other Counsel."

Late in the afternoon, McKeon said he wished to make a motion that may save time, and he might do it now before the jury returned from recess. Judge Wright agreed.

Wall asked that it wait until the next morning.

McKeon continued, "To protect the record I would ask that the document in question, the bind over file, be marked for identification."

To which the judge asked, "Are there such files?"

Wall said, "There certainly is a bind over file, Your Honor. It's my file and the only one in existence. It has been furnished to me by the State Police, and it's my file."

Another argument started over the file. Should it be marked, and did it exist at all?

Wall said, "The case related only to evidence. It's ridiculous to think it could be offered in evidence."

The judge agreed, even if Wall was right, this was a ridiculous request. Still an aggrieved person couldn't appeal unless there was some marking.

McKeon said, "The efficiency of a witness would be impaired if he was unable to see his own records. He could not go before the Supreme Court with the claim unless the records were marked for identification." Then, the judge asked where the records were, and McKeon asked to call Lieutenant Fuessenich to find out.

Wall said, "Your Honor, I'm not sure what they have in mind. A full bindover file was furnished to me, and there is another file that was—well, I won't go into that."

The judge then said, "Well, I will mark them and give them right back to you."

Wall addressing the judge, said, "Might this be done in an orderly procedure, Your Honor, there is a witness on the stand. The only purpose in this, at this time of day, is to get a headline in The Hartford Courant in the morning."

The argument continued. The judge said, "If they produced the files I will mark, and return them, but, you won't see them."

Wall said, "Someone should be there to present them."

McKeon said, "I will have a witness right away, Your Honor."

The judge said, "These are his working papers, Mr. McKeon. Meanwhile, we will continue with Mr. Stadler's testimony."

The next witness was Mrs. Burdick, who had been in Court all day, every day. She looked exhausted. She cried as she leaned forward in the chair to tell about receiving as many as three or four telephone calls a day from Dorothy. Then she fainted. Her husband and the sheriff hurried to her with some pills, and water. Wall asked if she would like to come back another day. She thanked him, and said, "No, I would like to get it over with." She sat up, and answered the now familiar questions. Yes, She was close to her daughter, Yes, Dorothy did have a schedule of doing things, especially the lunch with Christa, putting her down for her nap, watching the Soap Operas, and doing the ironing at 1:30, in the afternoon, every day the same."

Cross examination by McKeon.

As usual, a repetition of questioning and answering. He was especially interested in the telephone calls.

"Did Mrs. Thompsen ever answer the phone when you called Dorothy, I'm sure she could hear it upstairs."

"She used to, but Dorothy told her not to, because she might fall and get hurt. Mrs. Burdick was extremely nervous, and began giving answers before questions were asked, so much so, she was excused.

The judge said, "It's late now, it would be better to start with the next witness in the morning." He then dismissed the Jury.

Wall replied, "I could finish with Carole Stadler by five o'clock, but I know why Counsel wants this, at this time, I know why it's important."

McKeon, not to let Wall get away with that wise crack said, "Your Honor, if the State's Attorney thinks that we are doing this for headlines, we will do it at such time as the State's Attorney would like to have it done."

The judge, finally getting fed up with the childish behavior of the lawyers said, "This is ridiculous. I will mark certain files if you produce them, and I will return them to the State's Attorney."

Wall continuing with his typical manner, said, "I object to any such procedure, because, Your Honor has already made a ruling. This was done this morning, in spite of the fact it was obvious, not to have it this morning, but in the afternoon. It's a postponement until the proper time, for obvious purposes, Your Honor."

McKeon said, "Your Honor, at two o'clock I asked to go into this and put a witness on."

Wall, being true to form, said, "The deadlines of the Newspapers were over at that time."

McKeon called the lieutenant to the stand, and asked him in very simple terms, "Is there a bind over file?"

The lieutenant answered, "I believe there is, sir."

Wall objected to any questions relating to the evidence the State has. Judge Wright interrupted, "If it gets to that, I will sustain you, overruled."

The constant sparring continued. McKeon asked the lieutenant if he had seen the file within this past two weeks. The lieutenant said, he had never seen it. He explained that the file is a collection of reports assembled for the Special Services Division, and sent to the State's Attorney.

"Does it contain reports of the Hartford Division?"

Wall objected, "I see no relevancy at all, Your Honor."

McKeon, showing his irritation with Wall said, "I will do it through another witness in Chambers, or in secrecy, whatever Mr. Wall suggests, as long as I have it on record."

The judge responded with, "Where are they? Let's mark these files, and I'll give them back to you."

Wall once again objected.

The judge, finally fed up with the constant objections by Wall, turned to him and said, "I request you, and order you, to give it to the clerk for marking, and he will return it to you immediately! The record will show that the file was returned promptly to the State's Attorney, without having been seen by anybody."

32

The next morning, with the jury seated and Detective Rebillard on the stand, Wall showed proof that the Black 59 Ford was registered to Thorbjorn Solberg. Detective Rebillard agreed that he and Officer Pennington went to the Solberg home three days after the murder, and glanced at the car before they went in the house. Inside were Harry, his mother, brother and sister. "We just had an ordinary conversation, in which the mother took part."

Wall asked, "Was there anything else that you noticed relating to Harry, during this interview?"

McKeon objected, "I have no way of knowing what he observed and what he meant."

At this time, Judge Wright excused the jury, temporally, and asked, "Before we go any further, gentlemen, it was Judge MacDonald's hope that these excursions and delays be surmounted by agreement. Is that impossible?"

Shew responded with, "I offered to agree to all suggestions, Your Honor, and Mr. Wall said, "Nothing doing." "Now, I feel we have to go on. He's asking for the substance of conversation between the officer and defendant. Suppose he said, Harry admitted to me that he killed Dorothy. How do I know that he is not going to say that?"

The judge then asked, "Did he testify to that at the first trial?"

McKeon answered, "Your Honor, Rebillard reported conversations, that Harry gave them, of his movements on the day of the murder. Coming home on the school bus, eating lunch, going to the Hayes' Store, going to the lawn mower shop, and going to Mr. Zimmer's house in North Granby, to work with his father."

"Prior to talking to him, did you give any indication as to his right of silence?"

With the jury still out, McKeon continued, "What they are accomplishing here is to get a story from the accused's own mouth, then knock it down."

Wall stepped forward, "Your Honor, Mr. Shew quoted me as saying, 'nothing doing'. I never said, 'nothing doing', I feel it is my duty to go ahead with the matter. The questions were addressed to the accused in the presence of his brother. The Miranda has no application in this particular matter."

Then Judge Wright asked questions concerning restrictions placed on Harry's freedom, such as, who was there, did he flash a badge on him, did you make him sit down or stand, was he free to come and go, and did you pose any words of stern import?

"It was a general conversation in which his Mother took part."

The Jury was permitted to return, and the Attorneys agreed about what was observed, and what was meant by the word observation.

The Jury was excused once again while Detective Rebillard explained observations.

"Harry was barefoot, he was rocking back, and forth, and appeared fidgety and nervous."

After lunch, the Jury returned and Rebillard returned to the stand. He testified that he and Pennington went to Sharon's house, and found that Harry was there also. Wall asked about the conversation.

"Objection."

Once again the Jury was excused.

The conversation was about Harry visiting Sharon on the afternoon of the murder about 2:00 P.M., in his black Ford.

The Jury returned, and Detective Rebillard was asked, and answered the same questions. About Harry being there at 2:00 p.m., in the black Ford. He repeated his dialogue with Harry. He stated that, "Lieutenant Fuessenich and Lieutenant Riemer also interviewed Harry on the 13th., and 14th., and Lieutenant Fuessenich interviewed Harry once again."

Wall interrupted and asked, "Were all these interviews on tape?"

The answer was, "Yes."

"And are these tapes in the custody of the Court, and have they all been heard by Counsel for the Defendant?"

"Yes, sir," was the answer.

"May we have the tapes?" At this time the Sheriff left, to retrieve the tapes.

"How many tapes are there? Were all the interviews made voluntarily?"

"Seven, I believe," was the answer.

Shew objected.

McKeon also objected and said, "This is improper, Your Honor."

The judge sustained the objections.

Shew remarked, "Mr. Wall, that certainly is one of the most dastardly things I have ever heard in a Courtroom. Your Honor, this man knew better than to say that."

The judge replied, "Well, it's not that bad, Mr. Shew."

Shew said, "Your Honor, excuse me, I think it's worse than that."

The judge answered, "Objection sustained."

Wall then offered the tapes, and turning to the judge said, "Your Honor, I ask that they be played to the jury."

McKeon questioned the admissibility, and Wall said they should be offered as a whole, as one exhibit, at which McKeon objected. He said, "They should be marked separately."

Judge Wright agreeing said, "I think they should, too, Mr. Wall."

Wall then said, "I am offering them as one exhibit, Your Honor. They are not offered piecemeal. They are offered as a whole. They may have different numbers, but the offer is for the exhibit as a whole."

The attorneys went to their chairs as the tapes were marked, and the jury was recessed again. Back on the stand, the officer was asked by McKeon, "Is it your sworn testimony that every conversation, or interview, to your knowledge, between Harry Solberg and the people you described, is on these tapes made on the 13th, 14th., and part of 15th."

Officer Rebillard answered, "To the best of my knowledge, yes, sir."

"And you listened in on all the conversations?"

"Yes, sir."

"There was no other interview, other than what is recorded on the tapes?"

"No, I couldn't say that."

In a surprised tone, McKeon asked, "What is your recollection?. I thought that was your testimony"

McKeon approached the bench and spoke to the judge, "Your Honor, I ask that Detective Holden and Lieutenant Fuessenich, be sequestered from the room for the next question."

Wall said, he had no objection.

McKeon then asked, "Were there any interviews between the State Police and Harry Solberg, between five minutes to nine and eleven forty five on the evening of March 14?"

Wall objected to that. He said, "There was nothing about that on direct. The question is, admissibility of these tapes, Your Honor."

McKeon remarked, "He said on direct, that these tapes cover all the conversations or interviews."

Officer Rebillard replied, "All that I heard."

"Did you hear any other interviews or conversations other than those recorded on the tapes now offered?"

"Yes, sir."

"And when did they take place?"

"On the 14$^{th.}$ It would have been between 8:00 and 9:00 a.m., in Hartford." "How about 9:30? Was there any conversation between you and Lieutenant Fuessenich and Harry Solberg that was not recorded?"

"There would be some, but I'm not sure of the time. There was one interview before we left for East Hartland with Harry."

"And to the best of your knowledge, that was not on the tapes?"

"That's correct, Lieutenant Fuessenich, Sergeant Kielty, Rebillard and Harry were present."

"You were the first to initiate the interrogation process?"

"Yes, sir."

Attorney McKeon addressing the judge said, "Your Honor, I submit under Miranda, that none of these conversations after that time are admissible." Then he turned to Rebillard. "You became aware within the first hour of questioning that this man was in financial difficulty, did you not, officer? During the interrogation you learned of his numerous bills, and that he was paying $60.00 a month rent, and his house had bugs."

Officer Rebillard asked, "In great financial difficulty? I don't recall that, exactly the way you put it. You also left out part of the warning I gave him."

McKeon said, "Let's hear the rest."

"I asked him if he understood it, and I also told him that he had a right to have an attorney. I also asked him if he understood these rights and, I told him he did not have to talk to me."

"You said, you have a right to counsel? Those are your exact words, correct?"

"I believe so, yes."

"Did you tell him he had a right to have an attorney present in the interrogation room, and if he wished to make that choice no interrogation would begin until the attorney was present?"

"No, Sir, 'Miranda' was not in effect then."

"You did not advise him, then, that before questioning began, he was entitled to have Counsel present with him in the interrogation room?"

"I advised him that he had a right to Counsel."

"Could you answer my question, sir?"

Wall said, "I submit he has answered it, Your Honor."

McKeon asked, "Did you say he had the right to consult with an attorney before the interrogation started?"

"Not in those words, no sir."

"The exact words you used were, "You have a right to Counsel, and did you tell him, sir, that if he could not afford counsel, one would be appointed for him before the interrogation began if he so desired?"

"No, sir."

McKeon said, "Your Honor, I claim all these tapes are inadmissble. An individual held for interrogation must be clearly informed that he has a right to consult with a lawyer, and to have a lawyer with him during interrogation. This warning is an absolute prerequisite to interrogation. Your Honor, it is necessary to inform an accused that if he cannot afford Counsel, one will be appointed for him, if he so desires, and no interrogation will take place before the appointment, Your Honor, it is clear, the record speaks for itself, these tapes are not admissible for admissions, exculpatory statements, or what purports to be confessions."

Wall said, "Your Honor, I have not laid a foundation under Miranda. I believe I can lay a foundation for their admissibility under what the law was at that time."

McKeon started to reply, however, was interrupted by Wall, who said, "I made no statements until Counsel was finished. I submit, Your Honor, that I can lay a foundation for these tapes to be admitted, if it becomes necessary to do so. I say it is not necessary for me to comply with Miranda, because of actions of council, in that there was newspaper publicity about the tapes."

Then, Wall recalled the day when Shew mentioned the tapes before the jury. It was the day they finished the examination of Lieutenant Fuessenich, and Mr. Shew said, "They had been up late last night listening to the tapes." Wall said, "I objected in Chambers, and said to Your Honor and Counsel, that I felt it was improper to bring the tapes in at this particular stage, relating to whether Counsel was listening to them. Mr. Shew said, before the jury, that we were all tired because, "We had been listening to tapes." Those tapes were then brought before the jury. Wall then said, "I made an objection in Chambers requesting Counsel not to mention the tapes, because it could become prejudicial to the case. Not because they would hurt the State's case, Your Honor. I feel that the door has been opened to the introduction of these tapes, by the conduct of the defense in bringing them in over my objections. I feel the jury should hear them."

McKeon then said, "The Miranda applies to all cases going to trial after June 16, 1966. This trial did not go to Court until September 1966, and the second trial began this month."

Wall said, "The present argument is not related to Miranda, Your Honor. I feel that the Defense has waived any such thoughts by opening the door, insisting that these tapes be brought forth, and by emphasizing them before the Jury. I feel the door has been opened by them. Other considerations and objections have been put aside by them deliberately, these are therefore admissible."

After lunch, Shew answered Mr. Wall's charges of impropriety in having mentioned the tapes. He stated, "I explained it so that the Jury would understand. I merely wish to call that to Your Honor's attention."

Wall said, "Your Honor, it was stated in Chambers by me, that the impropriety of mentioning was pointed out to Mr. Shew. I agree there had been some conversation between Counsel and Your Honor relating to it. I feel that the door has been opened, for the tapes to be admitted."

Shew countered with, "Your Honor, most of Mr. Wall's argument is beneath notice and childish. Mr. Wall interpreted the statements that way. Your Honor did not, and Your Honor is presiding in this Court. The characterizations made by Mr. Wall are in his own mind."

Wall answered, "I would like to inquire, Your Honor, whether Counsel is withdrawing his charges of my talking through my hat, and he now feels it's merely childish?"

The judge evidently totally confused by all the lengthy rhetoric asked, "What's before me now?"

McKeon answered, "Your Honor, I object to the admissibility of the tapes."

Wall then stated, "I claim them, Your Honor. The door has been opened."

The judge answered, "I'm not concerned with that aspect, Mr. Wall. A fundamental constitutional right protected under the Miranda ruling, certainly cannot be waived by Counsel by some injudicious remark." Then the judge asked Officer Rebillard, who was still on the stand, "Officer, at the time these seven tapes were taken, was Mr. Solberg under arrest?"

Officer Rebillard replied, "He was under arrest after the fifth or sixth tape. I'm not sure, Your Honor."

Judge Wright's next question was, "Where did he spend the night of March 13?

Did he go home under custody, or at his own free will? Had his freedom been infringed in any way?"

"You mean had he asked to go, or had we detained him by force?"

"Or any other way, by moral force, even."

"Moral force?"

"How did he happen to come to Police Headquarters for the making of these tapes?"

Officer Rebillard again told of picking Harry up at his house that Sunday morning and taking him to the Canaan Barracks. He told Harry he was not under arrest. The judge asked Rebillard if he took Harry home again, Rebillard said, "Harry went home from Hartford with either his parents or his wife."

The judge then said, "Gentlemen, my inquiry at this juncture is whether or not during the taking of these tapes, Harry was under custodial interrogation?"

McKeon then asked, "Officer, at that time were you were reasonably convinced that Harry was the author of the letter?"

"Yes, sir."

"And your investigation into the murder of Dorothy Thompsen had focused on him at this point?"

"It had focused on him in the sense that he was the author of this letter and we wanted to find out why."

McKeon read from Miranda: By custodial interrogation we mean questioning initiated by law enforcement officers after having been taken into custody or otherwise deprived of his freedom of action in any significant way. "I submit the mere fact that the police sought in an emasculated way to advise him of his rights, indicates a police attitude that he was an accused at that point. Your Honor, this is a boy who had not achieved majority. It took him six years to complete High School, and he has an I Q below average. He was held incommunicado for three to four hours at the Canaan Barracks, and his parents were told he was being held on some matter unrelated to the murder. Your Honor, I submit this is exactly what the Supreme Court contemplated in its terms "custodial interrogation", of being deprived of his freedom of action. Therefore, none of these tapes should be admitted. I will show that the so-called lie-detector examination was nothing but a device to carry out an almost vicious interrogation, lasting for six hours. If I may, Your Honor, I would like to get that before the Court now—relative to the lie-detector examination."

The judge asked for Wall's response.

Wall said, "Rebillard's answer was that the investigation had focused on the accused for having written the Letter. The police had learned this man had written the letter, therefore, they had a right to find out what he knew. The attention of the police was focused on him, only as a witness, Your Honor."

The judge restated his position. "The one question remaining in my mind as to admissibility of the tapes, is whether or not at the time Harry Solberg was under custodial interrogation, or whether his freedom of action had been infringed in any way. Any evidence you want to give me on either side, I'll listen to."

Wall turned to the witness, "Mr. Rebillard, were you in uniform at any time on March 13?"

"No, sir."

"On March 13 did you indicate to Harry Solberg that you had the authority to keep him in custody?"

"No, sir."
"Did he go with you voluntarily?"
Yes, he came voluntarily.
"During the questioning on the day of the 13, did he ever express the wish to be other than where he was?"
"He may at one point said he wanted to go home, or something of that nature. He mentioned something about wanting to see his father, and I asked him if he wanted his father to come down and see him, or his pastor, he said, no, he didn't want them to come down."
"Was any restraint placed on him that day?"
"No, I saw no restraint put on him."
"And was he deprived at any time on the 13th., of his freedom of action?"
"No, sir."
Wall stated that Harry had discussed the lie-detector test, first with his parents, and then they spoke to Lieutenant Fuessenich. He then made the decision to take the polygraph test. Wall then showed the polygraph form, signed both by Harry, and his parents.
"Did he sign it of his own accord?"
"Yes, sir."
McKeon then asked what the parents had agreed to, and what was told to them. "They agreed that Harry take a lie-detector examination and nothing else, isn't that true, sir?"
Detective Rebillard answered, "No. He was asked and urged by his parents to take this test to show whether he was involved in any way other than writing this letter, and to get at the truth of the matter."
McKeon then said, "The polygraph form was not admissible, because it contained an inadequate warning of rights."
Wall replied, "Your Honor, it's the claim of the State that at this particular stage, this was voluntary, and was not custodial interrogation, and no warning whatsoever was necessary. Your Honor, in view of the fact that this was not custodial interrogation."

The judge interrupted him and said, "Wholly apart from these points about warning, how can any lie-detector test become a part of this trial? Our courts have never recognized the validity of a polygraph examination."

"Wall stated, "I am not trying to introduce the results of the test, Your Honor, I am merely trying to introduce the interrogation that took place in connection with it."

The judge, not about to give in to this particular ploy said, "Again I ask you, sir, what bearing does an agreement to take a lie-detector test have upon these tapes?"

Wall answered, "Your Honor, the consensual nature of what happened, the fact of there being no custodial interrogation, indicates that this was agreed upon after a consultation with his father and mother. It shows that he remained there without restraint. He had a choice to go home, or stay there. There was no restriction on his freedom of action."

McKeon then offered his thoughts on the subject, "Your Honor, if Mr. Wall wants to put in just the responses to the lie-detector questions, there is no objection on our part. But that is submerged in a complete interrogation The lie-detector test was nothing but a device, almost a fraud, to keep this boy there and wear him out. He went home in fear and indicated he didn't sleep at all that night. As a matter of fact the next day when he returned he said, "I wasn't going to go to work today, but I was so scared you'd be over to pick me up, that I went anyhow."

He was questioned from 5:00 to 8:30 P.M., during which time; something like an exculpatory statement was elicited from him. Your Honor, Lieutenant Riemer in that examination did not let up on the boy. He kept asking him why? Why? Why?, almost two hundred times, under the pretext of a lie-detector examination. Lieutenant Riemer is here in the courtroom to deny it. I'd be happy to put him on the stand."

Wall said, "Your Honor, these statements made by Counsel are untrue, and reckless. He is attempting to testify. There is no such evidence before the Court."

The judge said, "For the first time I'm getting a glimmering, Mr. Wall."

Wall said, "There were two lie-detector tests, Your Honor, and there were other interviews by policemen."

Judge Wright said the case cited by Mr. Wall, the lie-detector test, did not rule out the subsequent confession, but did not itself, come into evidence."

Wall said, "And I didn't intend to have it."

Then the judge said, "But you are offering these tapes now."

Wall's reply was. "I offered them originally for another reason. It may be that any portions of them, where results are indicated, might be deleted. In administering a lie-detector test there are certain discussions, questions and answers, and these would be admissible apart from any results. I concede the possibility of certain portions not being admissible, where results were being shown. As far as the questions and answers are concerned, I don't agree with what Counsel said about the evidence. I can say without any question, that on occasions, Lieutenant Riemer stated to the accused, that the last thing he wanted him to do was confess to something he didn't do. When they talked about wearing down the Defendant being questioned, he said, "This was the third lie-detector test that Lieutenant Riemer had given that day. If anyone was to be worn down, it would have been the lieutenant. Your Honor. Right now we are talking about the admissibility of this present document, and I submit, Your Honor that it is part of the totality of circumstances showing the voluntariness of the act of the accused in entering this discussion or taking this lie-detector test."

The judge, in trying to clear up this question asked, "Detective at one point, you said he wanted to go home, is that correct?" Detective Rebillard answered, "Yes, sir, he wanted to see his father. I told him I would call his father, and have him come down."

"How soon thereafter did his father arrive?"

"Well his father went to Hartford, and we went to Hartford to meet him."

"Did he ever say he wanted to go home?"

"Yes, I believe he did."

"Did you refuse him the right to go home?"

"Not as such, no. He didn't press the point. If he stood up and said, I'm going home, he would have gone home. He finally went home at about 8:30. that night."

Judge Wright asked Rebillard to examine the marked tapes, to identify those included in the lie-detector test. Then he said, "Well, now, can we agree on this, gentlemen? At a certain time, somewhere on the fifth or sixth tape, Harry Solberg was placed under arrest. Do you agree, Mr. Wall, that at that point, the Miranda rule was not satisfied and those tapes must go out?"

"No, Your Honor, I don't."

"Why not?"

"Because I believe that Miranda was satisfied. We haven't come to the evidence on that yet. This evidence related to what was said on the 13th., at a time when the State contends no warning was necessary, because of the lack of detention. There was at a time after the arrest, a warning of the accused of his rights, which did satisfy Miranda and that will be testified to. It relates to the stenographic report taken by the Court Reporter on the 14th."

McKeon said, "Your Honor, That's a misrepresentation. The language before Stenographer Roberts is identical language used by Rebillard."

The judge asked, "Where is this evidence, Mr. Wall?"

"It is one of the exhibits from the previous trial. Wall handed the judge the transcript of the "confession", and the judge asked him to point out the warning.

"It is on page one, Your Honor."

The judge read page one, "Well, the same three warnings were given but there are other warnings that Miranda requires."

Wall's reply was, "We intended to have evidence, that there was no other one required under those circumstances, Your Honor."

The judge responded with, "Well, sometime on the 14th, of March, Harry Solberg was placed under arrest. Now certainly after that he is under custodial interrogation, correct?, therefore, the three old requirements are not enough."

Wall answered, "I believe this is sufficient, in connection with other evidence we intend to produce."

"Well, go ahead and offer the evidence." was his reply.

Judge Wright reviewed the three additional warnings required under Miranda. "That if a man cannot afford a lawyer, the State will provide one for him. That the interrogated party has the right to terminate the questioning at any time. He should be told this. Finally, the State must prove that he knowledgeably, with full knowledge and acquiescence and understanding, waived his right to remain silent. So now there are six requirements that must be satisfied. You have satisfied only three of them so far."

Wall's answer was, "Your Honor, as the matter of affording a lawyer, that's the evidence that I intend to bring out. Miranda says this isn't necessary if the questioner has knowledge of the fact that the man does not need counsel and does not need to have one hired for him. That is the case and it was so found in the previous trial—that was the situation. And the fact that he knowledgeably waived his right to remain silent is set forth on the first page here of exhibit "RR", where there was a response made by the accused to the question in which he indicated—when such a well-worded and understandable notice to him was given, he acquiesced and said, "Yes."

The judge then said, "That's only the third requirement—the old-fashioned requirement—the right to remain silent."

"Your Honor, actually, my interpretation of Miranda is, that the offer to have a lawyer appointed for him is only on the basis where it is definitely required, or on the basis that the questioner has no knowledge of the man's ability to hire a lawyer on his own. Miranda so states."

Judge Wright then read the fourth requirement. "It is necessary to warn him not only that he has a right to consult with an attorney, but also that if he is indigent, a lawyer will be appointed to represent him. Without this additional warning the right to consult would often be understood as meaning, only that he can consult with a lawyer, if he has one, or has the funds to obtain one. The warning of a right to counsel would be hollow if not couched in terms that would convey to the indigent, the knowledge that he, too, has the right to have counsel present. So, your warning in this statement is only the old-fashioned third warning."

Wall said, "The passage referred to an indigent. Evidence will show that this man was no indigent. He was employed in one of the best-paying factories in the State. We intend to have evidence here that will show he was certainly no indigent, that he was well employed here."

The judge told him, he would give him time to find the reference, he then called for a recess. As a result of the recess the jury had been out of the courtroom most of the day.

There was such an air of anticipation throughout the Courtroom, you could hear a pin drop, as, Shew, McKeon, Major Rome, and the reporters stood in the press room, anxiously waiting.

Just before four o'clock, Shew and McKeon were summoned to Chambers. It was reported that Wall had entered Chambers several minutes earlier, from which indistinct voices could be heard from the room. Major Rome stood over by the courtroom window. Suddenly, someone said, "Shew and McKeon just went down the corridor, they're talking to the family." The press room door was left open, and the reporters were leaning into the corridor watching. Shew came back, with McKeon a few paces behind him, while the judge and Wall remained in chambers.

The reporters came out in the corridor, and Shew and McKeon walked right past them, without speaking a word, down the hall to the room where Harry's family waited. Major Rome remained in the press room, while Shew and McKeon returned. The door to the Chambers opened, and closed.

Court was called to order, and Rebillard returned to the stand. Holden and Fuessenich sat in the back of the court, and Major Rome stood across the aisle from them.

Wall withdrew the offer of the tapes, and instead offered a transcript of the confession. McKeon objected to the confession on the basis of Miranda. The judge examined the document, then said, "In view of all the evidence, I must rule that this exhibit does not satisfy the Miranda rules, and therefore the Court cannot accept this offer. It is inadmissible."

The State's case had finally come to an end, and the entire Courtroom was stunned by the judge's decision.

Wall requested a recess to confer with the Defense Counsel. The State offered a substitute charge based on the threatening letter. Wall said, "Your Honor, in view of your ruling relating to the confession, I ask permission to file a substituted information, charging the Defendant with malicious threatening under the blackmail statute."

In the late afternoon, Harry Solberg was put to plea. He stood before the bench, his attorney standing next to him. The Clerk asked the question that demanded an explicit answer, "To the information charging you with malicious threatening, how do you plead—guilty or not guilty?"

"Guilty."

Judge Wright said, "Before the plea is accepted, Mr. Solberg, I must ask you a few questions." "How old are you?"

"I'm twenty-one."

The judge then stated, "This statute under which you are now charged, has a possible penalty of up to ten years in prison, or a fine of not more than five thousand dollars, or both. Do you understand that possibility, sir?"

"Yes, sir, I do."

"Are you doing this freely, and voluntarily?"

"Yes, sir, I am."

"And have you any understanding about promises being made to you?"

"Nobody made any promises."

The judge replied with, "All right, sir, the plea is accepted. You may sit down."

Harry Solberg returned to his seat, sobbing and shaking.

The State nolled the charge of first degree murder. Harry would spend the night in the Bridgeport jail, and be returned to Litchfield in the morning. Bond was set for $5,000.00 and sentencing would take place in Litchfield, the following Friday.

Harry's mother was crying, as Wall went over and shook hands with her and Mr. Solberg. Sharon, again burst into tears, and repeated, "Thank the Lord, it's over, praise the Lord."

In the press room, Major Rome called the State Police Headquarters. "Tell the Commissioner that the State's Attorney just nolled the case." The reporters followed him, pestering him with questions, however, he ignored them, as he put on his hat and walked to his car.

The next day Tobey Solberg, put up his home and cottage as collateral, to produce bond, and Harry went home for eight days. Judge Wright sentenced him to not less than a year and a day, and not more than ten years in State's Prison. He served little more than eight months of the sentence and was paroled, with credit for exceptional good behavior.

33

Solberg Goes Free On Murder Charge. Evidence Barred, Faces Second count. Mr. Gerald Demeusy's article was quite long, and included several photos. It read: *The trial of accused slayer, Harry A. Solberg, 21, ended abruptly in Superior Court here Wednesday when State's Attorney Thomas F. Wall nolled a first degree murder indictment returned against the East Hartland youth by a grand jury last year.*

Wall's prosecution collapsed when he was unable to get into evidence, Solberg's alleged confession to the June 15, 1965 killing of Mrs. Dorothy Thompsen, a 30-year-old Barkhamsted housewife.

Judge Douglas B. Wright agreed with the defense counsel that the statement was inadmissible because State Police had failed to fully advise Solberg of his constitutional rights as required by a 1966 decision of the United States Supreme Court.

"Nolle" is derived from the Latin words "nolle prosequi" which mean literally "do not prosecute" The term describes the dropping of a case by a prosecutor when he can no longer proceed legally. It does not prevent future opening of the case should circumstances change. Solberg did not walk out of the court a free man, however. Wall drafted a, "New Information", charging the 21-year-old plumber's helper with "malicious threatening," which is part of the state's blackmail statute. The charge arises from Solberg's admitted act of posing as the killer in sending a threatening letter to Mrs. Thompsen's husband two days after the mutilated body was found under the back porch of her home. Mr. Demeusy's article detailed the entire day's procedures, as accurately as in the court transcript, including, *"Before accepting Solberg's plea of guilty to the charge of "malicious threatening" Judge Wright asked him point blank if he was aware of the penalty.*

Solberg said he was.

The judge inquired if the plea of guilty was being made, freely and voluntarily.

Yes, sir, replied Solberg.

All right, plea accepted, said the judge.

The nolle ended the bizarre capital case. It came after two weeks of bitterly-contested trial often punctuated by legal skirmishes, accusations, and personality clashes between counsel. This was described by Judge Wright as "name-calling" that he did not intend to tolerate.

It was reminiscent of Solberg's first trial in Litchfield. The trial received so much publicity that the retrial was switched to Bridgeport because both the State and the defense felt it would be impossible to impanel an impartial jury in Hartford or Litchfield Counties."

Now that the two trials were over, and Harry was out of prison, the families and relatives would have to get their lives together. Time would ease the pain, however, the heartbreak and tragic memories would remain. Take little Christa for example, what would she remember? What could she remember?

Residents of Barkhamsted and surrounding towns, however, were not happy at all with the verdict. Many expressed publicly that they thought Harry was guilty. He was once again walking around town, a free man, and this caused them concern. The question bothering everyone was, if Harry didn't commit the murder, then the person who did is still around. Woman couldn't dispel the nervousness of being alone in the house. They were still afraid to go out to the barn, or stable alone. It would take time for the families of this community to regain their equanimity.

High up on Louse Hill, Margaret wasn't worrying about being alone in the country anymore. Her suitcases were packed, she hid the house keys in the old cabinet on the back wall of the barn, put the car in the barn, and locked the barn door. She was now ready and waiting for John to come and take her to the airport, where she would be off to a new life in London. All the time, however, she wondered, if some day, there would be another women waiting for John, "To come up on one of his business trips."

Driving over the back roads through Granby and Windsor Locks to the airport, they were too choked up to speak. Just casual talk about passport, tickets, changing money, warm clothes for the dampness in London, and so on. But, when she kissed him goodbye at the boarding gate, all emotions let loose.

The End

0-595-26960-5